A STUDY OF FAIRY TALES

BY

LAURA F. KREADY, B.S.

WITH AN INTRODUCTION

By HENRY SUZZALLO, Ph.D.

President of the University of Washington
Seattle

HOUGHTON MIFFLIN COMPANY

BOSTON NEW YORK CHICAGO

The Riverside Press Cambridge

The Riverside Press
CAMBRIDGE . MASSACHUSETTS
U . S . A.

TO THE CHILDREN

WHO, BECAUSE OF IT, MAY RECEIVE ANY GOOD

PREFACE

One of the problems of present-day education is to secure for the entire school system, from the kindergarten to the university, a curriculum which shall have a proved and permanent value. In this curriculum literature has established itself as a subject of unquestioned worth. But children's literature, as that distinct portion of the subject literature written especially for children or especially suited to them, is only beginning to take shape and form. It seems necessary at this time to work upon the content of children's literature to see what is worthy of a permanent place in the child's English, and to dwell upon its possibilities. A consideration of this subject has convinced me of three points: (1) that literature in the kindergarten and elementary school should be taught as a distinct subject, accessory neither to reading nor to any other subject of the curriculum, though intimately related to them; (2) that it takes training in the subject to teach literature to little children; (3) that the field of children's literature is largely untilled, inviting laborers, embracing literature which should be selected from past ages down to the present.

A single *motif* of this children's literature, *Fairy Tales*, is here presented, with the aim of organizing this small portion of the curriculum for the child of five, six, or seven years, in the kindergarten and the first grade. The purpose has been to show this unit of literature in its varied connection with those subjects which bear an essential relation to it. This presentation incidentally may serve as an example of one method of giving to teachers a course in literature by showing what training may be given in a single *motif*, *Fairy Tales*. Incidentally also it may set forth a few theories of education, not isolated from practice, but united to the everyday problems where the teacher will recognize them with greatest impression.

In the selection of the subject no undue prominence is hereby advocated for fairy tales. We know fairy tales about which we could agree with Maria Edgeworth when she said: "Even if children do prefer fairy tales, is this a reason why their minds should be filled with fantastic visions instead of useful knowledge?" However, there is no danger that fairy tales will occupy more than a fair share of the child's interest, much as he enjoys a tale; for the little child's main interest is centered in the actual things of everyday life and his direct contact with them. Yet there is a part of him untouched by these practical activities of his real and immediate life; and it is this which gives to literature its unique function, to minister to the spirit. Fairy tales, in contributing in their small way to this high service, while they occupy a position of no undue prominence, nevertheless hold a place of no mean value in education.

In the study of fairy tales, as of any portion of the curriculum or as in any presentation of subject-matter, three main elements must unite to form one combined whole: the child, the subject, and the teaching of the subject. In behalf of the child I want to show how fairy tales contain his interests and how they are means for the expression of his instincts and for his development in purpose, in initiative, in judgment, in organization of ideas, and in the creative return possible to him. In behalf of the subject I want to show what fairy tales must possess as classics, as literature and composition, and as short-stories; to trace their history, to classify the types, and to supply the sources of material. In behalf of the teaching of fairy tales I want to describe the telling of the tale: the preparation it involves, the art required in its presentation, and the creative return to be expected from the child.

In the consideration of the subject the main purpose has been to relate fairy tales to the large subjects, literature and composition. From the past those tales have come down to us which inherently possessed the qualities of true classics. In modern times so few children's tales have survived because they have been written mainly from the point of view of the subject and of the child without regard to the standards of literary criticism. In the school the teaching of literature in the kindergarten and elementary grades has been conducted largely also from the point of view of the child and of the subject without regard to the arts of literature and composition. In bookshops counters are filled with many books that lack literary value or artistic merit. The object in this book has been to preserve the point of view of the child and of the subject and yet at the same time relate the tale to the standards of literature and of composition. The object has been to get the teacher, every time she selects or tells a tale, to apply practically the great underlying principles of literature, of composition, and of the short-story, as well as those of child-psychology and of pedagogy.

This relating of the tale to literary standards will give to the teacher a greater respect for the material she is handling and a consequent further understanding of its possibilities. It will reveal what there is in the tale to teach and also how to teach it. In teaching literature as also other art subject-matter in the kindergarten and first grade, the problem is to hold fast to the principles of the art and yet select, or let the child choose, material adapted to his simplicity. As the little child uses analysis but slightly, his best method of possessing a piece of literature is to do something with it.

The fairy tale is also related to life standards, for it presents to the child a criticism of life. By bringing forward in high light the character of the fairy, the fairy tale furnishes a unique contribution to life. Through its repeated impression of the idea of fairy-hood it may implant in the child a desire which may fructify into that pure, generous, disinterested kindness and love of the grown-up, which aims to play fairy to another, with sincere altruism to make appear before his eyes his heart's desire, or in a twinkling to cause what hitherto seemed impossible. Fairy tales thus are harbingers of that helpfulness which would make a new earth, and as such afford a contribution to the religion of life.

In stressing the history of fairy tales the purpose has been to present fairy tales as an evolution. The kindergarten and first-grade teacher must therefore look to find her material anywhere in the whole field and intimately related with the whole. Special attention has been placed upon the English fairy tale as the tale of our language. As we claim an American literature since the days of Washington Irving, the gradual growth of the American fairy tale has been included, for which we gratefully acknowledge the courtesy of the Librarian of the United States Bureau of Education and the Bibliographer of the Library of Congress. A particular treatment of some North American Indian folk-tales would also be desirable. But a study of these tales reveals but one unimportant *pourquois* tale, of sufficient simplicity. This study of the natural history of the fairy tale as an art form is not necessary for the child. But for the teacher it reveals the nature of fairy tales and their meaning. It is an aid to that scholarly command of subject-matter which is the first essential for expertness in teaching. Only when we view the American fairy tale of to-day in the light of its past history can we obtain a correct standard by which to judge of its excellence or of its worth.

In the classification of fairy tales the purpose has been to organize the entire field so that any tale may be studied through the type which emphasizes its distinguishing features. The source material endeavors to furnish a comprehensive treatment of fairy tales for the kindergarten and elementary school.

In the preparation of this book the author takes pleasure in expressing an appreciation of the criticism and helpful suggestions given by the Editor, Dr. Henry Suzzallo, under whose counsel, coöperation, and incentive the work grew. The author wishes also to make a general acknowledgment for the use of many books which of necessity would be consulted in organizing and standardizing any unit of literature. Special acknowledgment should be made for the use of *Grimm's Household Tales*, edited by Margaret Hunt, containing valuable notes and an introduction by Andrew Lang; of *English Fairy Tales*, *More English Fairy Tales*, *Indian Fairy Tales*, and *Reynard the Fox*, and their scholarly introductions and notes, by Joseph Jacobs; of *Norse Tales* and its full introduction, by Sir George W. Dasent; of *Tales of the Punjab* and its Appendix, by Mrs. F. A. Steel; of the *Uncle Remus Books*, by J. C. Harris; of *Fairy Tales*, by Hans C.

Andersen; of *Fairy Mythology* and *Tales and Popular Fictions*, by Thomas Keightley; of *Principles of Literary Criticism*, by Professor C. T. Winchester, for its standards of literature; of *English Composition*, by Professor Barrett Wendell, for its standards of composition; of Professor John Dewey's classification of the child's instincts; and of the *Kindergarten Review*, containing many articles of current practice illustrating standards emphasized here.

Recognition is gratefully given for the use of various collections of fairy tales and for the use of any particular fairy tale that has been presented in outline, descriptive narrative, criticism, or dramatization. Among collections special mention should be made of *The Fairy Library*, by Kate D. Wiggin and Nora A. Smith; the *Fairy Books*, by Clifton Johnson; and the *Fairy Books*, by Andrew Lang. Among tales, particular mention should be made for the use, in adaptation, made of *Oeyvind and Marit*, given in Whittier's *Child Life in Prose;* of *The Foolish Timid Rabbit*, given in *The Jataka Tales*, by Ellen C. Babbit; of *The Sheep and the Pig*, in Miss Bailey's *For the Children's Hour;* of *Drakesbill*, in *The Fairy Ring*, by Wiggin and Smith; of *The Magpie's Nest*, in *English Fairy Tales*, by Joseph Jacobs; of *How the Evergreen Trees Lose their Leaves*, in *The Book of Nature Myths*, by Miss Holbrook; of *The Good-Natured Bear*, described by Thackeray in "On Some Illustrated Christmas Books"; and of *The Hop-About-Man*, by

Agnes Herbertson, given in *The Story-Teller's Book*, by Alice O'Grady (Moulton) and Frances Throop.

The author wishes also to express thanks to the many teachers and children whose work has in any way contributed to *A Study of Fairy Tales*.

LAURA F. KREADY

LANCASTER, PENNSYLVANIA
August, 1916

CONTENTS

Introduction. By Henry Suzzallo xv

I. The Worth of Fairy Tales 1

II. Principles of Selection for Fairy Tales . 13

III. The Telling of Fairy Tales 90

IV. The History of Fairy Tales 158

V. Classes of Fairy Tales 204

VI. Sources of Material for Fairy Tales . . 245

Appendix 265

Outline 291

Index 305

INTRODUCTION

The fairy tale has a place in the training of children which common sense and a sympathetic attitude toward childhood will not deny. Some rigid philosophers, who see no more of life than is to be found in logical science, condemn the imaginative tale. They regard the teaching of myths and stories as the telling of pleasant lies, which, if harmless, are wasteful. What the child acquires through them, he must sooner or later forget or unlearn.

Such arguments carry conviction until one perceives that their authors are measuring the worth of all teaching in terms of strictly intellectual products. Life is more than precise information; it is impulse and action. The fairy tale is a literary rather than a scientific achievement. Its realities are matters of feeling, in which thought is a mere skeleton to support the adventure. It matters little that the facts alleged in the story never were and never can be. The values and ideals which enlist the child's sympathy are morally worthy, affording a practice to those fundamental prejudices toward right and wrong which are the earliest acquisitions of a young soul. The other characteristics of the tale — the rhythmic, the grotesque, the weird, and the droll — are mere recreation, the abundant playfulness which children require to rest them from the dangers and terrors which fascinate them.

The fairy tale, like every other literary production, must be judged by the fitness of its emotional effects. Fairyland is the stage-world of childhood, a realm of vicarious living, more elemental and more fancy-free than the perfected dramas of sophisticated adults whose ingrained acceptance of binding realities demands sterner stuff. The tales are classics of a particular kind; they are children's classics, artful adaptations of life and form which grip the imaginations of little folks.

The diet of babes cannot be determined by the needs of grown-ups. A spiritual malnutrition which starves would soon set in if adult wisdom were imposed on children for their sustenance. The truth is amply illustrated by those pathetic objects of our acquaintance, the men and women who have never been boys and girls.

To cast out the fairy tale is to rob human beings of their childhood, that transition period in which breadth and richness are given to human life so that it may be full and plastic enough to permit the creation of those exacting efficiencies which increasing knowledge and responsibility compel. We cannot omit the adventures of fairyland from our educational program. They are too well adapted to the restless, active, and unrestrained life of childhood. They take the objects which little boys and girls know vividly and personify them so that instinctive hopes and fears may play and be disciplined.

While the fairy tales have no immediate purpose other than to amuse, they leave a substantial by-product which has a moral significance. In every reaction which the child has for distress or humor in the tale, he deposits another layer of vicarious experience which sets his character more firmly in the mould of right or wrong attitude. Every sympathy, every aversion helps to set the impulsive currents of his life, and to give direction to his personality.

Because of the important æsthetic and ethical bearings of this form of literary experience, the fairy stories must be rightly chosen and artfully told. In no other way can their full worth in education be realized. They are tools which require discrimination and skill. Out of the wisdom of one who knows both tales and children, and who holds a thoughtful grasp on educational purpose, we offer this volume of unusually helpful counsel.

HENRY SUZZALLO

A STUDY OF FAIRY TALES

CHAPTER I

THE WORTH OF FAIRY TALES

In olde dayes of the kyng Arthour,
Of which that Britouns speken gret honour,
Al was this lond fulfilled of fayrie;
The elf-queen, with hir joly compaignye,
Daunced ful oft in many a grene mede.

CHAUCER

I. TWO PUBLIC TRIBUTES

ONLY a few years ago, in the gardens of the Tuileries, in Paris, a statue was erected in memory of Charles Perrault, to be placed there among the sculptures of the never-to-be-forgotten fairy tales he had created, — *Red Riding Hood, Sleeping Beauty, Puss-in-Boots, Hop-o'-my-Thumb, Bluebeard,* and the rest, — so that the children who roamed the gardens, and in their play gathered about the statues of their beloved fairy friends, might have with them also a reminder of the giver of all this joy, their friend Perrault. Two hundred years before, Perrault truly had been their friend, not only in making for them fairy tales, but in successfully pleading in their behalf when he said, "I am persuaded that the gardens of the King were made so great and spacious that all the children may walk in them."

Only in December, 1913, in Berlin, was completed the *Märchen Brunnen*, or "Fairy-Tale Fountain," at the entrance to Friedrichshain Park, in which the idea of the architect, Stadt-Baurat Ludwig Hoffmann, wholly in harmony with the social spirit of the times, was to erect an artistic monument to give joy to multitudes of children. This fairy entrance to the park is a decorative lay-out, a central ground surrounded by a high, thick lodge of beeches. Toward this central ground — which has been transformed into a joyous fairy world — many hedge walks lead; while in the sidewalks, to warn naughty children, are concealed fantastic figures. There is the huge *Menschenfresser*, who grasps a tender infant in each Titan hand and bears on his head a huge basket of children too young to have known much wrong. A humorous touch, giving distinct charm to the whole creation, pervades all. From lions' heads and vases, distributed at regular intervals in the semicircular arcade in the background, water gushes forth; while in the central basin, nine small water animals — seven frogs and two larger animals — appear spouting great jets of water. Clustered about the central fountain are the nine fairy characters of Professor Ignatius Taschner, among whom are Red Riding Hood, Hansel and Grethel each riding a duck, Puss-in-Boots, Cinderella, and Lucky Hans; and looking down upon them from the surrounding balustrade are the animal figures by Joseph Rauch. In these simple natural classic groups, fancy with what pleasure the children may look to find the friendly beasts and the favorite tales they love!

Such is the tribute to fairy tales rendered by two great nations who have recognized fairy tales as the joyous right of children. Any education which claims to relate itself to present child life can hardly afford to omit what is acknowledged as part of the child's everyday life; nor can it afford to omit to hand on to the child those fairy tales which are a portion of his literary heritage.

II. THE VALUE OF FAIRY TALES IN EDUCATION

In considering fairy tales for the little child, the first question which presents itself is, "Why are fairy stories suited to the little child, and what is their value for him?"

Fairy tales bring joy into child life. The mission of joy has not been fully preached, but we know that joy works toward physical health, mental brightness, and moral virtue. In the education of the future, happiness together with freedom will be recognized as the largest beneficent powers that will permit the individual of four, from his pristine, inexperienced self-activity, to become that final, matured, self-expressed, self-sufficient, social development — the educated man. Joy is the mission of art and fairy tales are art products. As such Pater would say, "For

Art comes to you, proposing to give nothing but the highest quality to your moments as they pass, and simply for those moments' sake. Not the fruit of experience, but experience, is the end." Such quality came from the art of the fairy tale into the walk of a little girl, for whom even the much-tabooed topic of the weather took on a new, fresh charm. In answer to a remark concerning the day she replied, "Yes, it 's not too hot, and not too cold, but just right." All art, being a product of the creative imagination, has the power to stimulate the creative faculties. "For Art, like Genius," says Professor Woodberry, "is common to all men, it is the stamp of the soul in them." All are creatures of imitation and combination; and the little child, in handling an art product, puts his thought through the artist's mould and gains a touch of the artist's joy.

2. **Fairy tales satisfy the play spirit of childhood.** Folk-tales are the product of a people in a primitive stage when all the world is a wonder-sphere. Most of our popular tales date from days when the primitive Aryan took his evening meal of yava and fermented mead, and the dusky Sudra roamed the Punjab. "All these fancies are pervaded with that purity by which children seem to us so wonderful," said William Grimm. "They have the same blue-white, immaculate bright eyes." Little children are in this same wonder-stage. They believe that the world about throbs with life and is peopled with all manner of beautiful, powerful folk.

All children are poets, and fairy tales are the poetic recording of the facts of life. In this day of commercial enterprise, if we would fit children for life we must see to it that we do not blight the poets in them. In this day of emphasis on vocational training we must remember there is a part of life unfed, unnurtured, and unexercised by industrial education. Moreover, whatever will be accomplished in life will be the achievement of a free and vigorous life of the imagination. Before it was realized, everything new had existed in some trained imagination, fertile with ideas. The tale feeds the imagination, for the soul of it is a bit of play. It suits the child because in it he is not bound by the law of cause and effect, nor by the necessary relations of actual life. He is entirely in sympathy with a world where events follow as one may choose. He likes the mastership of the universe. And fairyland — where there is no time; where troubles fade; where youth abides; where things come out all right — is a pleasant place.

Furthermore, fairy tales are play forms. "Play," Richter says, "is the first creative utterance of man." "It is the highest form in which the native activity of childhood expresses itself," says Miss Blow. Fairy tales offer to the little child an opportunity for the exercise of that self-active inner impulse which seeks expression in two kinds of play, the symbolic activity of free play and the concrete presentation of types. The play, *The Light Bird*, and the tale, *The Bremen*

Town Musicians, both offer an opportunity for the child to express that pursuit of a light afar off, a theme which appeals to childhood. The fairy tale, because it presents an organized form of human experience, helps to organize the mind and gives to play the values of human life. By contributing so largely to the play spirit, fairy tales contribute to that joy of activity, of achievement, of coöperation, and of judgment, which is the joy of all work. This habit of kindergarten play, with its joy and freedom and initiative, is the highest goal to be attained in the method of university work.

3. **Fairy tales give the child a power of accurate observation.** The habit of re-experiencing, of visualization, which they exercise, increases the ability to see, and is the contribution literature offers to nature study. In childhood acquaintance with the natural objects of everyday life is the central interest; and in its turn it furnishes those elements of experience upon which imagination builds. For this reason it is rather remarkable that the story, which is omitted from the Montessori system of education, is perhaps the most valuable means of effecting that sense-training, freedom, self-initiated play, repose, poise, and power of reflection, which are foundation stones of its structure.

4. **Fairy tales strengthen the power of emotion, develop the power of imagination, train the memory, and exercise the reason.** As emotion and imagination

are considered in Chapter II, in the section, "The Fairy Tale as Literature," and the training of the memory and the exercise of the reason in connection with the treatment of various other topics later on, these subjects will be passed by for the present. Every day the formation of habits of mind during the process of education is being looked upon with a higher estimate. The formation of habits of mind through the use of fairy tales will become evident during following chapters.

Fairy tales extend and intensify the child's social relations. They appeal to the child by presenting aspects of family life. Through them he realizes his relations to his own parents: their care, their guardianship, and their love. Through this he realizes different situations and social relations, and gains clear, simple notions of right and wrong. His sympathies are active for kindness and fairness, especially for the defenseless, and he feels deeply the calamity of the poor or the suffering and hardship of the ill-treated. He is in sympathy with that poetic justice which desires immediate punishment of wrong, unfairness, injustice, cruelty, or deceit. Through fairy tales he gains a many-sided view of life. Through his dramas, with a power of sympathy which has seemed universal, Shakespeare has given the adult world many types of character and conduct that are noble. But fairy tales place in the hands of childhood all that the thousands and thousands of the universe for ages have found excellent in character and conduct. They hold up for imitation all those cardinal virtues of love and self-sacrifice, — which is the ultimate criterion of character, — of courage, loyalty, kindness, gentleness, fairness, pity, endurance, bravery, industry, perseverance, and thrift. Thus fairy tales build up concepts of family life and of ethical standards, broaden a child's social sense of duty, and teach him to reflect. Besides developing his feelings and judgments, they also enlarge his world of experience.

In the school, the fairy tale as one form of the story is one part of the largest means to unify the entire work or play of the child. In proportion as the work of art, nature-study, game, occupation, etc., is fine, it will deal with some part of the child's everyday life. The good tale parallels life. It is a record of a portion of the race reaction to its environment; and being a permanent record of literature, it records experience which is universal and presents situations most human. It is therefore material best suited to furnish the child with real problems. As little children have their thoughts and observations directed mainly toward people and centered about the home, the fairy tale rests secure as the intellectual counterpart to those thoughts. As self-expression and self-activity are the great natural instincts of the child, in giving opportunity to make a crown for a princess, mould a clay bowl, decorate a tree, play a game, paint the wood, cut paper animals, sing a lullaby, or trip a dance, the tale affords many problems exercising all the child's accomplishments in the variety of his work. This does not make the story the central interest, for actual contact with nature is the child's chief interest. But it makes the story, because it is an organized experience marked by the values of human life, the unity of the child's return or reaction to his environment. The tale thus may bring about that "living union of thought and expression which dispels the isolation of studies and makes the child live in varied, concrete, active relation to a common world."

7. **In the home fairy tales employ leisure hours in a way that builds character.** Critical moments of decision will come into the lives of all when no amount of reason will be a sufficient guide. Mothers who cannot follow their sons to college, and fathers who cannot choose for their daughters, can help their children best to fortify their spirits for such crises by feeding them with good literature. This, when they are yet little, will begin the rearing of a fortress of ideals which will support true feeling and lead constantly to noble action. Then, too, in the home, the illustration of his tale may give the child much pleasure. For this is the day of fairy-tale art; and the child's satisfaction in the illustration of the well-known tale is limitless. It will increase as he grows older, as he understands art better, and as he becomes familiar with the wealth of beautiful editions which are at his command.

And finally, though not of least moment, fairy tales afford a vital basis for language training and thereby take on a new importance in the child's English. Through the fairy tale he learns the names of things and the meanings of words. One English fairy tale, *The Master of all Masters*, is a ludicrous example of the tale built on this very theme of names and meanings. Especially in the case of foreign children, in a tale of repetition, such as *The Cat and the Mouse*, *Teeny Tiny*, or *The Old Woman and Her Pig*, will the repetitive passages be an aid to verbal expression. The child learns to follow the sequence of a story and gains a sense of order. He catches the note of definiteness from the tale, which thereby clarifies his thinking. He gains the habit of reasoning to consequences, which is one form of a perception of that universal law which rules the world, and which is one of the biggest things he will ever come upon in life. Never can he meet any critical situation where this habit of reasoning to consequences will not be his surest guide in a decision. Thus fairy tales, by their direct influence upon habits of thinking, effect language training.

Fairy tales contribute to language training also by providing another form of that basic content which is furnished for reading. In the future the child will spend more time in the kindergarten and early first grade in acquiring this content, so that having enjoyed the real literature, when he reads later on he will be eager to satisfy his own desires. Then reading will take purpose for him and be accomplished almost without drill and practically with no effort. The reading book will gradually disappear as a portion of his literary heritage. In the kindergarten the child will learn the play forms, and in the first grade the real beginnings, of phonics and of the form of words in the applied science of spelling. In music he will learn the beginnings of the use of the voice. This will leave him free, when he begins reading later, to give attention to the thought reality back of the symbols. When the elements combining to produce good oral reading are cared for in the kindergarten and in the first grade, in the subjects of which they properly form a part, the child, when beginning to read, no longer will be needlessly diverted, his literature will contribute to his reading without interference, and his growth in language will become an improved, steady accomplishment.

REFERENCES

Allison, Samuel; and Perdue, Avis: *The Story in Primary Instruction.* Flanagan.

Blow, Susan; Hill, Patty; and Harrison, Elizabeth: *The Kindergarten.* Houghton.

Blow, Susan: *Symbolic Education.* Appleton.

Chamberlain, Alexander: "Folk-Lore in the Schools," *Pedagogical Seminary*, vol. VII, pp. 347–56.

Chubb, Percival: "Value and Place of Fairy Stories," *National Education Association Report*, 1905.

Dewey, John: *The School and the Child.* Blackie & Sons.

Ibid: The School and Society. University of Chicago Press.

"Fairy Tales," *Public Libraries*, 1906, vol. 11, pp. 175–78.

Palmer, Luella: "Standard for Kingergarten Training," *Kindergarten Review*, June, 1914.

Welsh, Charles: *Right Reading for Children.* Heath.

CHAPTER II

PRINCIPLES OF SELECTION FOR FAIRY TALES

All our troubles come from doing that in which we have no interest. — Epictetus.

That is useful for every man which is conformable to his own constitution and nature. — Marcus Aurelius.

Genuine interest means that a person has identified himself with, or found himself in, a certain course of activity. It is obtained not by thinking about it and consciously aiming at it, but by considering and aiming at the conditions that lie back of it, and compel it. — John Dewey.

I. THE INTERESTS OF CHILDREN

Now that the value of fairy tales in education has been made clear, let us consider some of those principles of selection which should guide the teacher, the mother, the father, and the librarian, in choosing the tale for the little child.

Fairy tales must contain what interests children. It is a well-known principle that selective interest precedes voluntary attention; therefore interest is fundamental. All that is accomplished of permanent good is a by-product of the enjoyment of the tale. The tale will go home only as it brings joy, and it will bring joy when it secures the child's interest. Now interest is the condition which requires least mental effort. And fairy tales for little children must follow that great law of composition pointed out by Herbert Spencer, which makes all language consider the audience and the economy of the hearer's attention. The first step, then, is to study the interests of the child. We do not wish to give him just what he likes, but we want to give him a chance to choose from among those things which he ought to have and, as good and wise guardians, see that we offer what is in harmony with his interests. Any observation of the child's interest will show that he loves the things he finds in his fairy tales. He enjoys —

A sense of life. This is the biggest thing in the fairy tales, and the basis for their universal appeal. The little child who is just entering life can no more escape its attraction than can the aged veteran about to leave the pathway. The little pig, Whitie, who with his briskly curling tail goes eagerly down the road to secure, from the man who carried a load of straw, a bit with which to build his easily destructible house; Red Riding Hood taking a pot of jam to her sick grandmother; Henny Penny starting out on a walk, to meet with the surprise of a nut falling on her head — the biggest charm of all this is that it is life.

The familiar. The child, limited in experience, loves to come in touch with the things he knows about. It soothes his tenderness, allays his fears, makes him feel at home in the world, — and he hates to feel strange, — it calms his timidity, and satisfies his heart. The home and the people who live in it; the food, the clothing, and shelter of everyday life; the garden, the plant in it, or the live ant or toad; the friendly dog and cat, the road or street near by, the brook, the hill, the sky — these are a part of his world, and he feels them his own even in a story. The presents which the Rabbit went to town to buy for the little Rabbits, in *How Brother Rabbit Frightens his Neighbors;* the distinct names, Miss Janey and Billy Malone, given to the animals of *In Some Lady's Garden,* just as a child would name her dolls; and the new shoes of the Dog which the Rabbit managed to get in *Why Mr. Dog Runs after Brother Rabbit* — these all bring up in the child's experience delightful familiar associations. The tale which takes a familiar experience, gives it more meaning, and organizes it, such as *The Little Red Hen,* broadens, deepens, and enriches the child's present life.

The surprise. While he loves the familiar, nothing more quickly brings a smile than the surprise. Perhaps the most essential of the fairy traits is the combination of the familiar and the unfamiliar. The desire for the unknown, that curiosity which brings upon itself surprise, is the charm of childhood as well as the divine fire of the scientist. The naughty little Elephant who asked "a new, fine question he had never asked before," and who went to answer his own question of "what the crocodile has for dinner," met with many surprises which were spankings; and as a result, he returned home with a trunk and experience. He is a very good example of how delightful to the child this surprise can be. The essence of the fairy tale is natural life in a spiritual world, the usual child in the unusual environment, or the unusual child in the natural environment. This combination of the usual and unusual is the chief charm of *Alice in Wonderland,* where a natural child wanders through a changing environment that is unusual. For an idle moment enjoy the task of seeing how many ideas it contains which are the familiar ideas of children, and how they all have been " made different." All children love a tea-party, but what child would not be caught by having a tea-party with a Mad Hatter, a March Hare, and a sleepy Dormouse, with nothing to eat and no tea! Red Riding Hood was a dear little girl who set out to take a basket to her grandmother. But in the wood, after she had been gathering a nosegay and chasing butterflies, " just as I might do," any child might say, she met a wolf! And what child's ears would not rise with curiosity? " Now something's going to happen! " The Three Bears kept house. That was usual enough; but everything was different, and the charm is in giving the child a real surprise at every step. The house was not like an ordinary house; it was in the wood, and more like a play-house than a real one. There was a room, but not much in it; a table, but there was not on it what is on your table — only three bowls. What they contained was usual, but unusually one bowl of porridge was big and hot, one was less big and cold, and one was little and just right. There were usual chairs, unusual in size and very unusual when Goldilocks sat in them. Upstairs the bedroom was usual, but the beds were unusual when Goldilocks lay upon them. The Bears themselves were usual, but their talk and action was a delightful mixture of the surprising and the comical. Perhaps this love of surprise accounts for the perfect leap of interest with which a child will follow the Cock in *The Bremen Town Musicians*, as he saw from the top of the tree on which he perched, a light, afar off through the wood. Certainly the theme of a light in the distance has a charm for children as it must have had for man long ago.

Sense impression. Good things to eat, beautiful flowers, jewels, the beauties of sight, color, and sound, of odor and of taste, all gratify a child's craving for sense impression. This, in its height, is the charm of the *Arabian Nights*. But in a lesser degree it appears in all fairy tales. Cinderella's beautiful gowns at the ball and the fine supper stimulate the sense of color, beauty, and taste. The sugar-panes and gingerbread roof of the Witch's House, in *Hansel and Grethel*, stir the child's kindred taste for sweets and cookies. The Gingerbread Boy, with his chocolate jacket, his cinnamon buttons, currant eyes, rose-sugar mouth, orange-candy cap, and gingerbread shoes, makes the same strong sense appeal. There is a natural attraction for the child in the beautiful interior of Sleeping Beauty's Castle, in the lovely perfume of roses in the Beast's Rose-Garden, in the dance and song of the

Elves, and in the dance of the Goat and her seven Kids about the well.

The beautiful. Closely related to this love of the material is the sense of the beautiful. "Beauty is pleasure regarded as the quality of a thing," says Santayana. Pleasures of the eye and ear, of the imagination and memory, are those most easily objectified, and form the groundwork on which all higher beauty rests. The green of the spring, the odor of Red Riding Hood's flowers, the splendor of the Prince's ball in *Cinderella* — these when perceived distinctly are intelligible, and when perceived delightfully are beautiful. Language is a kind of music, too; the mode of speaking, the sound of letters, the inflection of the voice — all are elements of beauty. But this material beauty is tied up in close association with things "eye hath not seen nor ear heard," the moral beauty of the good and the message of the true. The industry of the little Elves reflects the worth of honest effort of the two aged peasants, and the dance of the Goat and seven Kids reflects the triumph of mother wit and the sharpness of love. The good, the true, and the beautiful are inseparably linked in the tale, just as they forever grow together in the life of the child. The tales differ largely in the element of beauty they present. Among those conspicuous for beauty may be mentioned Andersen's *Thumbelina;* the Indian *How the Sun, the Moon, and West Wind Went Out to Dinner;* the Japanese *Mezumi, the Beautiful*; and the English *Robin's Christmas Song. Little Two-Eyes* stands out as one containing a large element of beauty, and *Oeyvind and Marit* represents in an ideal way the possible union of the good, the true, and the beautiful. This union of the good, the true, and the beautiful has been expressed by an old Persian legend: "In the midst of the light is the beautiful, in the midst of the beautiful is the good, in the midst of the good is God, the Eternal One."

Wonder, mystery, magic. The spirit of wonder, like a will-o'-the-wisp, leads on through a fairy tale, enticing the child who follows, knowing that something will happen, and wondering what. When magic comes in he is gratified because some one becomes master of the universe — Cinderella, when she plants the hazel bough, and later goes to the wishing-tree; the fairy godmother, when with her wand she transforms a pumpkin to a gilded coach and six mice to beautiful gray horses; Little Two-Eyes, when she says, —

> Little kid, bleat,
> I wish to eat!

and immediately her little table set with food so marvelously appears; or Hop-o'-my-Thumb when he steps into his Seven-League Boots and goes like the wind.

Adventure. This is a form of curiosity. In the old tale, as the wood was the place outside the usual habitation, naturally it was the place where things happened. Often there was a house in the wood, like the one "amidst the forest darkly green," where Snow White lived with the Dwarfs. This adventure the little child loves for its own sake. Later, when he is about eleven or twelve, he loves it for its motive. This love of adventure is part of the charm of *Red Riding Hood*, of the *Three Bears*, of the *Three Pigs*, or of any good tale you might mention.

Success. The child likes the fairy tale to tell him of some one who succeeds. He admires the little pig Speckle who outwitted the Wolf in getting to the field of turnips first, or in going to the apple tree at Merry-Garden, or to the fair at Shanklin; who built his house of brick which would defy assault; and whose cleverness ended the Wolf's life. This observation of success teaches the child to admire masterliness, to get the motto, *Age quod agis*, stamped into his child life from the beginning. It influences character to follow such conduct as that of the Little Red Hen, who took a grain of wheat, — her little mite, — who planted it, reaped it, made it into bread, and then ate it; who, in spite of the Goose and the Duck, secured to herself the reward of her labors.

Action. Akin to his love of running, skipping, and jumping, to his enjoyment in making things go and in seeing others make things go, is the child's desire for action in his fairy tales; and this is just another way of saying he wants his fairy tales to parallel life. Action is the special charm of the Gingerbread Boy, who opened the oven door and so marvelously ran along, outrunning an old Man, an old Woman, a little Boy, two Well-Diggers, two Ditch-Diggers, a Bear, and a Wolf, until he met the Fox waiting by the corner of the fence. *Dame Wiggins of Lee and Her Seven Wonderful Cats* — a humorous tale written by Mrs. Sharp, a lady of ninety, edited by John Ruskin, who added the third, fourth, eighth, and ninth stanzas, and illustrated by Kate Greenaway — has this pleasing trait of action to a unique degree. So also has *The Cock, the Mouse, and the Little Red Hen,* a modern tale by Félicité Lefèvre. This very popular tale among children is a retelling of two old tales combined, *The Little Red Hen* and the Irish *Little Rid Hin.*

Humor. The child loves a joke, and the tale that is humorous is his special delight. Humor is the source of pleasure in *Billy Bobtail,* where the number of animals and the noises they make fill the tale with hilarious fun. There is most pleasing humor in *Lambikin.* Here the reckless hero frolicked about on his little tottery legs. On his way to Granny's house, as he met the Jackal, the Vulture, the Tiger, and the Wolf, giving a little frisk, he said, —

To Granny's house I go,
Where I shall fatter grow,
Then you can eat me so!

Later, on returning, when the animals asked, " Have you seen Lambikin? " cozily settled within his Drumikin, laughing and singing to himself, he called out slyly —

Lost in the forest, and so are you,
On, little Drumikin! Tum-pa, tum-too!

Humor is the charm, too, of Andersen's *Snow Man.* Here the child can identify himself with the Dog and thereby join in the sport which the Dog makes at the Snow Man's expense, just as if he himself were enlightening the Snow Man about the Sun, the Moon, and the Stove. There is most delightful humor in *The Cat and the Mouse in Partnership*, where the Cat has the face to play upon the credulity of the poor housekeeper Mouse, who always " stayed at home and did not go out into the daytime." Returning home from his ventures abroad he named the first kitten Top-Off, the second one Half-Out, and the third one All-Out; while instead of having attended the christening of each, as he pretended, he secretly had been visiting the jar of fat he had placed for safe-keeping in the church.

Poetic justice. Emotional satisfaction and moral satisfaction based on emotional instinct appeal to the child. He pities the plight of the animals in the *Bremen Town Musicians*, and he wants them to find a refuge, a safe home. He is glad that the robbers are chased out, his sense of right and wrong is satisfied. Poetic justice suits him. This is one reason why fairy tales make a more definite impression often than life — because in the tale the retribution follows the act so swiftly that the child may see it, while in life " the mills of the gods grind slowly," and even the adult who looks cannot see them grind. The child wants Cinderella to gain the reward for her goodness; and he wishes the worthy Shoemaker and his Wife, in the *Elves and the Shoemaker*, to get the riches their industry deserves.

The imaginative. Fairy tales satisfy the activity of the child's imagination and stimulate his fancy. Some beautiful spring day, perhaps, after he has enjoyed an excursion to a field or meadow or wood, he will want to follow Andersen's Thumbelina in her travels. He will follow her as she floats on a lily pad, escapes a frog of a husband, rides on a butterfly, lives in the house of a field-mouse, escapes a mole of a husband, and then rides on the back of a friendly swallow to reach the south land and to become queen of the flowers. Here there is much play of fancy. But even when the episodes are homely and the situations familiar, as in *Little Red Hen*, the act of seeing them as distinct images and of following them with interest feeds the imagination. For while the elements are familiar, the combination is unusual; and this nourishes the child's ability to remove from the usual situation, which is the essential element in all originality. By entering into the life of the characters and identifying himself with them, he develops a large sympathy and a sense of power, he gains insight into life, and a care for the interests of the world. Thus imagination grows " in flexibility, in scope, and in sympathy, till the life which the individual lives is informed with the life of nature and of society," and acquires what Professor John Dewey calls Culture.

Animals. Very few of the child's fairy tales contain no animals. Southey said of a home: "A house is never perfectly furnished for enjoyment unless there is in it a child rising three years old and a kitten rising six weeks; kitten is in the animal world what a rose-bud is in a garden." In the same way it might be said of fairy tales: No tale is quite suited to the little child unless in it there is at least one animal. Such animal tales are *The Bremen Town Musicians*, *Henny Penny*, *Ludwig and Marleen* and *The Elephant's Child.* The episode of the hero or heroine and the friendly animal, as we find it retained in Two-Eyes and her little Goat, was probably a folk-lore convention — since dropped — common to the beginning of many of the old tales. It indicates how largely the friendly animal entered into the old stories.

A portrayal of human relations, especially with children. In *Cinderella* the child is held by the unkind treatment inflicted upon Cinderella by her Stepmother and the two haughty Sisters. He notes the solicitude of the Mother of the Seven Kids in guarding them from the Wolf. In the *Three Bears* he observes a picture of family life. A little child, on listening to *The Three Pigs* for the first time, was overwhelmed by one thought and cried out, "And did n't the Mother come home any more?" Naturally the child would be interested especially in children, for he is like the older boy, who, when looking at a picture-book, gleefully exclaimed, "That 's me!" He likes to put himself in the place of others. He can do it most readily if the character is a small individual like Red Riding Hood who should obey her mother; or like Goldilocks who must not wander in the wood; or like Henny Penny who went to take a walk and was accosted by, "Where are you going?" In *Brother Rabbit and the Little Girl* the Little Girl takes the keenest enjoyment in putting herself in the customary grown-up's place of granting permission, while the Rabbit takes the usual child's place of mentioning a request with much persuasion. The child is interested, too, in the strange people he meets in the fairy tales: the clever little elves who lived in the groves and danced on the grass; the dwarfs who inhabited the earth-rocks and the hills; the trolls who dwelt in the wild pine forest or the rocky spurs, who ate men or porridge, and who fled at the noise of bells; the fairies who pleased with their red caps, green jackets, and sprightly ways; the beautiful fairy godmother who waved her wonderful wand; or those lovely fairy spirits who appeared at the moment when most needed — just as all best friends do — and who could grant, in a twinkling, the wish that was most desired.

The diminutive. This pleasure in the diminutive is found in the interest in the fairy characters, Baby Bear, Little Billy-Goat, Little Pig, the Little Elves, Teeny Tiny, Thumbelina, and Tom Thumb, as well as in tiny objects. In the *Tale of Tom Thumb* the child is captivated by the miniature chariot drawn by six small mice, the tiny butterfly-wing shirt and chicken-skin boots worn by Tom, and the small speech produced by him at court, when asked his name: —

> My name is Tom Thumb,
> From the Fairies I come;
> When King Arthur shone,
> This court was my home.
> In me he delighted,
> By him I was knighted.
> Did you never hear of
> Sir Thomas Thumb?

Doll i' the Grass contains a tiny chariot made from a silver spoon and drawn by two white mice, and *Little Two-Eyes* gives a magic table. The child takes keen delight in the fairy ship which could be folded up and put into a pocket, and in the wonderful nut-shell that could bring forth beautiful silver and gold dresses. The little wagon of Chanticleer and Partlet that took them a trip up to the hill, and the tiny mugs and beds, table and plates, of Snow White's cottage in the wood — such as these all meet the approval of child-nature.

Rhythm and repetition. The child at first loves sound; later he loves sound and sense, or meaning. Repetition pleases him because he has limited experience and is glad to come upon something he has known before. He observes and he wants to compare, but it is a job. Repetition saves him a task and boldly proclaims, "We are the same." Such is the effect of the repetitive expressions which we find in *Teeny Tiny*: as, "Now when the teeny-tiny woman got home to her teeny-tiny house, she was a teeny-tiny bit tired"; or, in *Little Jack Rollaround*, who cried out with such vigorous persistence, "Roll me around!" and called to the moon, "I want the people to see me!" In *The Little Rabbit Who Wanted Red Wings*, one of the pleasantest tales for little children, the White Rabbit said to his Mammy, "Oh, Mammy, I wish I had a long gray tail like Bushy Tail's; I wish I had a back full of bristles like Mr. Porcupine's; I wish I had a pair of red rubbers like Miss Puddleduck's." At last, when he beheld the tiny red-bird at the Wishing-Pond, he said, "Oh, I wish I had a pair of little red wings!" Then, after getting his wings, when he came home at night and his Mammy no longer knew him, he repeated to Mr. Bushy Tail, Miss Puddleduck, and old Mr. Ground Hog, the same petition to sleep all night, "Please, kind Mr. Bushy Tail, may I sleep in your house all night?" etc. Repetition here aids the child in following the characters, the story, and its meaning. It is a distinct help to unity and to clearness.

The Elephant's Child is an example of how the literary artist has used this element of repetition, and used it so wonderfully that the form is the matter and the tale cannot be told without the artist's words. "'Satiable curtiosity," "the banks of the great, grey-green, greasy, Limpopo River, all set about with fever-trees," and "'Scuse me," are but a few of those expressions for which the child will watch as eagerly as one does for a signal light known to be due. The repetition of the one word, "curtiosity," throughout the tale, simply makes the point of the whole story and makes that point delightfully impressive.

Rhythm and repetition also make a bodily appeal, they appeal to the child's motor sense and instinctively get into his muscles. This is very evident in *Brother Rabbit's Riddle*: —

> De big bird bob en little bird sing;
> De big bee zoon en little bee sting,
> De little man lead en big hoss foller —
> Kin you tell wat's good fer a head in a holler?

The song in *Brother Rabbit and the Little Girl* appeals also to the child's sense of sound: —

> De jay-bird hunt de sparrer-nes;
> De bee-martin sail all 'roun';
> De squer'l, he holler from de top er de tree,
> Mr. Mole, he stay in de ground;
> He hide en he stay twel de dark drap down —
> Mr. Mole, he hide in de groun'.

The simple and the sincere. The child's taste for the simple and the sincere is one reason for the appeal which Andersen's tales make. In using his stories it is to be remembered that, although Andersen lacked manliness in being sentimental, he preserved the child's point of view and gave his thought in the true nursery story's mode of expression. Since real sentiment places the emphasis on the object which arouses feeling and the sentimental places the emphasis on the feeling, sincerity demands that in using Andersen's tales, one lessen the sentimental when it occurs by omitting to give prominence to the feeling. Andersen's tales reflect what is elementary in human nature, childlike fancy, and emotion. His speech is characterized by the simplest words and conceptions, an avoidance of the abstract, the use of direct language, and a naïve poetic expression adapted to general comprehension. He is not to be equaled in child conversations. The world of the fairy tale must be simple like the world Andersen has given us. It must be a world of genuine people and honest occupations in order to form a suitable background for the supernatural. Only fairy tales possessing simplicity are suited to the oldest kindergarten child of five or six years. To the degree that the child is younger than five years, he should be given fewer and fewer fairy tales. Those given should be largely realistic stories of extreme simplicity.

Unity of effect. The little child likes the short tale, for it is a unity he can grasp. If you have ever listened to a child of five spontaneously attempting to tell you a long tale he has not grasped, and have observed how the units of the tale have become confused in the mind that has not held the central theme, you then realize how harmful it is to give a child too long a story. Unity demands that there be no heaping up of sensations, but neat, orderly, essential incidents, held together by one central idea. The tale must go to the climax directly. It must close according to Uncle Remus's idea when he says, " De tale ain't persoon atter em no furder don de place whar dey [the characters] make der disappear'nce." It will say what it has to say and lose no time in saying it; and often it will attempt to say only one thing. It will be remarkable as well for what it omits as for what it tells. The Norse *Doll i' the Grass* well illustrates this unity. Boots set out to find a wife and found a charming little lassie who could spin and weave a shirt in one day, though of course the shirt was tiny. He took her home and then celebrated his wedding with the pleasure of the king. This unity, which is violated in Grimm's complicated *Golden Bird*, appears pleasantly in *The Little Pine Tree that Wished for New Leaves*. Here one feeling dominates the tale, the Pine Tree was no longer contented. So she wished, first for gold leaves, next for glass leaves, and then for leaves like those of the oaks and maples. But the robber who stole her gold leaves, the storm that shattered her glass leaves, and the goat that ate her broad green leaves, changed her feeling of discontent, until she wished at last to have back her slender needles, green and fair, and awoke next morning, happy and contented.

Fairy tales for little children must avoid certain elements opposed to the interests of the very young child. Temperaments vary and one must be guided by the characteristics of the individual child. But while the little girl with unusual power of visualization, who weeps on hearing of Thumbling's travels down the cow's mouth in company with the hay, may be the exception, she proves the rule: the little child generally should not have the tale that creates an emotion of horror or deep feeling of pain. This standard would determine what tales should not be given to the child of kindergarten age:—

The tale of the witch. The witch is too strange and too fearful for the child who has not learned to distinguish the true from the imaginative. This would move *Hansel and Grethel* into the second-grade work and *Sleeping Beauty* preferably into the work of the first grade. The child soon gains sufficient experience so that later the story impresses, not the strangeness.

The tale of the dragon. This would eliminate *Siegfried and the Dragon.* A dragon is too fearful a beast and produces terror in the heart of the child. Tales of heroic adventure with the sword are not suited to his strength. He has not yet entered the realm of bold adventure where Perseus and Theseus and Hercules display their powers. The fact that hero-tales abound in delightful literature is not adequate reason for crowding the *Rhinegold Legends, Wagner Stories,* and *Tales of King Arthur,* into the kindergarten. Their beauty and charm do not make it less criminal to present to little children such a variety of images as knighthood carries with it. These tales are not sufficiently simple for the little child, and must produce a mental confusion and the crudest of returns.

Giant tales. This would omit *Jack and the Beanstalk, Jack the Giant-Killer,* and *Tom Hickathrift,* moving them up into the primary field. A little girl, when eating tongue, confidingly asked, "Whose tongue?" and when told, "A cow's," immediately questioned with tenderness, "Don't he feel it?" Thereafter she insisted that she did n't like tongue. To a child of such sensibilities the cutting off of heads is savage and gruesome and should not be given a chance to impress so prominently. Life cannot be without its strife and struggle, but the little child need not meet everything in life at once. This does not mean that absolutely no giant tale would be used at this time. The tale of *Mr. Miacca*, in which "little Tommy could n't always be good and one day went round the corner," is a giant tale which could be used with young children because it is full of delightful humor. Because of the simplicity of Tommy's language and his sweet childishness it appeals to the child's desire to identify himself with the character. Tommy is so clever and inventive and his lively surprises so brimful of fun that the final effect is entirely pleasing.

Some tales of transformation. The little child is not pleased but shocked by the transformation of men into animals. A little girl, on looking at an illustration of *Little Brother and Sister*, remarked, "If my Sister would turn into a fawn I would cry." When the animals are terrifying, the transformation contains horror for the child. This, together with the length and complexity of the story, would move

Beauty and the Beast up into the second grade where the same transformation becomes an element of pleasure. A simple tale of transformation, such as *The Little Lamb and the Little Fish,* in which Gretchen becomes a lamb and Peterkin a little fish, is interesting but not horrible, and could be used. So also could a tale such as Grimm's *Fundevogel,* in which the brother and sister escape the pursuit of the witch by becoming, one a rosebush and the other a rose; later, one a church and the other a steeple; and a third time, one a pond and the other a duck. In both these tales we have the witch and transformation, but the effect contains no horror.

The tale of strange animal relations and strange creatures. *Tom Tit Tot,* which Jacobs considers the most delightful of all fairy tales, is brimful of humor for the older child, but here the tailed man is not suited to the faith and understanding of six years. *Rumpelstiltskin,* its parallel, must also be excluded. *The House in the Wood,* and its Norse parallel, *The Two Step-Sisters,* are both very beautiful, but are more suited to the second grade. In the kindergarten it is much better to present the tale which emphasizes goodness, rather than the two just mentioned, which present the good and the bad and show what happens to both. Besides there is a certain elation resulting from the superior reward won by the good child which crowds out any pity for the erring child. Such elation is a form of selfishness and ought not to be emphasized. *Snow White and Rose Red* contains the strange dwarf, but it is a tale so full of love and goodness and home life that in spite of its length it could be used in the first grade.

Unhappy tales. The very little child pities, and its tender heart must be protected from depressing sadness as unrelieved as we find it in *The Little Match Girl.* The image of suffering impressed on a child, who cannot forget the sight of a cripple for days, is too intense to be healthful. The sorrow of the poor is one of the elements of life that even the very little child meets, and it is legitimate that his literature should include tales that call for compassion. But in a year or two, when he develops less impressionability and more poise, he is better prepared to meet such situations, as he must meet them in life.

The tale of capture. This would eliminate *Proserpine.* No more beautiful myth exists than this one of the springtime, but its beauty and its symbolism do not make it suitable for the kindergarten. It is more suited to the elementary child of the fourth grade. In fact, very few myths of any sort find a legitimate place in the kindergarten, perhaps only a few of the simpler *pourquois* tales. *The Legend of the Pied Piper of Hamelin,* which is very beautiful, and appeals to little children because of the piping and of the children following after, should be omitted from the kindergarten because the capture at the close — the disappearance of the children in the hill — is tragic in pathos. It is better to leave the literature as it is and offer it later when the child reaches the second grade. The effect of this tragic end has been realized by Josephine Scribner Gates, who (*St. Nicholas*, November, 1914) has given to the children, "And Piped Those Children Back Again." This is a modern completion of *The Pied Piper*. It most happily makes the little lame boy who was left in Hamelin when the Piper closed the door of the mountain, the means of the restoration of the other children to their parents.

The very long tale. This would omit *The Ugly Duckling. The Ugly Duckling* is a most artistic tale and one that is very true to life. Its characters are the animals of the barn-yard, the hens and ducks familiar to the little child's experience. But the theme and emotional interest working out at length through varied scenes, make it much better adapted to the capacities of a third-grade child. *The White Cat*, a feminine counterpart of *Puss-in-Boots* — which gives a most charming picture of how a White Cat, a transformed princess, helped a youth, and re-transformed became his bride — because of its length, is better used in the first grade at the same time with *Puss-in-Boots*. The same holds true of *Peter, Paul, and Espen*, or its parallel, Laboulaye's *Poucinet*. This is a fine tale telling how the youngest of three sons succeeded in winning the king's favor and finally the princess and half the kingdom. First, Espen had to cut down the giant oak that shadowed the palace and dig a well in the courtyard of the castle deep enough to furnish water the entire year. But after winning in these tests, he is required to conquer a great Ogre who dwells in the forest, and later to prove himself cleverer in intellect than the princess by telling the greater falsehood. It is evident that not only the subject-matter but the working out of the long plot are much beyond kindergarten children.

The complicated or the insincere tale. This would eliminate a tale of complicated structure, such as Grimm's *Golden Bird*; and many of the modern fairy tales, which will be dealt with later on.

The fairy tales mentioned above are all important tales which the child should receive at a later time when he is ready for them. They are mentioned because they all have been suggested for kindergarten use. The whole field of children's literature is largely unclassified and ungraded as yet, and such arrangements as we possess show slight respect for standards. There is abundant material for the youngest, and much will be gained by omitting to give the very young what they will enjoy a little later, much better and with freshness. It is true that a few classics are well-suited to the child at any age, such as *Alice in Wonderland*, *The Jungle Books*, and *Uncle Remus Tales*. In regard to this grading of the classics, Lamb in *Mackery End*, speaking of his sister's education, said, " She was tumbled early, by accident or design, into a spacious closet of good old English reading, without much selection or prohibition, and browsed at will upon that fair and wholesome pasturage. Had I twenty girls they should be brought up exactly in this fashion." Lamb would have argued: Set the child free in the library and let him choose for himself, and feed on great literature, those stories which give general types of situation and character, which give the simplest pictures of a people at different epochs. But with all due respect to Lamb it must be said that Lamb is not living in this scientific day of discovery of the child's personality and of accurate attention to the child's needs. Because the *Odyssey* is a great book and will give much to any child does not prove at all that the same child would not be better off by reading it when his interests reach its life. This outlook on the problem would eliminate the necessity of having the classics rewritten from a new moral viewpoint, which is becoming a custom now-a-days, and which is to be frowned upon, for it deprives the literature of much of its vigor and force.

II. THE FAIRY TALE AS LITERATURE

From the point of view of the child, we have seen that in a subjective sense, fairy tales must contain the interests of children. In an objective sense, rather from the point of view of literature, let us now consider what fairy tales must contain, what are the main standards which determine the value of fairy tales as literature, and as such, subject-matter of real worth to the child.

The old tale will not always be perfect literature; often it will be imperfect, especially in form. Yet the tale should be selected with the standards of literature guiding in the estimate of its worth and in the emphasis to be placed upon its content. Such relating of the tale to literary standards would make it quite impossible later in the primary grades when teaching the reading of *Three Pigs*, to put the main stress on a mere external like the expression of the voice. A study of the story as literature would have centered the attention on the situation, the characters, and the plot. If the voice is receiving training in music and in the phonics of spelling, then when the reading of the tale is undertaken it will be a willing servant to the mind which is concentrating on the reality, and will express what the thought compels.

The fairy tale first must be a classic in reality even if it lacks the crowning touch of perfect form given through the re-treatment of a literary artist. In *Reynard the Fox* we have an exact example of the folk-tale that has been elevated into literature. But this was possible only because the tales originally possessed the qualities of a true classic. " A true classic," Sainte-Beuve has said, " is one which enriches the human mind, has increased its treasure and caused it to advance a step, which has discovered some moral and unequivocal truth or revealed some eternal passion in that heart where all seemed known and discovered; which is an expression of thought, observation, or invention, in no matter what form, only provided it be broad and great, refined and sensible, sane and beautiful in itself; which speaks in its own peculiar style which is found to be also that of the whole world, a style new and old, easily contemporary with all time." Immediately some of the great fairy tales stand out as answering to this test — *Red Riding Hood, Sleeping Beauty, Jack and the Beanstalk, Cinderella, Jack the Giant-Killer,* — which has been said to be the epitome of the whole life of man — *Beauty and the Beast,* and a crowd of others. Any fairy tale which answers to the test of a real classic must, like these, show itself to contain for the child a permanent enrichment of the mind.

Fairy tales must have certain qualities which belong to all literature as a fine art, whether it is the literature of knowledge or the literature of power. Literature is not the book nor is it life; but literature is the sense of life, whose artist is the author, and the medium he uses is words, language. It is good art when his sense of life is truth, and fine art when there is beauty in that truth. The one essential beauty of literature is in its essence and does not depend upon any decoration. As words are the medium, literature will distinguish carefully among them and use them as the painter, for particular lights and shades. According to Pater literature must have two qualities, mind and soul. Literature will have mind when it has that architectural sense of structure which foresees the end in the beginning and keeps all the parts related in a harmonious unity. It will have soul when it has that "vagrant sympathy" which makes it come home to us and which makes it suggest what it does not say. Test the *Tale of Cinderella* by this standard. As to mind, it makes one think of a bridge in which the very keystone of the structure is the condition that Cinderella return from the ball by the stroke of twelve. And its "vagrant sympathy" is quite definite enough to reach a maid of five, who remarked: "If I'd have been Cinderella, I would n't have helped those ugly sisters, would you?"

If the fairy tale stands the test of literature it must have proved itself, not only a genuine classic according to Sainte-Beuve's standard, and a tale possessing qualities of mind and soul according to Pater's *Style*, but it must have shown itself also a work owning certain features distinguishing it as literature. These particular literary marks which differentiate the literary tale from the ordinary prose tale have been pointed out by Professor Winchester in his *Principles of Literary Criticism.* They apply to the old tale of primitive peoples just as well as to the modern tale of to-day. As literature the tale must have: (1) a power to appeal to the emotions; (2) a power to appeal to the imagination; (3) a basis of truth; and (4) a form more or less perfect.

(1) A power to appeal to the emotions. This appeal to the emotions is its unique distinguishing literary trait. Literature appeals, not to the personal emotions but to the universal ones. For this reason, through literature the child may come in time to develop a power of universal sympathy, which is not the least value literature has to bestow upon him, for this sympathy will become a benediction to all those with whom he may have to deal. In order that emotion in the tales may be literary — make a permanent appeal — according to Professor Winchester's standards, it must have justness given by a deep and worthy cause; vividness so that it may enlarge and thrill; a certain steadiness produced by everything in the tale contributing to the main emotion; a variety resulting from contrasts of character; and a high quality obtained through its sympathy with life and its relation to the conduct of life, so that the feeling for the material beauty of mere sights and sounds is closely related to the deepest suggestions of moral beauty. The best literary tales will possess emotion having all five characteristics. Many tales will exhibit one or more of these traits conspicuously. No tale that is literature will be found which does not lay claim to some one of these qualities which appeal to the broadly human emotions.

Applying the test of emotion to fairy tales, *Cinderella* possesses a just emotion, Cinderella's cause is the cause of goodness and kindness and love, and deserves a just reward. *The Town Musicians of Bremen* exhibits vivid emotion, for all four characters are in the same desperate danger of losing life, all four unite to save it, and to find a home. Andersen's *Steadfast Tin Soldier* is a good example of steadiness of emotion, as it maintains throughout its message of courage. The Tin Soldier remained steadfast, whether on the table just escaped from the toy-box, or in the street after a frightful fall from the window, or spinning in a paper boat that bobbed, or sailing under the crossing, or lying at full length within the fish that swallowed him, or at last melting in the full glare of the hearth fire. It is a very good example, too, of vividness of emotion. *The Little Elves* illustrates steadiness of emotion, it is pervaded by the one feeling, that industry deserves reward. The French tale, *Drakesbill*, is especially delightful and humorous because "Bill Drake" perseveres in his happy, fresh vivacity, at the end of every rebuff of fortune, and triumphantly continues his one cry of, "Quack, quack, quack! When shall I get my money back?" *Lambikin* leaves the one distinct impression of light gaiety and happy-heartedness; and *The Foolish, Timid Rabbit* preserves steadily the one effect of the credulity of the animals, made all the more prominent by contrast to the wisdom of the Lion. Variety of emotion appears in tales such as *Cinderella, Little Two-Eyes, Sleeping Beauty*, and *Three Pigs*, where the various characters are drawn distinctly and their contrasting traits produce varied emotional effects. All the great fairy tales appeal to emotion of a high moral quality and it is this which is the source of their universal appeal. It is this high moral quality of the spiritual truth, which is the center of the tale's unity, holding together all the parts under one emotional theme. This is the source of the perennial freshness of the old tale; for while the immortal truth it presents is old, the personality of the child that meets it is new. For the child, the tale is new because he discovers in it a bit of himself he had not known before, and it retains for him a lasting charm so that he longs to hear it again and again. The beauty of truth, the reward of goodness, and the duty of fairness, give a high emotional quality to *Little Two-Eyes*; and *Sleeping Beauty* illustrates the blighting power of hatred to impose a curse and the saving power of love to overcome the works of hatred.

Considering folk-tales from the standpoint of emotion, if asked to suggest what author's work would rank in the same class, one is rather surprised to find, that for high moral quality, variety, and worthy cause, the author who comes to mind is none other than Shakespeare. Perhaps, with all due respect to literature's idol, one might even venture to question which receives honor by the comparison, Shakespeare or the folk-tales? It might be rather a pleasant task to discover who is the Cordelia, the Othello, the Rosalind, and the Portia of the folk-tales; or who the Beauty, the Bluebeard, the Cinderella, the Puss-in-Boots, and the Hop-o'-my-Thumb, of Shakespeare.

The little child is open to emotional appeal, his heart is tender and he is impressionable. If he feels with the characters in his tales he develops a power of emotion. In Andersen's *Snow Man* it is hard to say which seems more human to him or which makes more of an emotional appeal, the Snow Man or the Dog. He is sorry for the poor Shoemaker in *The Little Elves*, glad when he grows rich, delighted for the Elves when they receive their presents, and satisfied at the happy end. Since literature depicts life and character in order to awaken noble emotions, it follows that one must omit to present what awakens repulsive or degrading emotions. And it is for this reason, as has been mentioned under the heading "Elements to be avoided," that the tales of the witch and the dragon must be excluded, not for all time, but for the earliest years, when they awaken horror.

Through fairy tales we have seen that the emotional power of the child is strengthened. This has been effected because, in the tale just as truly as in life, action is presented in real situations; and back of every action is the motive force of emotion. This cumulative power of emotion, secured by the child through the handling of tales, will serve daily a present need. It will be the dynamic force which he will require for anything he wishes to accomplish in life. It will give the child the ability to use it in any situation similar to that in which it was acquired. It will make a difference in his speech; he will not have to say so much, for what he does say will produce results. This growing power of emotion will carry over into feelings of relation and thus lead to judgment of values. This evaluation is the basis of reasoning and answers to the child's daily call to think from causes to consequences. This increasing power of emotion develops into the æsthetic sensibilites and so results in a cultivation of taste and an understanding of life. Emotion therefore leads to appreciation, which, when logically developed, becomes expression. Fairy tales, thus, in conducting emotional capacity through this varied growth and toward this high development, hold an educational value of no mean order.

(2) **The power to appeal to the imagination.** Emotion can be aroused by showing the objects which excite emotion. Imagination is this power to see and show things in the concrete. Curry says, "Whenever the soul comes vividly in contact with any fact, truth, etc., whenever it takes them home to itself with more than common intensity, out of that meeting of the soul and its object there arises a thrill of joy, a glow of feeling. It is the faculty that can create ideal presence." When through imagination we select spontaneously from the elements of experience and combine into new wholes, we call it creative imagination. — The creative imagination will be viewed here as it appears in action in the creative return given

by the child to his fairy tales. — When we emphasize a similarity seen in mere external or accidental relations or follow suggestions not of an essential nature in the object, we call it fancy. Ruskin, in his *Modern Painters*, vol. I, part III, *Of the Imaginative Faculty*, would distinguish three classes of the imagination: —

(*a*) *The associative imagination.* This is the power of imagination by which we call into association other images that tend to produce the same or allied emotion. When this association has no common ground of emotion it is fancy. The test for the associative imagination, which has the power to combine ideas to form a conception, is that if one part is taken away the rest of the combination goes to pieces. It requires intense simplicity, harmony, and absolute truth. Andersen's *Fairy Tales* are a perfect drill for the associative imagination. Literature parallels life and what is presented calls up individual experience. Any child will feel a thrill of kinship with the experiences given in *The Tin Soldier* — a little boy's birthday, the opening of the box, the counting of the soldiers, and the setting of them upon the table. And because here Andersen has transformed this usual experience with a vivacity and charm, the tale ranks high as a tale of imagination. *Little Ida's Flowers* and *Thumbelina* are tales of pure fancy. Grimm's *The Straw, the Coal, and the Bean* and *The Spindle, the Shuttle, and the Needle* rank in the same class, as also do the Norse *The Doll i' the Grass* and the English *Tom Thumb*.

(*b*) *The penetrative imagination.* This power of imagination shows the real character of a thing and describes it by its spiritual effects. It sees the heart and inner nature of things. Through fancy the child cannot reach this central viewpoint since fancy deals only with externals. Through the exercise of this power the child develops insight, intuition, and a perception of spiritual values, and gains a love of the ideal truth and a perpetual thirst for it. He develops genuineness, one of the chief virtues of originality. He will tend not to have respect for sayings or opinions but will seek the truth, be governed by its laws, and hold a passion for perfection. This power of imagination makes of him a continual seeker, " a pilgrim upon earth." Through the penetrative imagination the child forgets himself and enters into the things about him, into the doings of Three Pigs or the adventures of Henny Penny.

(*c*) *The contemplative imagination.* This is that special phase of the imagination that gives to abstract being consistency and reality. Through the contemplative imagination the child gains the significance of meaning and discerns the true message of the tale. When merely external resemblance is caught, when the likeness is forced, and the image created believed in, we have fancy. The contemplative imagination interprets the past in the tale and relates it to the future. It shows what is felt by indicating some aspect of what is seen. Through the exercise of this power the child develops the capacity to see. This capacity has received a high estimate from Ruskin, who said, "Hundreds of people can talk for one who can think, thousands can think for one who can see." For language-training the capacity to see gives that ability to image words which results in mental growth.

The labor of the spirit seeking the full message of the fairy tale, often is rewarded with bits of philosophy which are the essence of its personal wisdom. Even the Woman Suffragists of our day might be amused to find, in *The Cat and Mouse in Partnership*, this side-light on one of their claims. The Mouse said she did not know what to think of the curious names, Top-off, Half-Out, and All-Out, which the Cat had chosen. To which the Cat replied, "That is because you always stay at home. You sit here in your soft gray coat and long tail, and these foolish whims get into your head. It is always the way when one does not go out in the daytime." Sometimes the philosophy of the tale is expressed not at all directly. This is the case in Andersen's *The Emperor's New Suit*, a gem in story-telling art — more suited to the second grade — where the purpose of the story is veiled, and the satire or humor is conveyed through a very telling word or two. — "'I will send my *old, honest* minister to the weavers,' thought the Emperor. And the old, honest minister went to the room where the two swindlers sat working at empty looms.

'Heaven preserve me!' thought the old minister, opening his eyes wide. 'Why, I cannot see anything!' — But he did not say so." The entire tale is a concrete representation of one point; and the concreteness is so explicit that at the close of the story its philosophy easily forms itself into the implied message of worldly wisdom: People are afraid to speak truth concerning much through cowardice or through fear of acting otherwise than all the world. The philosophy underlying *The Steadfast Tin Soldier* is even finer as a bit of truth than the perfect art of the literary story: That what happens in life does not matter so much as the way you take it. The Tin Soldier always remained steadfast, no matter what happened. Kipling's *Elephant's Child* is more charming than ever when looked at from the standpoint of its philosophy. It might be interpreted as an allegory answering the question, "How should one get experience?" a theme which cannot be said to lack in universal appeal. *The Ugly Duckling* is full of sayings of philosophy that contribute to its complete message. The Cat and the Hen to whom the Duckling crept for refuge said, "We and the world," and could not bear a difference of opinion. "You may believe me," said the Hen, "because I tell you the truth. That is the way to tell your friends." Their treatment of the Duckling expressed the philosophy: "If you can't do what I can you 're no good." The Hen said to him, "You have nothing to do, that 's why you have such strange ideas." The

Duckling expressed his philosophy by saying quietly, "You don't understand me."

These bits of philosophy often become compressed into expressions which to-day we recognize as proverbs. The words of the Mother Duck, "Into the water he goes if I have to kick him in," became a Scandinavian proverb. "A little bird told it," a common saying of to-day, appears in Andersen's *Nightingale* and in *Thumbelina.* But this saying is traceable at least to the third story of the fourth night in Straparola, translated by Keightley, *The Dancing Water, the Singing Apple, and the Beautiful Green Bird,* in which the bird tells the King that his three guests are his own children. "Even a cat may look at a king," is probably traceable to some fairy tale if not to *Puss-in-Boots.* The philosophy in the fairy tales and the proverbs that have arisen in them, are subjects which offer to the adult much pleasure and fruitfulness.

But one must ask, "Does this philosophy appeal to the child? Is it not adult wisdom foreign to his immaturity?" The old folk-tales are the products of adult minds; but the adults were grown-ups that looked upon the world with the eyes of children, and their philosophy often was the philosophy of childhood. For childhood has its philosophy; but because it meets with repression on so many sides it usually keeps it to itself. When given freedom and self-activity and self-expression, the child's philosophy appears also. And it is the inner truth of the tale rather than the outer forms of sense and shapes of beauty which, when suited to the little child, appeals to this child-philosophy and makes the deepest impression upon him.

In the literary fairy tale there often appears a philosophy which is didactic and above and beyond the child's knowledge of the world. It remains a question how much this adult philosophy appeals to him. Although his tales were written for his grandchildren, so finished a telling of the tale as we find in Laboulaye, with its delightful hits of satire, appeals more to the grown-up versed in the ways of the world. But the sage remarks of worldly wisdom of Uncle Remus could not fail to impress a little boy: " Go where you will and when you may, and stay long ez you choosen ter stay, en right dar en den you 'll sholy fin' dat folks what git full er consate en proudness is gwine ter git it tuck out 'm um." — Uncle Remus treated the little boy as if he was "pestered with sense, like grown-ups," and surely the little boy gained much amusement from sayings such as these: " If you know the man that would refuse to take care of himself, I 'd like mighty well if you 'd point him out." — " Well, well," said Uncle Remus soothingly, " in deze low groun's er sorrer, you des got to lean back en make allowances fer all sorts er folks. You got ter low fer dem dat knows too much same ez dem what knows too little. A heap er sayin's en a heap er doin's in dis roun' worl' got ter be tuck on trus'. " — The child does not get the full force of the philosophy but he gets what he can and that much sinks in.

It is through the contemplative imagination that the child realizes the meaning of particular tales. He learns: that *Cinderella* means that goodness brings its own reward; that *Three Pigs* means that the wise build with care and caution, with foresight; that *Star Dollars* means compassion for others and kindness to them; and that *Red Riding Hood* means obedience.

The power of the contemplative imagination is based on the indistinctness of the image. It suggests, too, the relation between cause and effect, which reason afterwards proves; and therefore it is a direct aid to science. In the tales there are expressed facts of truth symbolically clothed which science since then has discovered. And now that folk-lore is being studied seriously to unfold all it gives of an earlier life, perhaps this new study may reveal some new truths of science hidden in its depths. The marvels of modern shoe manufacture were prophesied in *The Little Elves*, and the power of electricity to hold fast was foretold in *Dummling and his Golden Goose*. The wonders of modern machinery appeared in the magic axe of Espen that hit at every stroke; and the miracle of modern canals sees a counterpart in the spring which Espen brought to the giant's boiling-pot in the wood. The magic sleep from which there was an awakening, even after a hundred years, may have typified hypnotism and its strange power upon man. These are realizations of some of the wonders of fairyland. But there may be found lurking in its depths many truths as yet undiscovered by science. Perhaps the dreams of primitive man may suggest to the present-day scientist new possibilities. — What primitive man has done in fancy present-day man can do in reality.

(3) **A basis of truth.** All fine emotional effects arise from truth. The tale must hold the mirror and show an image of life. It must select and combine facts which will suggest emotion but the facts must be a true expression of human nature. The tale, whether it is realistic in emphasizing the familiar, the commonplace, and the present, or romantic in emphasizing the strange, the heroic, and the remote, must be idealistic to interpret truly the facts of life by high ideals. If the tale has this basis of truth the child will gain, through his handling of it, a body of facts. This increases his knowledge and strengthens his intellect. And it is to be remembered that, for the child's all-round development, the appeal of literature to the intellect is a value to be emphasized equally with the appeal to the emotions and to the imagination. Speaking of the nature of the intellect in his essay on *Intellect*, Emerson has said: "We do not determine what we will think. We only open our senses, clear away as we can all obstruction from the fact, and suffer the intellect to see." Attention to the intellectual element in literature gives a power of thought. The consideration of the truth of the fairy tale aids the child

to clear, definite thinking because the experience of the tale is ordered from a beginning, through a development, to a climax, and to a conclusion. It assists him to form conclusions because it presents results of circumstances and consequences of conduct. Continued attention to the facts, knowledge, and truth presented in the tales, helps the child to grow a sincerity of spirit. This leads to that love of actual truth, which is one of the armors of middle life, against which false opinion falls harmless.

(4) **A form, more or less perfect.** Form is the union of all the means which the writer employs to convey his thought and emotion to the reader. Flaubert has said, " Among all the expressions of the world there is but *one*, one form, one mode, to express what I want to say." — " Say what you have to say, what you have a will to say, in the simplest, the most direct and exact manner possible, with no surplusage," Walter Pater has spoken. Then the form and the matter will fit each other so perfectly there will be no unnecessary adornment.

In regard to form it is to be remembered that feeling is best awakened incidentally by suggestion. Words are the instruments, the medium of the writer. Words have two powers: the power to name what they mean, or denotation; and the power to suggest what they imply, or connotation. Words have the power of connotation in two ways: They may mean more than they say or they may produce emotional effect not only from meaning but also from sound. To make these two suggestive powers of words work together is the perfect art of Milton. Pope describes for us the relation of sound to sense in a few lines which themselves illustrate the point: —

> Soft is the strain when zephyr gently blows,
> And the smooth stream in smoother numbers flows.
> But when loud surges lash the sounding shore,
> The hoarse, rough verse, should like the torrent roar.
> When Ajax strives some rock's vast weight to throw,
> The line too labors, and the words move slow:
> Not so when swift Camilla scours the plain,
> Flies o'er the unbending corn and skims along the main.

When a kindergarten child, the most timid one of a group, on listening to the telling of *The Bremen Town Musicians*, at the description of the Donkey and the Dog coming to the Cat, sitting in the road with a face "dismal as three rainy Sundays," chuckled with humor at the word "dismal," it was not because she knew the meaning of the word or the significance of "three rainy Sundays," but because the sounds of the words and the facial expression of the story-teller conveyed the emotional effect, which she sensed.

The connection between sound and action appears in *Little Spider's First Web:* The Fly said, "Then I will *buzz*"; the Bee said, "Then I will *hum*"; the Cricket said, "Then I will *chirp*"; the Ant said, "Then I will *run* to and fro"; the Butterfly said, "Then I will *fly*"; and the Bird said, "Then I will *sing*." The effect is produced here because the words selected are concrete ones which visualize. Repetitive passages in the tales often contribute this effect of sound upon meaning, as we find in *The Three Billy-Goats Gruff:* "Trip, trap; trip, trap! went the bridge as the youngest Billy-Goat Gruff came to cross the bridge." The sound of the words in this entire tale contributes largely to the meaning. The Troll roared and said, "Now I 'm coming to gobble you up!" Usually the bits of rhyme interspersed throughout the tales, illustrate this contribution of sound to meaning; as in the *Three Pigs:* —

> Then I'll huff,
> And I'll puff,
> And I'll blow your house in!

Especially is this the case in tales dignified by the cante-fable form; such as Grimm's *Cinderella:* —

> Rustle and shake yourself, dear tree,
> And silver and gold throw down to me!

Or in *Little Two-Eyes:* —

> Little kid, bleat,
> I wish to eat!

Or in *The Little Lamb and the Little Fish:* —

> Ah, my brother, in the wood
> A lamb, now I must search for food!

The suggestive power of words to convey more than they mean, is produced, not only by the sounds contained in the words themselves, but also largely by the arrangement of the words and by the speech-tunes of the voice in speaking them. Kipling's *Elephant's Child* is a living example of the suggestive power of words. The "new, fine question" suggests that the Elephant's Child had a habit of asking questions which had not been received as if they were fine. "Wait-a-bit thorn-bush," suggests the Kolokolo Bird sitting alone on the bush in placid quiet. "And *still* I want to know what the crocodile has for dinner" implies that there had been enough spankings to have killed the curiosity, but contrary to what one would expect, it was living and active. When Kolokolo Bird said with a *mournful* cry, "Go to the banks of the great, grey-green, greasy Limpopo River," etc., the implication of *mournful* is, that there the Elephant's Child would have a sorry time of it. The expression, "dear families," which occurs so often, is full of delightful irony and suggests the vigorous treatment, anything but dear, which had come to the Elephant's Child from them.

Perfect form consists in the "ability to convey thought and emotion with perfect fidelity." The general qualities characteristic of perfect form, which have been outlined by Professor Winchester, in his *Principles of Literary Criticism*, are: (1) precision or clearness; (2) energy or force; (3) delicacy or emotional harmony; and (4) personality. Precision or clearness demands the precise value and meaning of words. It requires that words have the power of denotation. It appeals to the intellect of the reader or listener and demands that language be neither vague nor ambiguous nor obscure. Energy or force demands that perfect form have the quality of emotion. It requires that words have especially the power of connotation. It appeals to the emotions of the reader or listener and has the power to hold the attention. It demands of language that sympathy which will imply what it would suggest. Delicacy or emotional harmony demands that perfect form please the taste. It requires that an emotional harmony be secured by a selection and arrangement of the melody of words and of the emotional associations which, together with the meanings, are tied up in words. It demands that words have the power of perfect adaptation to the thought and feeling they express, that words have both the power of denotation and of connotation. It appeals to the æsthetic sense of the reader or listener, it gives to form beauty and charm. Personality is the influence of the author, the charm of individuality, and suggests the character of the writer.

At the same time that perfect form is characterized by the general qualities of precision, energy, delicacy, and personality, as composition consisting of words, sentences, paragraphs, or large wholes, its elements must be controlled by certain main principles, which have been presented by Professor Barrett Wendell in *English Composition.* Perfect form cannot possess the four general qualities above mentioned unless its elements are controlled by these main principles. These are: (1) the principle of sincerity; (2) the principle of unity; (3) the principle of mass; and (4) the principle of coherence. Sincerity demands of perfect form that it be a just expression. Unity demands that every composition should group itself about a central idea. There must be one story, all incidents subordinated, one main course of action, one main group of characters, and one tone of feeling to produce an emotional effect. Variety of action must lead to one definite result and variety of feeling to one total impression. Unity demands that the tale must have a plan that is complete, with no irrelevant material, and that there must be a logical order and a climax. Mass demands that the chief parts of every composition should readily catch the eye. It maintains a harmonious proportion of all the parts. Coherence demands of any composition that the relation of each part to its neighbors should be unmistakable, and that the order, forms, and connections of the parts preserve this relation.

When form secures a perfect adaptation of the language to the thought and feeling expressed, it may be said to possess style, in a broad sense of the word. In a more detailed sense, when form is characterized by precision, energy, delicacy, and personality, and at the same time has the elements of its composition controlled by the principles of sincerity, unity, mass, and coherence, it is said to possess style. The fairy tale which is a classic characterized by that perfect form called style, will possess the general qualities of precision, energy, delicacy, and personality; and the elements of its structure, its words, its sentences, its paragraphs, will display a control of the principles of sincerity, unity, mass, and coherence.

A tale which well illustrates the literary form possible to the child's tale, which may be said to possess that perfection of form we call style, and which may be used with the distinct aim to improve the child's English and perfect his language expression, is the modern realistic fairy tale, *Oeyvind and Marit.*

Oeyvind and Marit is so entirely realistic as to be excluded here, but the talking rhymes which the Mother sings to Oeyvind bring in the fairy element of the talking animals. In the form of this tale, the perfect fidelity with which the words fit the meaning is apparent — nothing seems superfluous. When Oeyvind asked Marit who she was, she replied: —

"I am Marit, mother's little one, father's fiddle, the elf in the house, granddaughter of Ole Nordistuen of the Heidi farms, four years old in the autumn, two days after the frost nights, I!"

And Oeyvind replied: —

"Are you really?" — and drew a long breath which he had not dared to do so long as she was speaking.

The story is full of instances illustrating precision, energy, and delicacy. In fact, almost any passage exemplifies the general qualities of form and the qualities of composition. The personality of the writer has given to the tale a poetic and dramatic charm of simplicity. Note the precision and delicacy displayed in the opening paragraph: —

Oeyvind was his name. A low barren cliff overhung the house in which he was born; fir and birch looked down on the roof, and wild cherry strewed flowers over it. Upon this roof there walked about a little goat, which belonged to Oeyvind. He was kept there that he might not go astray; and Oeyvind carried leaves and grass up to him. One fine day the goat leaped down, and away to the cliff; he went straight up and came where he never had been before.

Energy is apparent in the following passage:—

"Is it yours, this goat?" asked the girl again.

"Yes," he said, and looked up.

"I have taken such a fancy to the goat. You will not give it to me?"

"No, that I won't."

She lay kicking her legs and looking down at him, and then she said, "But if I give you a butter-cake for the goat, can I have him then?"

The justness of expression, the sincerity, is especially impressive when Oeyvind's Mother came out and sat down by his side when the goat no longer satisfied him and he wanted to hear stories of what was far away. There is emotional harmony too, because the words suggest the free freshness of the mountain air and the landscape which rose round about the Boy and his Mother.

So she told him how once everything could talk: "The mountain talked to the stream, and the stream to the river, the river to the sea, and the sea to the sky." — But then he asked if the sky did not talk to any one: "And the sky talked to the clouds, the clouds to the trees, the trees to the grass, the grass to the flies, the flies to the animals, the animals to the children, the children to the grown-up people. . . ." Oeyvind looked at the mountain, the trees, and the sky and had never seen them before.

There is delicacy or emotional harmony also in the Mother's song. When Oeyvind asked, "What does the Cat say?" his Mother sang: —

At evening softly shines the sun,
The cat lies lazy on the stone.
Two small mice,
Cream, thick and nice,
Four bits of fish,
I stole behind a dish,
And am so lazy and tired,
Because so well I have fared.

The unity is maintained through the central interest of the two Children and the goat.

The tale is characterized by fairly good mass. As the

story aims to portray a natural picture of child life, obviously it could not maintain a style of too great solidity and force, but rather would seek one of ease and naturalness. Mass, as shown in *Oeyvind and Marit*, appears in the following description of Oeyvind's play with the goat, after he first realized its return:—

He jumped up, took it by the two fore-legs, and danced with it as if it were a brother; he pulled its beard, and he was just going in to his mother with it, when he heard someone behind him; and looking, saw the girl sitting on the greensward by his side. Now he understood it all, and let go the goat.

The story of child-friendship is told in distinct little episodes which naturally connect. That unmistakable relation of the parts which is essential to coherence, appears in the following outline of the story:—

1. A new acquaintance: Oeyvind and Marit meet.
   The exchange of a goat for a cake.
   The departure of the goat. Marit sings to the goat.
   The return of the goat. Marit accompanies the goat.
2. New interests.
   The stories of what the animals say, told to Oeyvind by his Mother.
   The first day of school.
3. An old acquaintance renewed: Oeyvind again meets Marit at school.

The Children's love of the goat, the comradeship of Oeyvind and Marit, of Oeyvind and his Mother, and of Marit and her Grandfather, are elements which assist in producing coherence. The songs of Marit, and the songs and stories of Oeyvind's Mother, especially preserve the relation of parts. In the following paragraphs, which give distinct pictures, note the coherence secured internally largely by the succession of verbs denoting action and also by the denotation of the words.

When he came in, there sat as many children round a table as he had ever seen at church; others were sitting on their luncheon-boxes, which were ranged round the walls; some stood in small groups round a large printed card; the school-master, an old gray-haired man, was sitting on a stool by the chimney-corner, filling his pipe. They all looked up as Oeyvind and his mother entered, and the mill-hum ceased as if the water had suddenly been turned off. . . .

As he was going to find his seat, they all wanted to make room for him. He looked round a long time, while they whispered and pointed; he turned round on all sides, with his cap in his hand and his book under his arm. . . .

Just as the boy is going to turn round to the school-master, he sees close beside him, sitting down by the hearthstone on a little red painted tub, Marit, of the many names; she had covered her face with both hands, and sat peeping at him through her fingers.

The imagination is appealed to continually through the simple concrete expressions which present an image; as, "He grew hot all over, looked around about, and called, 'Killy-killy-killy-goat!' "

The emotional element is distinct and pleasing and contributes to the total impression of admiration for the characters. We admire Oeyvind for his fondness for the goat and for his pain at losing it; for his dissatisfaction in keeping it after Marit returned it, though she wanted it; for his delight in his Mother's stories; and for his pleasure in Marit's friendship at school. We admire Marit for her appreciation of the beautiful goat; for her obedience to her Grandfather; for her sorrow at giving up the goat; for her generosity in giving the neck-chain with it; and for the childish comradeship she gave to Oeyvind. We admire the goat for his loyalty to his little master. We trust the Grandfather who trained Marit to be fair and courteous; who guarded her from the cliff; and who bought for her another goat. We have faith in the Mother who had feeling for the little goat her son bartered for a cake; and who had the wisdom to sing for her little boy and tell him stories when he was sorrowful and needed new interests.

Undoubtedly *Oeyvind and Marit* is a tale which conveys its thought clearly and makes you feel its feeling, and therefore may be said to possess style in a broad sense. In a particular sense, because its form is marked by the four general qualities: precision, energy, delicacy, and personality; and its elements are controlled by the principles of composition: sincerity, unity, mass, and coherence, it therefore may be said to possess style.

An old tale which has a literary form unusual in its approach to the perfect literary form, is the Norse, *The Three Billy-Goats Gruff*, told by Dasent in *Tales from the Norse.* Indeed after looking carefully at this tale one is tempted to say that, for perfection of style, some of the old folk-tales are not to be equaled. Note the simple precision shown in the very first paragraph: —

> Once on a time there were three Billy-Goats, who were to go up to the hill-side to make themselves fat, and the name of all three was "Gruff."

Energy or force appeals to the emotions in the words of the tiny Billy-Goat Gruff to the Troll: —

> "Oh, no! pray don't take me. I'm too little, that I am," said the Billy-Goat; "wait a bit till the second Billy-Goat Gruff comes, he's much bigger."

There is emotional harmony displayed in the second paragraph; the words used fit the ideas: —

> On the way up was a bridge over a burn they had to cross; and under the bridge lived a great ugly Troll, with eyes as big as saucers, and a nose as long as a poker.

The quality of personality is best described, perhaps, by saying that the tale seems to have impersonality. Any charm of the story-tellers of the ages has entered into the body of the tale, which has become an objective presentment of a reality that concentrates on itself and keeps personality out of sight. The character of the tellers is shown however in the qualities of the tale. The charm of the primitive story-tellers has given the tale inimitable morning-dew freshness. This seems to result from a fine simplicity, a sprightly visualization, a quaint picturesqueness, a pleasing terseness, and an Anglo-Saxon vigor.

Sincerity is displayed in the words of the Troll and of the three Billy-Goats. Note the sincerity of little Billy-Goat Gruff: —

"Oh! it is only I, the tiniest Billy-Goat Gruff; and I'm going up to the hillside to make myself fat," said the Billy-Goat, with such a small voice.

The unity in this tale is unusually good. The central idea which groups all the happenings in the tale is: Three Billy-Goats are crossing a bridge to go up to the hillside to make themselves fat. There are four characters, three Goats and the Troll. All that happens in the tale contributes to the one effect of a bridge going trip, trap! as a Goat crossed it on his way up the hillside; of a Troll roaring: "Who's that tripping over my bridge?" of the explanation of the Billy-Goat; of the answer of the Troll, "Now I'm coming to gobble you up"; and of the Billy-Goat's final petition. Unity is emphasized by the repetition in the tale, as the three Billy-Goats successively cross the bridge and reply to the Troll. The climax is the big Billy-Goat Gruff's tramp across the bridge.

This tale is characterized by perfect mass, the paragraphs always end with words that deserve distinction, and the sentences have their strongest words at the points where the eye would most readily see them; as, "But just then up came the big Billy-Goat Gruff." The coherence is fine, and is secured largely by the cumulative plan in a threefold sense. The relation of the parts is unmistakable. The similarity and contrast evident in the episodes of the three Billy-Goats makes this relation very clearly defined. To make doubly sure the end has been reached the tale concludes: —

Snip, snap, snout,
This tale's told out.

Let us examine the folk-tale generally as to its literary form. The folk-tale originally did not come from the people in literary form. The tale was first told by some nameless primitive man, who, returning from some adventure of everyday life, would narrate it to a group of his comrades. First told to astonish and interest, or to give a warning of the penalty of breaking Nature's laws, or to teach a moral lesson, or to raise a laugh, later it became worked up into the fabulous stories of gods and heroes. These fabulous stories developed into myth-systems, and these again into household tales. By constant repetition from one generation to another, incidents likely to happen in everyday life, which represented universal experiences and satisfied common needs of childhood, were selected and combined. These gradually assumed a form of simplicity and literary charm, partly because, just as a child insists on accuracy, savage people adhered strictly to form in repeating the tale, and because it is a law of permanence that what meets the universal need will survive. The great old folk-tales have acquired in their form a clearness and precision; for in the process of telling and re-telling through the ages all the episodes became clearly defined. And as irrelevant details dropped out, there developed that unity produced by one dominant theme and one dominant mood. The great old folk-tales, then, naturally acquired a good classic literary form through social selection and survival. But many of the tales as we know them have suffered either through translation or through careless modern re-telling. Many of the folk-tales take on real literary form only through the re-treatment of a literary artist. Mrs. Steel, who has collected the *Tales of the Punjab*, tells how the little boys of India who seek to hold their listening groups will vary the incidents in a tale in different tellings, proving that the complete tale was not the original unit, but that single incidents are much more apt to retain their stock forms than plots. The combination we now have in a given tale was probably a good form once hit upon and thereafter transmitted.

Jacob (1785–1863) and William (1786–1859) Grimm, both fine scholars, incapable of any but good work, did not undertake to put the tale into literary form suited to children. They were interested in preserving folk-lore records for scientific purposes. And we must distinguish between the tale as a means of reflecting the ideals of social and religious life, of displaying all the genius of primitive man for science to interpret, and the tale as a means of pleasing and educating the child. The Grimms obtained most of their tales from the lips of people in Hesse and Hanau, Germany. They were very fortunate in securing many of the tales they were thirteen years in collecting, from an old nurse, Frau Viehmannin, the wife of a cowherd, who lived at Niederzwehrn, near Cassel, who told her story with exactness and never changed anything in repeating. Grimm himself said, "Our first care was faithfulness to the truth. We strove to penetrate into the wild forests of our ancestors, listening to their noble language, watching their pure customs, recognizing their ancient freedom and hearty faith." The Grimms sought the purity of a straightforward narration. They were against reconstruction to beautify and poetize the legends. They were not opposed to a free appropriation for modern and individual purposes. They kept close to the original, adding nothing of circumstance or trait, but rendering the stories in a style and language and development of detail which was their own literary German.

Perrault (1628–1703) had taken the old tales as his son, Charles, a lad of ten or twelve, told them. The father had told them to the son as he had gathered them up, intending to put them into verse after the manner of La Fontaine. The lad loved the stories and re-wrote them from memory for his father with such charming naïveté that the father chose the son's version in preference to his own, and published it. But the tales of Perrault, nevertheless, show the embellishment of the mature master-Academician's touch in subduing the too marvelous tone, or adding a bit of court manners, or a satirical hit at the vanity and failings of man.

Dasent (1820–96) has translated the Norse tales from the original collection of Asbjörnsen and Moe. Comrades from boyhood to manhood, scholar and naturalist, these two together had taken long walks into the secluded peasant districts and had secured the tales from the people of the dales and fells, careful to retain the folk-expressions. Dasent, with the instinct, taste, and skill of a true scholar, has preserved these tales of an honest manly race, a race of simple men and women, free and unsubdued. He has preserved them in their folk-language and in their true Norse setting. Harris (1848–1908) has given his tales in the dialect of Uncle Remus. Jacobs (1854–) has aimed to give the folk-tales in the language of the folk, retaining nurses' expressions, giving a colloquial and romantic tone which often contains what is archaic and crude. He has displayed freedom with the text, invented whole incidents, or completed incidents, or changed them. His object has been to fill children's imaginations with bright images. Andrew Lang (1844–1912) has given the tale mainly to entertain children. He has accepted translations from many sources and has given a straightforward narration. He has collected fairy tales indefatigably in his rainbow *Fairy Books*, but they are not always to be recommended for children.

Andersen (1805–75), like Perrault, made his tale for the child as an audience, and he too has put the tale into literary form. Andersen's tale is not the old tale, but an original creation, a number of which are based on old folk-material. Preserving the child's point of view, Andersen has enriched his language with a mastery of perfection and literary style. And the "mantle of Andersen" has, so far, fallen on no one.

To-day it is to be questioned if the child should be given the tale in nurses' talk. To-day children are best cared for by mothers who feel ignorant if they cannot tell their children stories, and who, having an appreciation of their mother English, want their children to hear stories, not only told by themselves rather than by their servants, but also told in the best literary form possible. They recognize that these earliest years, when the child is first learning his language, are the years for a perfection of form to become indelibly impressed. The fairy tale, like every piece of literature, is an organism and "should be put before the youngest child with its head on, and standing on both feet." The wholesale re-telling of every tale is to be deplored. And stories which have proved themselves genuine classics, which have a right to live, which have been handed down by tradition, which have been preserved by folk-lore records, and which have been rescued from oblivion, — in this age of books should have a literary form, which is part of their message, settled upon them. The Grimm tales await their literary master.

III. THE FAIRY TALE AS A SHORT-STORY

The fairy tale, then, which in an objective sense, from the standpoint of literature, has proved itself subject-matter of real worth, must be a classic, must have the qualities of mind and soul, must possess the power to appeal to the emotions, a power to appeal to the imagination, and it must have a basis of truth and a perfection of form. But in addition to possessing these characteristics, because the fairy tale is a special literary form, — the short-story, — as literature it must stand the test of the short-story.

The three main characteristics of the short-story, as given by Professor Brander Matthews in his *Philosophy of the Short-Story*, are originality of theme, ingenuity of invention, and brevity, or compression. A single effect must be conceived, and no more written than contributes to that effect. The story depends for its power and charm on (1) characters; (2) plot; and (3) setting. In *The Life and Letters of Robert Louis Stevenson*, by Graham Balfour, Stevenson has said, concerning the short-story: —

"There are, so far as I know, three ways, and three ways only, of writing a story. You may take a plot and fit characters to it, or you may take a character and choose incidents and situations to develop it, or lastly — you must bear with me while I try to make this clear. . . . You may take a certain atmosphere and get action and persons to express and realize it. I'll give you an example — *The Merry Men*. There I began with the feeling of one of those islands on the west coast of Scotland, and I gradually developed the story to express the sentiment with which the coast affected me."

According to the method by which the story was made, the emphasis will be on character, plot, or setting. Sometimes you may have a perfect blending of all three.

(1) **Characters.** The characters must be unique and original, so that they catch the eye at once. They dare not be colorless, they must have striking experiences. The Elephant's Child, Henny Penny, Medio Pollito, Jack of the Beanstalk, the Three Pigs, the

Three Bears, and Drakesbill — the characters of the fairy tales have no equal in literature for freshness and vivacity. The very mention of the thought brings a smile of recognition; and it is for this reason, no doubt, that leading men in large universities turn aside from their high scholarly labors, to work or play with fairy tales. Besides the interesting chief characters, moreover, there are many more subordinate characters that are especially unique: the fairies, the fairy godmothers and wise women, the elves of the trees, the dwarfs of the ground, the trolls of the rocks and hills, and the giants and witches. Then that great company of toilers in every occupation of life bring the child in touch with many novel phases of life. At best we are all limited by circumstances to a somewhat narrow sphere and like to enter into all that we are not. The child, meeting in his tale the shoemaker, the woodcutter, the soldier, the fisherman, the hunter, the poor traveler, the carpenter, the prince, the princess, and a host of others, gets a view of the industrial and social conditions that man in simple life had to face. This could not fail to interest; and it not only broadens his experience and deepens his sympathy, but is the best means for acquiring a foundation upon which to build his own vocational training. This acquisition is one contribution of literature to industrial work. Those characters will appeal to the child which present what the child has noticed or can notice. They should appear as they do in life, by what they say and by what they do. This, in harmony with the needs of the young child, makes the tales which answer to the test of suitability, largely dramatic.

(2) **Plot.** The characters of the tales can be observed only in action. Plot is the synthesis of the actions, all the incidents which happen to the characters. The plot gives the picture of experience and allows us to see others through the events which come to them. According to Professor Bliss Perry, the plot should be entertaining, comical, novel, or thrilling. It should present images that are clear-cut and not of too great variety. It should easily separate itself into large, leading episodes that stand out distinctly. The sequence of events should be orderly and proceed without interruption. The general structure should easily be discerned into the beginning, the middle, and the end. Various writers of tales have their particular ways of beginning. Andersen loses no time in getting started, while Kipling begins by stating his theme. The old tales frequently began with the words, "Once upon a time," which Kipling modified to "In the High and Far-Off times, O Best Beloved," etc. Hawthorne begins variously with "Once upon a time", or, "Long, long ago"; or, "Did you ever hear of the golden apples?" etc. — Hawthorne has been omitted in this book because, so far as I can discover, he furnishes no tale for the kindergarten or first grade. His simplest tale, *Midas and the Golden*

Touch, properly belongs in the second grade when told; when read, in the fourth grade. — The introduction, in whatever form, should be simple and to the point. It should give the time and place and present the characters; and if good art it will be impatient of much preliminary delay. The great stories all show a rise of interest culminating in one central climax; and after that, sometimes following on its very heels, the conclusion where poetic justice is meted out. This climax is a very important feature in the tale, so important that it has been said, " The climax is the tale." It is the point where interest focuses. It makes the story because it is where the point of the story is made. In a good story this point always is made impressive and often is made so by means of surprise. The conclusion must show that the tale has arrived at a stopping place and in a moral tale it must leave one satisfied, at rest.

If the folk-tale is good narration, in answer to the question, " What? " it will tell what happened; in answer to the question, " Who? " it will tell to whom it happened; in answer to the question, " Where? " it will tell the place where, and the time when, it happened; and in answer to the question, " Why? " it will give the reason for telling the story, it will give the message, and the truth embodied in its form. As narration the tale must have truth, interest, and consistency. Its typical mood must be action and its language the language of suggestion. This language of suggestion appears when it shows an object by indicating how it is like something else; by telling what we feel when we see the object; and by telling what actions of the person or object make it hateful or charming. We learn to know Andersen's Snow Man through what the Dog says of him.

Description, in the sense of a static, detailed delineation of various qualities of objects, has no place in the child's story, for it bores the child, who is very persistent in wanting the main theme uninterrupted. But description that has touches of movement and action or that lays emphasis on a single effect and has point, distinctly aids visualization, and produces a pleasing result, as we have seen in Kipling's *Elephant's Child*. The young child of to-day, trained in nature study to look upon bird, tree, and flower with vital interest, to observe the color and the form of these, gains a love of the beautiful that makes him exclaim over the plumage of a bird or tint of a flower. To him beauty in the tale must make a direct appeal which the child unfamiliar with these things might not feel. *The Wonderful Adventures of Nils* makes an appeal to the modern child which could not possibly have been felt by the child living before 1850. The modern child brought up on phonics is sensitive to sound also, and open to an appreciation of the beauty of the individual word used in description. This description, when it occurs, should be characterized mainly by aptness and concreteness.

Having observed the general characteristics of the narrative contained in the plot, let us examine the structure of a few tales to see: What is the main theme of the plot and how it works itself out; what are the large, leading episodes, and how they culminate in the climax; and what is the conclusion, and how closely it follows the climax.

The Story of Three Pigs

I. *Introduction.* Time. Place. Characters: Mother and Three Pigs. Mother gone.

II. *Rise.*

1. First Pig's venture with a man with a load of straw.
   Builds a straw house. (Wolf enters.)
   Wolf comes and destroys him.
2. Second Pig's venture with a man with a load of furze.
   Builds a furze house.
   Wolf comes and destroys him.
3. Third Pig's venture with a man with a load of bricks.
   Builds a brick house.
   Wolf comes. (Climax.)

III. *Conclusion.* Third Pig outwits the Wolf.
At the turnip-field in Mr. Smith's home-field.
At the apple tree in Merry-Garden.
At the fair at Shanklin.
At his own brick house.

Evidently the climax here is when the Wolf comes to the third Pig's brick house. After that things take a turn; and the final test of strength and cleverness comes at the very end of the tale, at Little Pig's brick house.

Grimm's *Briar Rose* is a model of structure and easily separates itself into ten large episodes.

Briar Rose

1. *The Introduction.*
2. The Christening Feast.
   (*a*) The Fairies and their gifts.
   (*b*) The wicked Fairy and her curse.
3. The King's decree.
4. Princess Rose's birthday.
   (*a*) Princess Rose's visit to the old tower.
   (*b*) Princess Rose and the wicked Fairy spinning.
   (*c*) The magic sleep.
5. The hedge of briars.
6. The Prince and the old Man.
7. The Prince and the opening hedge.
8. The Prince in the castle. (Climax.)
9. The awakening.
10. The wedding. (Conclusion.)

The climax here is the Prince's awakening kiss. The blossoming of the hedge into roses prepares for the climax; and the conclusion — the awakening of all the life of the castle and the wedding — follow immediately after.

(3) **Setting.** The third element of the short-story that is essential to its power and charm is setting. The setting is the circumstances or events which surround the characters and action. The setting occupies a much more important place in the tale than we realize, for it is the source of a variety of sensations and feelings which it may arouse. It gives the poetic or artistic touch to a tale. In the old tale the setting is given often in a word or two which act like magic, to open to our eyes a whole vision of associations. The

road in the *Three Pigs*, the wood in *Red Riding Hood*, the castle in the *Sleeping Beauty*—these add charm. Often the transformation in setting aids greatly in producing effect. In *Cinderella* the scene shifts from the hearth to the palace ballroom; in the *Princess and the Pea*, from the comfortable castle of the Queen to the raging storm, and then back again to the castle, to the breakfast-room on the following morning. In *Snow White and Rose Red* the scene changes from the cheery, beautiful interior of the cottage, to the snow-storm from which the Bear emerged. In accumulative tales, such as *The Old Woman and her Pig*, *Medio Pollito*, and *The Robin's Christmas Song*, the sequence of the story itself is preserved mainly by the change of setting. This appears in the following outline of *The Robin's Christmas Song*, an English tale which is the same as the Scotch *Robin's Yule-Song*, which has been attributed to Robert Burns. This tale illustrates one main line of sequence: —

The Robin's Christmas Song

1. *Introduction.* A sunny morning. Waterside. A Gray Pussy. A Robin came along.
2. *Rise.*

   Pussy said, ... "See my white fur."
   Robin replied, ... "You ate the wee mousie."

   Change in setting. Stone wall on border of the wood. A greedy Hawk, sitting.

   Hawk said, ... "See the speckled feather in my wing."
   Robin replied, ... "You pecked the sparrow," etc.

Change in setting. Great rock. A sly Fox.
Fox said, ... "See the spot on my tail."
Robin replied, ... "You bit the wee lambie."
Change in setting. Banks of a rivulet. A small Boy.
Boy said, ... "See the crumbs in my pocket."
Robin replied, ... "You caught the goldfinch."
Change in setting. King's palace. The window sill. The King at the window.
Robin sang, ... "A song for the King."
King replied, ... "What shall we give Robin?"

3. *Conclusion.*
No change in setting. King's palace. The window sill. The King at the window.
King . . . . Filled a plate and set it on the window sill.
Robin . . . . Ate, sang a song again, and flew away.

Here, not only the sequence of the tale is held largely by the change in setting, but also the pleasure in the tale is due largely to the setting, the pictures of landscape beauty it presents, and the feelings arising from these images.

A Japanese tale, in which the setting is a large part of the tale, and a large element of beauty, is *Mezumi, the Beautiful*, or *The Rat Princess*.

A Grimm tale in which the setting is a very large element of pleasure and in which it preserves the sequence of the tale, is *The Spider and the Flea*, a lively accumulative tale that deserves attention for several reasons. — A Spider and a Flea dwelt together. One day a number of unusual occurrences happened, so that finally a little Girl with a water-pitcher broke it, and then the Streamlet from which she drew the water asked, " Why do you break your pitcher, little Girl? "

And she replied: —

> The little Spider 's burned herself,
> And the Flea weeps;
> The little Door creaks with the pain,
> And the Broom sweeps;
> The little Cart runs on so fast,
> And the Ashes burn;
> The little Tree shakes down its leaves,
> Now it is my turn!

And then the Streamlet said, " Now I must flow."

And it flowed on and on, getting bigger and bigger, until it swallowed up the little Girl, the little Tree, the Ashes, the Cart, the Broom, the Door, the Flea, and at last, the Spider — all together.

Here we have a tale, which, in its language, well illustrates Stevenson's " pattern of style," especially as regards the harmony produced by the arrangement of letters. From the standpoint of style, this tale might be named, *The Adventure of the Letter E;* it illustrates the part the phonics of the tale may contribute to the effect of the setting. Follow the letter *e* in the opening of the tale, both as to the eye and the ear: —

> A Spid*e*r and a Fl*e*a dw*e*lt tog*e*th*e*r in on*e* hous*e* and br*e*w*e*d th*e*ir b*ee*r in an *e*gg-sh*e*ll. On*e* day wh*e*n th*e* Spid*e*r was stirring it up sh*e* f*e*ll in and burn*e*d h*e*rs*e*lf. Th*e*r*e*upon th*e* Fl*e*a b*e*gan to scr*e*am. And th*e*n th*e* Door ask*e*d, "Why ar*e* you scr*e*aming, littl*e* Fl*e*a?"

If we follow the *e* sound through the tale, we find it in *Flea*, *beer*, *scream*, *creak*, *weeps*, *sweep*, *reason*, *heap*,

Tree, *leaves*, and *Streamlet*. This repetition of the one sound puts music into the tale and creates a center of the harmony of sound. But if we examine the next part of the tale we find a variety of sounds of *o* in *thereupon*, *Door*, *Broom*, *stood*, and *corner*. Later, in connection with *Cart*, we have *began*, *fast*, *past*, and *Ashes*. Other phonic effects are crowded into the tale; such as the sound of *l* in *violently*, *till*, *all*, *leaves*, and *fell;* the sound of *i* in *little* and *Girl;* of *p* in *pitcher* and *passing;* of *t* in *little* and *pitcher;* and of *ew* in *threw* and *drew*. Altogether this very effective use of sound is a fine employment of concrete language, words which present images that are clear-cut as a cameo. It also gives to the tale a poetical touch.

Titty Mouse and Tatty Mouse, an English tale, and a parallel of *The Spider and the Flea*, preserves the same beauty and sequence by means of its setting and illustrates the same very unusual contribution of the sounds of particular letters combined in the harmony of the whole. *The Phonics of the Fairy Tales* is a subject which yields much interest and, as yet, has been almost untouched.

In *The Adventures of Chanticleer and Partlet*, in part I, *The Trip to the Nut-Hill*, taken from Arthur Rackham's *Grimm Tales*, the setting contributes largely to the attractiveness of the tale, as is shown in Rackham's beautiful illustration. The setting is given throughout the tale often in a telling word or two. Chanticleer and Partlet went up the *nut-hill* to gather nuts before the *squirrel* carried them all away. The *day* was *bright* and they stayed till *evening.* The *carriage* of *nut-shells;* the *Duck* they met; the *dirty road* they traveled in the *pitch dark;* the *Inn* they arrived at; the *night* at the Inn; the early *dawn;* the *hearth* where they threw the egg-shells; the Landlord's *chair* whose *cushion* received the Needle; the *towel* which received the Pin; the *heath* over which they hurried away; the *yard* of the Inn where the Duck slept and the *stream* he escaped by; the Landlord's *room* where he gained experience with his towel; the *kitchen* where the egg-shells from the *hearth* flew into his face; and the *arm-chair* which received him with a Needle — these are all elements of setting which contribute largely to the humor and the beauty of the tale.

A blending of the three elements, characters, plot, and setting, appears in the following outline of *The Elves and the Shoemaker:* —

The Elves and the Shoemaker

1. *Introduction.* A poor Shoemaker. A poor room containing a bed and a shoemaker's board. Leather for one pair of shoes.
2. *Development.*
   First night......Cut out shoes. Went to bed. Shoes ready next morning. Sold them. Bought leather for two pairs.
   Second night......Cut out shoes. Went to bed. Shoes ready next morning. Sold them. Bought leather for four pairs.
   One night......Conversation of Shoemaker and his wife: "I should like to sit up to-night to see who it is that makes the shoes." They sat up. Two Elves

ran in, sewed, rapped, and tapped, and ran away when the shoes were made.

Day after......Conversation. "These Elves made us rich. I should like to do something for them. You make each of them a little pair of shoes, and I will make them each a little shirt, a coat, a waistcoat, trousers, and a pair of stockings."

Christmas Eve..Finished shoes and clothes put on the table. Shoemaker and Wife hid in the corner of the room behind clothes, and watched. (Climax.)

Elves came in and put on clothes.

3. *Conclusion.*

Happy end. Elves danced and sang, —

> "Smart and natty boys are we,
> Cobblers we'll no longer be."

Shoemaker and Wife became happy and prosperous.

The characters of this tale are usual, a poor Shoemaker and his Wife; and unusual, the dainty Elves who made shoes in a twinkling. But the commonplace peasants become interesting through their generosity, kindness, and service to the Elves; and the Elves become human in their joy at receiving gifts. The structure of the tale is so distinct as to be seen a thing itself, apart from the story. The framework is built on what happens on two nights and following nights, the conversation of the next day, and what happens on Christmas Eve. The climax evidently is what the Shoemaker and his Wife hid in the corner to see — the entrance of the Elves on Christmas Eve — which episode has been interpreted charmingly by the English illustrator, Cruikshank. The joy of the Elves and of the two aged people, the gifts received by the one and the riches won by the other, form the conclusion, which follows very closely upon the climax. The commonplace setting, the poor room with its simple bed and table, becomes transformed by the unusual happenings in the place. If we should take away this setting, we see how much the tale would suffer. Also without the characters the tale would be empty. And without the interesting, human, humorous, and pleasing plot, characters and setting would be insufficient. Each element of the short-story contributes its fair share to the tale, and blends harmoniously in the whole.

Various standards for testing the folk-tale have been given by writers. One might refer to the standards given by Wilman in his *Pedagogische Vorträge* and those mentioned by William Rein in *Das Erste Schuljahr*. We have seen here that the fairy tale must contain the child's interests and it must be able to stand the test of a true classic. It must stand the test of literature in its appeal to emotion and to imagination, in its appeal to the intellect through its basis of truth, and to the language-sense through its perfection of form; it must stand the test of the short-story and of good narration and of description. Let us now examine a few of the old tales to see how they stand the complete test: —

How the Sun, Moon, and West Wind went out to Dinner

This story of How the Sun, Moon, and West Wind Went out to Dinner appeals to the children's interest in a family dinner — they went to dine with their Uncle and Aunt,

Thunder and Lightning. The characters are interesting to the child, for they are the inhabitants of his sky that cause him much wonder: the star, the sun, the moon, the thunder, and the lightning. To the little child, who as she watched a grown-up drying her hands, remarked, "I would n't like to be a towel, would you?" the idea of the moon, sun, and wind possessing personality and going to a dinner-party will amuse and please. The theme of the story finds a place in the experience of children who go to a party; and secretly they will enjoy making comparisons. When they go to a party they too like to bring something home; but they would n't think of hiding goodies in their hands. They are fortunate enough to have their hostess give them a toy animal or a box of sweetmeats, a tiny dolly or a gay balloon, as a souvenir. The greediness and selfishness of the Sun and Wind impress little children, for these are perhaps the two sins possible to childhood; and all children will fully appreciate why the Sun and the Wind received so swiftly the punishment they deserved. The thoughtfulness of the loving gentle Moon to remember her Mother the Star, appeals to them. The rapid punishment, well-deserved, and the simplicity of the story with its one point, make it a very good tale for little children. The whole effect is pleasing. What children recall is the motherly Star; and the beautiful Moon, who was cool and calm and bright as a reward for being good.

The structure of the tale is neat and orderly, dominated by a single theme. The form of the tale, as given in Jacobs's *Indian Tales*, shows a good use of telling expressions; such as, "the Mother waited *alone* for her children's return," "Kept watch with her *little bright eye*," "the Moon, *shaking* her hands *showered* down such a *choice* dinner," etc. Here we have too, the use of concrete, visualized expressions and direct language. There is also a good use of repetition, which aids the child in following the plot and which clarifies the meaning. The Mother Star, when pronouncing a punishment upon Sun, repeated his own words as he had spoken when returning from the dinner: "I went out to enjoy myself with my friends." In her speech to Wind she included his own remark: "I merely went for my own pleasure." — The examination of this tale shows that it stands well the complete test applied here to the fairy tale.

The Straw Ox

The Straw Ox is an accumulative tale which has sufficient plot to illustrate the fine points of the old tale completely. A poor woman who could barely earn a living had an idea and carried it out successfully. — Her need immediately wins sympathy in her behalf. — She asked her husband to make her a straw ox and smear it with tar. Then placing it in the field where she spun, she called out, "Graze away, little Ox, graze away, while I spin my flax!" First a Bear came out of the Wood and got caught by the tar so that the Straw Ox dragged him home. The old Man then put the Bear in the cellar. Then a Wolf, a Fox, and a Hare got caught in the same way and also were consigned to the cellar. — The plot has so far built itself up by an orderly succession of incidents. — But just when the Man is preparing to kill the animals, they save their lives by promising vicarious offerings: The Bear promises honey; the Wolf a flock of sheep; the Fox a flock of geese; and the Hare kale and cauliflower. — Then the plot, having tied itself into a knot, unties itself as the animals return, each with the gift he promised.

The setting is the field where the old Woman placed the Ox and where she spun, the wood from which the animals came, and the peasant home. The characters are two poor people who need food and clothing and seek to secure both; and the animals of the forest. The peasants need the Bear for a coat, the Wolf for a fur cap, the Fox for a fur collar, and the Hare for mittens. This human need produces an emotional appeal so that we wish to see the animals caught. But when the plot unties itself, the plight of the animals appeals to us equally and we want just as much to see them win their freedom. Each animal works out his own salvation by offering the old people a worthy substitute. Each animal is true to his nature in the substitute he offers, he promises what is only natural for him to procure, and what he himself likes best. The conclusion is satisfying because in the end everybody is happy: the old people who have all they need; and the animals who have life and freedom. The distinct pictures offered to the imagination are the capture of the four animals and their return with their life-substitutes. The form of the tale is a good example of folk-story style, with its vivid words, direct language, and repetition. This is one of the tales which is finer than at first appears because it has a strong sense of life. It touches the present-day problem: "How can the inhuman slaughter of animals for man's use be avoided?" Its underlying message is: Self-help is a good way out of a difficulty. — *The Straw Ox* also answers the complete test of the tale with much satisfaction.

REFERENCES

The Child

Barnes, Earl: *Study of Children's Stories.* ("Children's Interests.")

Dewey, John: *Interest and Effort in Education.* Houghton.

King, Irving: *Psychology of Child Development.* University of Chicago Press.

Lawrence, Isabel: "Children's Interests in Literature." *N. E. A. Report,* 1899, p. 1044.

McCracken, Elizabeth: "What Children Like to Read." *Outlook,* Dec., 1904, vol. 78.

Tyler, John M.: *Growth in Education.* Houghton.

Vostrovsky, Clara: "A Study of Children's Own Stories." *Studies in Education,* vol. I, pp. 15–17.

Literature

Baldwin, Charles S.: *Specimens of Prose Description.* Holt.

Brewster, William T.: *English Composition and Style.* Century.

Ibid: Specimens of Prose Narration. Holt.

Gardiner, John H.: *Forms of Prose Literature.* Scribner.

Matthews, Brander: *The Philosophy of the Short-Story.* Longmans.

Pater, Walter: *Appreciations.* (*Essay on Style*). Macmillan.

Perry, Bliss: *A Study of Prose Fiction.* ("The Short Story.") Houghton.

Sainte-Beuve, Charles A.: *Essays.* ("What is a Classic?") Dutton.

Santayana, George: *The Sense of Beauty.* Scribner.

Wendell, Barrett: *English Composition.* Scribner.

Winchester, Caleb T.: *Principles of Literary Criticism.* Macmillan.

Emotion

Bain, Alexander: *The Emotions and the Will.* Appleton.

Darwin, Charles R.: *Expression of the Emotions in Man and Animals.* Appleton.

Imagination

Colvin, Stephen: *The Learning Process.* Macmillan.

Curry, S. S.: *Imagination and the Dramatic Instinct.* Expression Co.

Ruskin, John: *Modern Painters,* vol. I. ("Of the Imagination.")

Children's Literature

Baker, Franklin T.: *Bibliography of Children's Reading.* (*Introduction.*) Teachers College, Columbia University.

Day, Mary B., and Wilson, Elisabeth: *Suggestive Outlines on Children's Literature.* S. Illinois Normal, Carbondale.

Dodd, C. F.: "Fairy Tales in the Schoolroom." *Living Age,* Nov. 8, 1902, vol. 235, pp. 369–75.

Fay, Lucy, and Eaton, Anne: *Instruction in the Use of Books and Libraries.* (Chap. xv, "Fairy Tales.") Boston Book Co.

Field, Mrs. E. M.: *The Child and His Book.* Wells Gardner, Darton & Co.

Field, Walter T.: *Finger-Posts to Children's Reading.* A. C. McClurg.

Harron, Julia; Bacon, Corinne; and Dana, J. C.: *A Course*

of Study on Literature for Children. Newark Public Library.

Hosic, James F.: "The Conduct of a Course in Literature for Children." *N. E. A. Report,* 1913.

Ibid: The Elementary Course in English. University of Chicago.

Hunt, Clara: *What shall we Read to the Children?* Houghton.

Kready, Laura F.: "Picture-Books for Little Children." *Kindergarten Review,* Sept., 1914.

Lowe, Orton: *Literature for Children.* Macmillan.

MacClintock, Porter L.: *Literature in the Elementary School.* University of Chicago.

Moore, Annie E.: "Principles in the Selection of Stories for the Kindergarten." *I. K. U. Report,* 1913.

Moses, Montrose: *Children's Books and Reading.* M. Kennerley.

Olcott, Frances J.: *The Children's Reading.* Houghton.

CHAPTER III

THE TELLING OF FAIRY TALES

The telling of stories refreshes the mind as a bath refreshes the body. It gives exercise to the intellect and its powers. It tests the judgments and feelings. The story-teller must wholly take into himself the life of which he speaks, must let it live and operate in himself freely. He must reproduce it whole and undiminished, yet stand superior to life as it actually is. — FROEBEL.

The purpose of the story. — To look out with new eyes upon the many-featured, habitable world; to be thrilled by the pity and the beauty of this life of ours, itself brief as a tale that is told; to learn to know men and women better, and to love them more. — BLISS PERRY.

Expertness in teaching consists in a scholarly command of subject-matter, in a better organization of character, in a larger and more versatile command of conscious modes of transmitting facts and ideals, and in a more potent and winsome, forceful and sympathetic manner of personal contact with other human beings. — HENRY SUZZALLO.

Story-telling as an art. No matter how perfectly the tale, in a subjective sense, may contain the interests of the child, or how carefully it may avoid what repels him; though in an objective sense it may stand the test of a true classic in offering a permanent enrichment of the mind and the test of literature in appealing to the emotions and the imagination, in giving a contribution of truth and an embodiment of good form; though it may stand the test of the short-story — furnishing interesting characters, definite plot, and effective setting; though its sequence be orderly and its climax pointed, its narration consistent and its description apt — the tale yet remains to be told. The telling of the tale is a distinct art governed by distinct principles because the life of the story must be transmitted and rendered into voice.

Story-telling is one of the most ancient and universal of arts. Concerning this art Thackeray has said: —

> Stories exist everywhere: there is no calculating the distance through which stories have come to us, the number of languages through which they have been filtered, or the centuries during which they have been told. Many of them have been narrated almost in their present shape for thousands of years to the little copper-colored Sanskrit children, listening to their mothers under the palm-trees by the banks of the yellow Jumna — their Brahmin mother, who softly narrated them through the ring in her nose. The very same tale has been heard by the northern Vikings as they lay on their shields on deck; and the Arabs couched under the stars on the Syrian plains when their flocks were gathered in, and their mares were picketed by the tents.

In his *Roundabout Papers,* Thackeray gives a picture of a score of white-bearded, white-robed warriors or grave seniors of the city, seated at the gate of Jaffa or Beyrout, listening to the story-teller reciting his marvels out of *Arabian Nights.* "A Reading from Homer," by Alma Tadema, is a well-known picture which portrays the Greeks listening to the *Tales of Homer.* In the *Lysistrata* of Aristophanes, the chorus of old men begins with, "I will tell ye a story!" Plutarch, in his *Theseus* says, "All kinds of stories were told at the festival Oschophoria, as the mothers related such things to their children before their departure, to give them courage." In his *Symposium* he mentions a child's story containing the proverb, " No man can make a gown for the moon." —

> The Moon begged her Mother to weave her a little frock which would fit her.
>
> The Mother said, "How can I make it fit thee, when thou art sometimes a Full Moon, and then a Half Moon, and then a New Moon? " —

In the works of the German, Schuppius (1677), appeared this: —

> Your old folks can remember how, in the olden times, it was customary at vespers on Easter day, to tell some Easter tidings from the pulpit. These were foolish fables and stories such as are told to children in the spinning-room. They were intended to make people merry.

In England, *Chaucer's Tales* reflect the common custom of the times for the pilgrim, the traveler, the lawyer, the doctor, the monk, and the nun, to relate a tale. *The Wife of Bathes Tale* is evidently a fairy tale. In Peele's *Old Wives' Tale* we learn how the smith's goodwife related some nursery tales of Old England to the two travelers her husband brought to the cottage for the night. In Akenside's *Pleasures of Imagination* we find: —

> Hence, finally by night,
> The village matres, round the blazing hearth
> Suspend the infant audience with their tales,
> Breathing astonishment.

The custom of Florentine mothers has been described by the poet, Dante, when he says: —

> Another, drawing tresses from her distaff,
> Told o'er among her family the tales
> Of Trojans, and of Fesole and Rome.

The French troubadours and the Italian counts of Boccaccio's time told tales. It is recorded of the French Galland, the first translator of *The Arabian Nights*, how the young men of his day would gather under his windows at night and shout for him until he showed himself and told them stories. The German Luther paid a high tribute to stories; and Goethe's mother, in giving her experience in telling stories to her children, has shown how the German mother valued the story in the home. To-day, savage children, when the day of toil is ended with the setting sun, gather in groups to listen to the never-dying charm of the tale; and the most learned of men, meeting in the great centers of civilization to work out weighty problems, find relief and pleasure when wit and culture tell the tale.

In the home the tale is the mother's power to build in her little children ideals of life which will tower as a fortress when there come critical moments of decision for which no amount of reasoning will be a sufficient guide, but for which true feeling, a kind of unconscious higher reasoning, will be the safest guide. In the library the story is the greatest social asset of the librarian, it is her best means of reaching the obscure child who seeks there some food for his spirit, it is her best opportunity to lead and direct his tastes. In the school it is the teacher's strongest personal ally. It is her wishing-ring, with which she may play fairy to herself in accomplishing a great variety of aims, and incidentally be a fairy godmother to the child.

Story-telling is an art handling an art and therefore must be pursued in accordance with certain principles. These principles govern: (1) the teacher's preparation; (2) the presentation of the tale; and (3) the return from the child.

I. THE TEACHER'S PREPARATION

1. The teacher's preparation must be concerned with a variety of subjects. The first rule to be observed is: *Select the tale for some purpose, to meet a situation.* This purpose may be any one of the elements of value which have been presented here under "The Worth of Fairy Tales." The teacher must consider, not only the possibilities of her subject-matter and what she wishes to accomplish through the telling of the tale, but also what the child's purpose will be in listening. She may select her tale specifically, not just because it contains certain interests, but because through those interests she can direct the child's activity toward higher interests. She must consider what problems the tale can suggest to the child. She may select her tale to develop habits in the child, to clarify his thinking, to give a habit of memory or to develop emotion or imagination. She may select her tale "just for fun," to give pure joy, or to teach a

definite moral lesson, to make a selfish child see the beauty of unselfishness or to impress an idea. The *Story of Lazy Jack*, like the realistic *Epaminondas*, will impress more deeply than any word of exhortation, the necessity for a little child to use "the sense he was born with."

In the selection of the tale the teacher is up against the problem of whether she shall choose her tale psychologically or logically. As this is the day of the psychologic point of view in education, the teacher realizing this feels that she must select a tale for a particular purpose, according to the child's interests, his needs, and the possibilities it offers for his self-activity and self-expression. Looking freely over the field she may choose any tale which satisfies her purposes. This is psychologic. But in a year's work this choice of a tale for a particular purpose is followed by successive choices until she has selected a wide variety of tales giving exercise to many forms of activity, establishing various habits of growth. This method of choice is the psychologic built up until, in the hands of the teacher who knows the subject, it becomes somewhat logical. It is the method which uses the ability of the individual teacher, alone and unaided. There is another method. The teacher may be furnished with a course of tales arranged by expert study of the full subject outlined in large units of a year's work, offering the literary heritage possible to the child of a given age. This is logical. From this logical course of tales she may select one which answers to the momentary need, she may use it according to its nature, to develop habits, to give opportunity for self-activity and self-expression, and to enter into the child's daily life. This method of choice is the logical, which through use and adaptation has become psychologized. It uses the ability of the individual teacher in adaptation, not unaided and alone, but assisted by the concentrated knowledge and practice of the expert. Such a logical course, seeking uniformity only by what it requires at the close of a year's work, would give to the individual teacher a large freedom of choice and would bring into kindergarten and elementary literature a basis of content demanding as much respect as high school or college literature. It is in no way opposed to maintaining the child as the center of interest. The teacher's problem is to see that she uses the logical course psychologically.

2. Having selected the tale then, from a logical course, and psychologically for a present particular purpose, the next step is: *Know the tale.* Know the tale historically, if possible. Know it first as folk-lore and then as literature. Read several versions of the tale, the original if possible, selecting that version which seems most perfectly fitted to express what there is in the tale. As folk-lore, study its variants and note its individual motifs. Note what glimpses it gives of the social life and customs of a primitive people. The best way to dwell on the life of the story, to realize

it, is to compare these motifs with similar motifs in other tales. It has been said that we do not see anything clearly until we compare it with another; and associating individual motifs of the tales makes the incidents stand out most clearly. Henny Penny's walk appears more distinctly in association with that of Medio Pollito or that of Drakesbill or of the Foolish Timid Rabbit; the fairy words in *Sleeping Beauty* and the good things they bestowed upon Briar Rose in association with the fairy wand in *Cinderella* and the good things it brought her; the visit of the Wolf in *The Wolf and Seven Kids* with the visit of the Wolf in *Three Pigs* and of the Fox in *The Little Rid Hin.* It is interesting to note that a clog motif, similar to the motif of shoes in *The Elves and the Shoemaker*, occurs in the Hindu *Panch-Rhul Ranee*, told in *Old Deccan Days.*

All the common motifs which occur in the fairy tales have been classified by Andrew Lang under these heads: —

(1) Bride or bridegroom who transgresses a mystic command.
(2) Penelope formula; one leaves the other and returns later.
(3) Attempt to avoid Fate.
(4) Slaughter of monster.
(5) Flight, by aid of animal.
(6) Flight from giant or wizard.
(7) Success of youngest.
(8) Marriage test, to perform tasks.
(9) Grateful beasts.

(10) Strong man and his comrades.
(11) Adventure with Ogre, and trick.
(12) Descent to Hades.
(13) False bride.
(14) Bride with animal children.

From a less scientific view some of the common motifs noticeable in the fairy tales, which however would generally fall under one of the heads given by Lang, might be listed: —

(1) Child wandering into a home; as in *Three Bears* and *Snow White.*
(2) Transformation; simple, as in *Puss-in-Boots;* by love, as in *Beauty and the Beast,* by sprinkling with water, as in *Beauty and the Beast* or by bathing, as in *Catskin;* by violence, as in *Frog Prince* and *White Cat.*
(3) Tasks as marriage tests; as in *Cinderella.*
(4) Riddle test; as in *Peter, Paul, and Espen;* questions asked, as in *Red Riding Hood.*
(5) Magic sleep; as in *Sleeping Beauty.*
(6) Magic touch; as in *Golden Goose.*
(7) Stupid person causing royalty to laugh; as in *Lazy Jack.*
(8) Exchange; as in *Jack and the Beanstalk.*
(9) Curiosity punished; as in *Bluebeard* and *Three Bears.*
(10) Kindness to persons rewarded; as in *Cinderella, Little Two-Eyes,* and *The House in the Wood.*
(11) Kindness to animals repaid; as in *Thumbelina, Cinderella,* and *White Cat.*
(12) Industry rewarded; as in *Elves and the Shoemaker.*
(13) Hospitality rewarded; as in *Tom Thumb.*
(14) Success of a venture; as in *Dick Whittington.*

After studying the tale as folk-lore, know it as literature. Master it as a classic, test it as literature, to see wherein lies its appeal to the emotions, its power of imagination, its basis of truth, and its quality of form; study it as a short-story and view it as a piece of narration. It is rather interesting to note that you can get all there is in a tale from any one point of view. If you follow the sequence as setting, through association you get the whole, as may be seen by referring to *Chanticleer and Partlet* under the heading, "Setting," in the chapter on the "Short-Story." Or, if you follow the successive doings of the characters you get the whole, as may be observed in the story of *Medio Pollito*, described later in the "Animal Tale" in the chapter, "Classes of Tales." Or if you follow the successive happenings to the characters, the plot, you get the whole, as may appear in the outline of *Three Pigs* given in the chapter which handles "Plot." Note the beauty of detail and the quality of atmosphere with which the setting surrounds the tale; note the individual traits of the characters and their contrasts; observe how what each one does causes what happens to him. Realize your story from the three points of view to enter into the author's fullness. Get a good general notion of the story first.

3. The next step is: *Master the complete structure of the tale.* This is the most important step in the particular study of the tale, for it is the unity about which any perfection in the art of telling must center. To discern that repose of centrality which the main theme of the tale gives, to follow it to its climax and to its conclusion, where poetic justice leaves the listener satisfied —

this is the most fundamental work of the story-teller. The teacher must analyze the structure of her tale into its leading episodes, as has been illustrated in the handling of structure, under the subject, "Plot," in the chapter on the "Short-Story."

4. The next step is: *Secure the message of the tale.* The message is what we wish to transmit, it is the explicit reason for telling the tale. And one evidently must possess a message before one can give it. As the message is the chief worth of the tale, the message should dominate the telling and pervade its life. A complete realization of the message of the tale will affect the minutest details giving color and tone to the telling, and resulting so that what the child does with the story will deepen the impression of the message he receives.

5. The next step is: *Master the tale as form.* This means that if the tale is in classic form, not only the message and the structure must be transmitted, but the actual words. Words are the artist's medium, Stevenson includes them in his pattern of style, and how can we exclude them if we wish to express what they have expressed? A tale like Kipling's *The Elephant's Child* would be ruined without those clinging epithets, such as "the wait-a-bit thorn-bush," "meresmear nose," "slushy squshy mud-cap," "Bi-Colored-Python-Rock-Snake," and "'satiable curtiosity." No one could substitute other words in this tale; for contrasts of feeling and humor are so tied up with the

words that other words would fail to tell the real story. If an interjection has seemed an insignificant part of speech, note the vision of tropical setting opened up by the exclamation, " O Bananas! Where did you learn that trick? " This is indeed a tale where the form is the matter, the form and the message are one complete whole that cannot be separated. But it is a proof that where any form is of sufficient perfection to be a classic form, you may give a modified tale by changing it, but you do not give the real complete tale. You cannot tell Andersen's *Tin Soldier* in your own words; for its sentences, its phrases, its sounds, its suggestive language, its humor, its imagination, its emotion, and its message, are so intricately woven together that you could not duplicate them.

When the fairy tale does not possess a settled classic form, select, as was mentioned, that version in which the language best conveys the life of the story, improving it yourself, if you can, in harmony with the standards of literature, until the day in the future when the tale may be fortunate enough to receive a settled form at the hands of a literary artist. Sometimes a slight change may improve greatly an old tale. In Grimm's *Briar Rose* [1] the episode of the Prince and the old Man contains irrelevant material. The two paragraphs following, "after the lapse of many years there came a king's son into the country," easily may be re-written to preserve the same unity and simplicity

[1] McLoughlin edition.

which mark the rest of the tale. This individual retelling of an old tale demands a careful distinction between what is essential and internal and what may have been added, what is accidental and external. The clock-case in *The Wolf and Seven Kids* evidently is not a part of the original story, which arose before clocks were in use, and is a feature added in some German telling of the tale. It may be retained but it is not essential to the tale that it should be. Exact conversations and bits of dialogue, repetitive phrases, rhymes, concrete words which visualize, brief expressions, and Anglo-Saxon words — these are all bits of detail which need to be mastered in a complete acquirement of the story's form, because these are characteristics of the form which time has settled upon the old tales. Any literary form bestowed upon the tales worthy of the name literature, will have to preserve these essentials.

II. THE PRESENTATION OF THE TALE

In the oral presentation of the tale new elements of the teacher's preparation enter, for here the voice is the medium and the teacher must use the voice as the organist his keys. The aim of the oral presentation is to give the spiritual effect. This requires certain conditions of effectiveness — to speak with distinctness, to give the sense, and to cause to understand; and certain intellectual requirements — to articulate with perfection, to present successive thoughts in clear outline, and to preserve relative values of importance.

The production of the proper effect necessitates placing in the foreground, with full expression, what needs emphasis, and throwing back with monotony or acceleration parts that do not need emphasis. It requires slighting subordinate, unimportant parts, so that one point is made and one total impression given. This results in that flexibility and lightsomeness of the voice, which is one of the most important features in the telling of the tale. The study of technique, when controlled by these principles of vocal expression, is not opposed to the art of story-telling any more than the painter's knowledge of color is opposed to his art of painting. To obtain complete control of the voice as an instrument of the mind, there is necessary: (1) training of the voice; (2) exercises in breathing; (3) a knowledge of gesture; and (4) a power of personality.

(1) **Training of the voice.** This training aims to secure freedom of tone, purity of tone, fullness of tone, variety of volume, and tone-color. It will include a study of phonetics to give correct pronunciation of sounds and a knowledge of their formation; freeing exercises to produce a jaw which is not set, an open throat, a mobile lip, and nimble tongue; and exercises to get rid of nasality or throatiness. The art of articulation adds to the richness of meaning, it is the connection between sound and sense. Open sounds are in harmony with joy, and very distinct emotional effects are produced by arrangements of consonants. The

effect created by the use of the vowels and consonants in *The Spider and the Flea* has already been referred to under "Setting." The open vowels of "*Ŏn*, little Drumikin! Tum-p*ä*, tum-t*o͞o!*" help to convey the impression of lightsome gaiety in *Lambikin.* The effect of power displayed by "Then I'll huff and I'll puff, and I'll blow your house in," is made largely by the sound of the consonants *ff* and the *n* in the concluding *in*, the force of the rough *u* of *huff* and *puff*, and the prolonged *o* in *blōw.* The effect of walking is produced by the *p* of "*Trip, trap*," and of varied walking by the change of vowel from *ĭ* to *ă.* The action of "I have come to gobble you up," is emphasized and made realistic by the *bb* of *gobble* and the *p* of *up.* Attention to the power of phonics to contribute to the emotional force and to the strength of meaning in the tale, will reveal to the story-teller many new beauties.

(2) **Exercises in breathing.** Training in breathing includes exercises to secure the regulation of proper breathing during speech and to point out the relation between breathing and voice expression. The correct use of the voice includes also ability to place tone. — Find out your natural tone and tell the story in that tone. — Many of the effects of the voice need to be dealt with from the inside, not externally. The use of the pause in story-telling is one of the subtlest and most important elements that contribute to the final effect. The proper placing of the pause will follow un-

consciously as a consequence when the structure of the story is realized in distinct episodes and the proper emphasis given mentally to the most important details of action, while less emphasis in thought is given to subordinate parts. Therefore, the study of the pause must be made, not artificially and externally, but internally through the elements of the story which produce the pause. Tone-color, which is to ordinary speech what melody is to music — those varied effects of intonation, inflection, and modulation — is to be sought, not as a result from an isolated study of technique, but from attention to those elements in association with the complete realization of the life of the story. Genuine feeling is worth more than mere isolated exercises to secure modulation, and complete realization eliminates the necessity of "pretending to be." The study of the fairy tale as literature, as has been indicated in the chapter on "Principles of Selection," will therefore be fundamental to the presentation of the tale. Entering into the motives of the story gives action, entering into the thought gives form, and entering into the feeling gives tone-color to the voice. The sincere desire to share the thought will be the best aid to bring expression.

(3) **A knowledge of gesture.** The teacher must understand the laws of gesture. The body is one means of the mind's expression. There is the eloquence of gesture and of pose. The simplest laws of gesture may be stated: —

(*a*) All gesture precedes speech in proportion to the intense realization of emotion.

(*b*) All expression begins in the face and passes to some other agent of the body in proportion to the quality of the emotion. The eye leads in pointing.

(*c*) Hands and arms remain close to the body in gesture when intensity of emotion is controlled.

In regard to gesture, a Children's Library pamphlet, dealing with the purpose of story-telling, has said, "The object of the story-teller is to present the story, not in the way advocated usually in the schools, but to present it with as little dramatic excitement and foreign gesture as possible, keeping one's personality in the background and giving all prominence to the story itself, relying for interest in the story alone." The schools have perhaps been misinterpreted. It is clear that only that personality is allowable which interprets truly the story's life. The listening child must be interested in the life of the story, not in the story-teller; and therefore gesture, tone, or sentiment that is individual variation and addition to the story itself, detracts from the story, is foreign to its thought, and occupies a wrong place of prominence. It is possible to tell a story, however, just as the author tells it, and yet give it naturally by realizing it imaginatively and by using the voice and the body artistically, as means of expression.

(4) **A power of personality.** What rules shall be given for the making of that personality which is to bring with it force in the telling of the tale and

which must override phonetics, inflection, and gesture?

The very best help towards acquiring that personality which is the power of story-telling, is to have a power of life gained through the experience of having lived; to have a power of emotion acquired through the exercise of daily affairs; a power of imagination won from having dwelt upon the things of life with intentness, a power of sympathy obtained from seeing the things of others as you meet them day by day; and a first-hand knowledge of the sights and sounds and beauties of Nature, a knowledge of bird and flower, tree and rock, their names and some of their secrets — a knowledge accumulated from actual contact with the real physical world. This power of life will enable the story-teller to enter, at the same time, into the life of the story she tells, and the life of those listening, to see the gift of the one and the need of the other.

The ideal position for the story-teller is to be seated opposite the center of the semicircle of listeners, facing them. The extreme nearness of the group, when the teller seeks the fingers of the listeners to add force to the telling, seems an infringement upon the child's personal rights. A strong personality will make the story go home without too great nearness and will want to give the children a little room so that their thoughts may meet hers out in the story.

Suggestions for telling. Now that the teacher is ready to speak, her first step in the art of story-telling, which is the first step in the art of any teaching, which lies at the very foundation of teaching, which is the most important step, and which is the step that often is neglected, is the *establishing of the personal relation between herself and the listener*. This is one of those subtleties which evades measuring, but its influence is most lasting. It is the setting to the whole story of teaching. It must play so important a part because, as teacher and listener are both human beings, there must be between them a common bond of humanity. How do you wish to appear to this group of listeners? As a friend to be trusted, a brother or sister to give help, or as a good comrade to be played with; as "master, expert, leader, or servant"? If you wish to be as real and forceful as the characters in your story, you must do something which will cause the personal relation you desire, to be established; and moreover, having established it, you must live up to it, and prove no friend without faith. You must do this before you presume to teach or to tell a story. You need not do it before each individual story you present to a group you meet often; you may do it so effectively, with a masterstroke, at the beginning when you first meet your class, that all you need do at successive meetings will be but to add point to your first establishment.

A student-teacher, in telling a story to a group of kindergarten children who were complete strangers, and telling it to them as they sat in a semicircle in front of her comrades, adult students, established this personal relation by beginning to tell the little children her experience with the first telling of *Three Bears* to a little girl of four: — Seated before a sand-box in the yard, after hearing the story of *Three Bears*, M—— had been asked, "Would n't this be a good time for you to tell me the story?" In reply, she paused, and while the story-teller was expecting her to begin, suddenly said, "Do you think M——'s big enough for all that?" and refused to tell a word. Then turning to the group before her, the student-teacher made the direct appeal. "But you are the biggest little people in the kindergarten, and you would n't treat a story like that, would you?" The children, through the personal picture of friendly story-telling with a little child, that paralleled their own situation somewhat, immediately felt at home with the teller; it was just as if they were the same intimate friends with her that the little girl portrayed to them was. The human bond of good comradeship and intimacy was established. In the direct appeal at the end, the children were held up to an ideal they dare not disappoint, they must live up to their size, be able to get the story, and be the biggest little people in the kindergarten by showing what they could do with it. Again there was an undefined problem thrown at them, as it were — an element of wonder. They did not know just what was coming and they were mentally alert, waiting, on the lookout. The way for the story was open. — This is what you want, for no matter how perfect a gem of folk-lore you tell, it will fall heedless if the children do not listen to it.

The second step in the art of story-telling is one which grows naturally out of this first step. This second step, *to put the story in a concrete situation for the child*, to make the connection between the child and the literature you present, is the one which displays your unique power as an artist. It is the step which often is omitted and is the one which exercises all your individual ability and cleverness. It is the step which should speak comfort to the eager teacher of to-day, who is compelled to stand by, Montessori fashion, while many changing conceptions say to her: "Hands off! It is not what you do that helps the child develop; it is what he himself does!" Here at least is one of the teacher's chances to act. This step is the opening of the gateway so that the story you are about to tell may enter into the thoughts of your listeners. It is your means to organize the tale in the child's life. If in the school program you permit nature study, representing the central interest, to occupy the place of main emphasis, and if the game, occupation, and song work is related to the child's life, this organization of the child's tale in his life will be accomplished naturally.

In the example cited above, both the establishment of the personal relation and the placing of the story in a concrete situation, were managed partly at the one stroke. Your best help to furnish a concrete situation will be to preserve at the one end a sympathy for the life of your story and at the other to perceive the experience of the children in the listening group. Seeing both at once will result in a knowledge of what the children need most to make the story go home. If your children are good enough, and you and they sufficiently good friends to bear the fun of pantomime and the gaiety of hilarity, asking several boys, as they walk across the room before the children, to imitate some animals they had seen at a circus, and getting the children to guess the animal represented until they hit upon the elephant, would put certain children in a spirit of fun that would be exactly the wide-awake brightness and good humor needed to receive the story of *The Elephant's Child.* You can get children best into the story-telling mood by calling up ideas in line with the story. In the case of the story cited above, under the establishment of the personal relation, the story, *The Bremen Town Musicians,* was related to the child's experience by a few questions concerning kinds of music he knew, and what musician and kind of music the kindergarten had. In telling Andersen's *Tin Soldier* you must call up experience concerning a soldier, not only because of the relation of the toy to the real soldier, but because the underlying meaning of the tale is courage, and the emotional theme is steadfastness. And to preserve the proper unity between the tale and the telling of it, the telling must center itself in harmony with the message of the tale, its one dominant impression and its one dominant mood.

Every story told results in some return from the child. The teacher, in her presentation, must *conceive the child's aim in listening*. This does not mean that she forces her aim upon him. But it does mean that she makes a mental list of the child's own possible problems that the tale is best suited to originate, one of which the child himself will suggest. For the return should originate, not in imitation of what the teller plans, but spontaneously, as the child's own plan, answering to some felt need of his. But that does not prevent the story-teller from using her own imagination, and through it, from realizing what opportunities for growth the story presents, and what possible activities ought to be stimulated. A good guide will keep ahead of the children, know the possibilities of the material, and by knowledge and suggestion lead them to realize and accomplish the plans they crudely conceive. A consideration of these plans will modify the telling of the tale, and should be definitely thought about before the telling of the tale. A story told definitely to stimulate in the children dramatization, will emphasize action and dialogue; while one told to stimulate the painting of a water-color sketch, will emphasize the setting of the tale.

The telling of the tale. With this preparation, directions seem futile. The tale should tell itself naturally. You must begin at the beginning, as your tale will if you have selected a good one. You must tell it simply, as your tale will have simplicity if it is a good one, and your telling must be in harmony with the tale you tell. You will tell it with joy; of course, if there is joy in it, or beauty, which is a "joy forever," or if you are giving joy to your listeners. Tell it, if possible, with a sense of bestowing a blessing, and a delicate perception of the reception it meets in the group before you, and the pleasure and interest it arouses in them, so that in the telling there is that human setting which is a quickening of the spirit and a union of ideas, which is something quite new and different from the story, yet born of the story.

The re-creative method of story-telling. This preparation for telling here described will result in a fundamental imitation of the author of the story. By participating in the life of the story; by realizing it as folklore; by realizing it as literature — its emotion, its imagination, its basis of truth, its message, its form; by paying conscious attention to the large units of the structure, the exact sequence of the plot, the characters, and the setting, the particular details of description, and the unique word — the story-teller reproduces the author's mode of thinking. She does with her mind what she wishes the child to do with his. With the very little child in the kindergarten and early first grade, who analyzes but slightly, this results consciously in a clear notion of the story, which shows itself in the child's free re-telling of the story as a whole. He may want to tell the story or he may not. Usually he enjoys re-telling it after some lapse of time; perhaps he tells it to himself, meanwhile. With the older child, who analyzes more definitely, this results in a re-telling which actually reproduces the teller's mode of thinking. If persisted in, it gives to one's mode of thinking, the *story-mode,* just as nature study gives to life the nature point of view. This mode of thinking is the *mode of re-creation,* of realization. It re-experiences the life, it reaches the processes of the mind, and develops free mind movement. It is a habit of thinking, and is at the basis of reading, which is thinking through symbols; at the basis of the memorization of poetry, which must first see the pictures the poet has portrayed; it is the best help toward the adult study of literature, and the narration of history and geography. It is the power to conceive a situation, which is most useful in science, mathematics, and the reasoning of logic. "For," says Professor John Dewey, "the mind which can make independent judgments, look at facts with fresh vision, and reach conclusions with simplicity, is the perennial power in the world."

This re-creative method of fundamental imitation was illustrated in the telling of Andersen's *Princess and the Pea,* in a student-teacher's class: —

The story was told by the Professor. After the telling of the story it was decided to have the story told again, but this time in parts and by those who had listened, in such a way that it would seem as if one person were telling the whole story.

The Professor named the first part of the story. A student was asked to tell the story from *the beginning* to the end of *the Prince's coming home again, sad at heart.* Another student told the second part, beginning with *the storm* and ending with *what the old Queen thought.* A third student told the third part, beginning with *the next morning* and ending with the close of the story, *Now this is a true story.*

The Professor next asked students to think over the entire story, to see if each student could find any weak places in the remembering of the story. Several students reported difficulty — one failed to remember the exact description of the storm. A number of details were thus filled in, in the exact words of the author. After this intimate handling of the separate parts of the story, a final re-telling by one student — omitted in this case because of lack of time — would bring together what had been contributed by individual students, and would represent the final re-creation of the entire story.

The simplicity of this selection, the simplicity of the plot, the few characters, the literary art of the story, the skillful use of the unique word, the art of presenting distinct pictures by means of vivid words, through suggestion rather than through illustration, together with the delicate humor that hovered about the tale, and the art of the Professor's telling — all combined in the final effect. The re-telling of the story in parts accomplished the analysis of the story into three big heads: —

(1) From *The Prince who wanted a real Princess* . . . to *his return home.*
(2) From *The storm, one dark evening* . . . to *what the old Queen thought.*
(3) From *What the Queen did next morning* . . . to *the end of the story.*

In the analysis of the story into parts, telling exactly what happened gave the framework of the story, gave its basis of meaning. Telling it in three steps gave a strong sense of sequence and a vivid conception of climax. — If the division into parts for re-telling corresponds with the natural divisions of the plot into its main episodes, this telling in steps impresses the structure of the tale and is in harmony with the real literary mastery of the story. — The re-telling of each part drew attention to the visualization of that part. Each hesitation on behalf of a student telling a part, led the class to fill in the details for themselves, and impressed the remembrance of the exact words of the author. This resulted in the mastery of each part through a visualization of it. Hand in hand with the visualization came the feeling aroused by the realization. This was more easily mastered because changes of feeling were noticeable in passing from one part of the story to another.

After a mastery of the structure of the story through analysis, after a mastery of the thought, imagination, and feeling of the story, after a mastery of the form, and the exact words of the author in the description of details embodied in that form, the story is possessed as the teller's own, ready to be given, not only to bestow pleasure, as in this case, but often to transmit a message of worth and to preserve a classic form.

The Foolish Timid Rabbit, a Jataka tale, might be prepared for telling by this same re-creative method of story-telling. It must be remembered — and because of its importance it will bear repetition, — that the separation of the story-structure into parts for separate telling should always be in harmony with the divisions of the plot so that there may be no departure from the author's original mode of thinking, and no break in the natural movement of sequence. A separation of the tale into parts for re-telling would result in the following analysis: —

(1) *Rabbit asleep under a palm tree* . . . to *his meeting hundreds of Rabbits.*
(2) *Rabbits met a Deer* . . . to *when the Elephant joined them.*
(3) *Lion saw the animals running* . . . to *when he came to the Rabbit who first had said the earth was all breaking up.*
(4) *Lion asked the Foolish Rabbit, 'Is it true the earth is all breaking up,'* . . . to *end of the story, 'And they all stopped running.'*

After the re-telling of these parts, each part should be filled in with the exact details so that in the final re-telling practically the whole tale is reproduced. This is a very good tale to tell by this method because the theme is attractive, the plot is simple, the sequence a very evident movement, the characters distinctive, the setting pleasing and rather prominent, and the details sufficiently few and separate to be grasped completely. The final re-telling therefore may be accomplished readily as a perfected result of this method of telling a tale.

During the telling, the charm here is in preserving the typical bits of dialogue, giving to the Lion's words that force and strength and sagacity which rank him the King of the Beasts. One must feel clearly the message and make this message enter into every part of the telling: That the Lion showed his superior wisdom by making a stand and asking for facts, by accepting only what he tested; while the Rabbit showed his credulity by foolishly accepting what he heard without testing it.

Adaptation of the fairy tale. Sometimes, in telling a story one cannot tell it exactly as it is. This may be the case when the story is too long for a purpose, or if it contains matter which had better be omitted, or if it needs to be amplified. In any case one must follow these general rules: —

(1) Preserve the essential story from a single point of view.
(2) Preserve a clear sequence with a distinct climax.
(3) Preserve a simplicity of plot and simple language.

In shortening a long story one may —

(1) Eliminate secondary themes.
(2) Eliminate extra personages.
(3) Eliminate passages of description.
(4) Eliminate irrelevant events.

It has been the practice to adapt such stories as Andersen's *Ugly Duckling* and Ruskin's *King of the Golden River*. In the *King of the Golden River* the description of Treasure Valley could be condensed into a few sentences and the character of South West Wind omitted; and in *The Ugly Duckling*, passages of description and bits of philosophy might be left out. But there is no reason why literature in the elementary school should be treated with mutilation. These stories are not suited to the kindergarten or first grade and may be reserved for the third and fourth grades where they may be used and enjoyed by the children as they are.

Andersen's *Thumbelina* might be adapted for kindergarten children because it is suitable for them yet it is very long. It could easily be analyzed into its leading episodes, each episode making a complete tale, and one or more episodes be told at one time. This would have the added attraction for the child of having one day's story follow naturally the preceding story. Adapted thus, the episodes would be: —

(1) Thumbelina in her Cradle.
(2) Thumbelina and the Toad.
(3) Thumbelina and the Fishes.
(4) Thumbelina and the Cockchafer in the tree.
(5) Thumbelina and the Field-Mouse.
(6) Thumbelina and the Mole.
(7) Thumbelina and the Swallow.
(8) Thumbelina as Queen of the Flowers.

Andersen's *Snow Man* as adapted for the kindergarten would require the episode of the lover omitted. It is irrelevant, not essential to the story, and is an illustration of the sentimental, which must be omitted when we use Andersen. To omit this episode one would cut out from "'That is wonderfully beautiful,' said a young girl," to the end of "'Why, they belong to the Master,' retorted the Yard Dog."

III. THE RETURN FROM THE CHILD[1]

The telling of the fairy tale is one phase of the teacher's art. And it is maintained that fairy tales are one portion of subject-matter suited to accomplish the highest greatness of the teaching art. For teaching is an art, an art of giving suggestions, of bearing influences, of securing adjustments, an art of knowing the best and of making it known. The material the artist works upon is the living child. The medium the artist uses is subject-matter. In the process the artist must ask, "What new connections or associations am I establishing in the child?" "To what power of curiosity and of problem-solving do these connections and associations lead?" The ideal which guides the teacher is the child's best self as she can interpret him. This ideal will be higher and larger than the child himself can know. In the manipulation of subject-matter,

[1] What if we could give the child that which is called education through his voluntary activities, and have him always as eager as he is at play! (*Froebel.*)

What if we could let the child be free and happy, and yet bring to him those things which he ought to have so that he will choose them freely!

What would be the possibilities for a future race if we would give the child mind a chance to come out and express itself, if we would remove adult repression, offer a stimulus, and closely watch the product, untouched by adult skill. (*Unknown.*)

The means by which the higher selective interest is aroused, is the exercise of selected forms of activity. (*Susan Blow.*)

through the practical application of principles, the artist aims to have the child awake, inquire, plan, and act, so that under her influences he grows by what he thinks, by what he feels, by what he chooses, and by what he achieves.

Teaching will be good art when the child's growth is a perfect fit to the uses of his life, when subject-matter brings to him influences he needs and can use. Teaching will be good art when it breaks up old habits, starts new ones, strengthens good traits, and weakens bad ones; when it gives a new attitude of cheerfulness in life or of thoughtfulness for others or of reason in all things. It will be good art when under it the child wants to do something and learns *how* to do it. Teaching will be great art when under it the child continually attains self-activity, self-development, and self-consciousness, when he continually grows so that he may finally contribute his utmost portion to the highest evolution of the race. Teaching will be great art when it touches the emotions of the child, — when history calls forth a warm indignation against wrong, when mathematics strengthens a noble love of truth or literature creates a strong satisfaction in justice. This is the poetry of teaching, because mere subject-matter becomes a criticism of life. Teaching will be great art when you, the teacher, through the humble means of your presentation of subject-matter, furnish the child at the same time with ideas, perceptions, and opinions which are your personal criticism of life. Teaching will be great art when you, the teacher, have worked up into your own character a portion of life which is of value, so that the child coming in touch with you knows an influence more powerful than anything you can do or say. Teaching will then awaken in the child a social relation of abiding confidence, of secure trust, of faith unshakable. And this relation will then create for the teacher the obligation to keep this trust inviolable, to practice daily, *noblesse oblige*. Teaching will be great art when with the subject-matter the artist gives love, a great universal kindness that thinks not of itself but, being no respecter of persons, looks upon each child in the light of that child's own best realization. This penetrating sympathy, this great understanding, will call forth from the child an answering love, which grows daily into a larger humanity of soul until the child, in time too, comes to have a universal sympathy. This is the true greatness of teaching. This it is which brings the child into harmony with the Divine love which speaks in all God's handiwork and brings him into that unity with God which is the mystery of Froebel's teaching.

During the story-telling one must ask, " In all this what is the part the child has to play? " In the telling the teacher has aimed to give what there is in the tale. The child's part is to receive what there is in the tale, the emotion, the imagination, the truth, and the form embodied in the tale. The content of feeling, of portrayal, of truth, and of language he receives, he will in some way transmit before the school day is ended, even if in forms obscure and hidden. Long years afterwards, he may exhibit this same emotion, imagination, truth and form, in deeds that proclaim loudly the return from his fairy tales. However, if the child is being surrounded by pragmatic influences through his teachers he will soon become aware that his feelings are useless unless he does something because of them; that what he sees is worthless unless he sees to some purpose; that it is somewhat fruitless to know the truth and not use it; and if words have in their form expressed the life of the tale, he is more dead than words not to express the life that teems within his own soul. The little child grows gradually into the responsibility for action, for expression, into a consciousness of purpose and a knowledge of his own problems. But each opportunity he is given to announce his own initiative breaks down the inhibition of inaction and aids him to become a free achieving spirit. As the child listens to the tale he is a thinking human creature; but in the return which he makes to his tale he becomes a quickened creator. The use which he makes of the ideas he has gained through his fairy tales, will be the work of his creative imagination.

Fairy tales, though perfectly ordinary subject-matter, may become the means of the greatest end in education, the development in the child of the power of consciousness. The special appeal to the various powers and capacities of the child mind, such as emotion, imagination, memory, and reason, here have been viewed separately. But in life action the mind is a unit. Thinking is therefore best developed through subject-matter which focuses the various powers of the child. The one element which makes the child manipulate his emotion, imagination, memory, and reason, is the presence of a problem. The problem is the best chance for the child to secure the adjustment of means to ends. This adjustment of means to ends in a problem situation, is real thinking and is the use of the highest power of which man is capable, that of functional consciousness. The real need of doing things is the best element essential to the problem. Through a problem which expresses such a genuine need, to learn to know himself, to realize his capacities and his limitations, and to secure for himself the evolution of his own character until it adapts, not itself to its environment, but its environment to its own uses and masters circumstances for its own purposes — this is the high hill to which education must look, "from which cometh its strength." The little child, in listening to a fairy tale, in seeing in it a problem of real need, and in working it out, may win some of this strength. We have previously seen that fairy tales, because of their universal elements, are subject-matter rich in possible problems.

During the story-telling what is the part the child has to play? The part of the child in all this may be to listen to the story because he has some problem of his own to work out through the literature, because he has some purpose of his own in listening, because he enjoys the story and wishes to find out what there is in it, or because he expects it to show him what he may afterwards wish to do with it. In any case the child's part is to see the characters and what they do, to follow the sequence of the tale, and to realize the life of the story through the telling. He may have something to say about the story at the close of the telling, he may wish to compare its motifs with similar motifs in other tales, or he may wish to talk about the life exhibited by the story. The various studies of the curriculum every day are following more closely the Greek ideal and giving the child daily exercise to keep the channels of expression free and open. And when the well-selected fairy tale which is art is told, through imitation and invention it awakens in the child the art-impulse and tends to carry him from appreciation to expression. If before the telling the story-teller has asked herself, "What variety of creative reaction will this tale arouse in the child?" and if she has told the story in the way to bring forward the best possibility for creative reaction the nature of the tale affords, she will help to make clear to the child what he himself will want to do with the story. She will help him to see a way to use the story to enter into his everyday life. The return of creative reaction possible to the child will be that in harmony with his natural instincts or large general interests. These instincts, as indicated by Professor John Dewey, in *The School and Society*, are: (1) the instinct of conversation or communication; (2) the instinct of inquiry or finding out things; (3) the instinct of construction or making things; and (4) the instinct of artistic expression or [of imitating and combining things].

(1) **The instinct of conversation.** The little child likes to talk. If you have ever listened to a little girl of five artlessly proceeding to tell a story, such as *Little Black Sambo*, which she had gathered from looking at a neighbor's book, but which she had not yet mastered sufficiently to grasp its central theme, reiterating the particular incidents with the enthusiasm and joy and narrative tone of the story-teller, you realized how the child likes to talk. For there appeared the charm of the story-telling mode distinct from the story it told.

Because of this instinct of conversation one form of creative reaction may be *language expression*. The oral reproduction of the story re-experiences the story anew. The teacher may help here by creating a situation for the re-telling. A teacher might put a little foreign boy through rapid paces in learning English by selecting a story like *The Sparrow and the Crow* and by managing that in the re-telling the little foreigner would be the Crow who makes the repetitive speeches, who must go to the Pond and say: —

> Your name, sir, is Pond
> And my name is Crow,
> Please give me some water,
> For if you do so

I can wash and be neat,
And the nice soup can eat,
Though I really don't know
What the sparrow can mean,
I'm quite sure, as crows go,
I'm remarkably clean.

As the Crow must go to the Deer, the Cow, the Grass, and the Blacksmith, and each time varies the beginning of his speech, four other children could represent the Crow successively, thus bringing in a social element which would relieve any one child's timidity. By that time any group of children would realize the fun they could get by playing out the simple tale; and there would be petitions to be the Deer, the Cow, etc. If the teacher sees that the characters place themselves as they should, carry out the parts naturally, and that the Crow begs with the correct rhyme, she is performing her legitimate task of suggestion and criticism that works toward developing from the first attempts of children, a good form in harmony with the story. Here, while there is free play, the emphasis is on the speeches of rhyme, so that the reaction is largely a language expression. The language expression is intimately related to all varieties of expression of which the child is capable, and may be made to dominate and use any of them, or be subordinated to them.

A most delightful form of creative reaction possible to the child in language expression, is the *formation of original little stories* similar to the "Toy Stories" written by Carolyn Bailey for the *Kindergarten Review* during 1915. A story similar to "The Little Woolly Dog" might be originated by the little child about any one of his toys. This would be related to his work with fairy tales because in such a story the child would be imitating his accumulative tales; and the adventures given the toy would be patterned after the familiar adventures of his tales.

A form of creative reaction, which will be a part of the language return given by the first-grade child from the telling of the tale, will be his *reading of the tale.* When the child re-experiences the life of the story as has been described, his mental realization of it will be re-creative, and his reading the tale aloud afterwards will be just as much a form of re-creative activity as his re-telling of the tale. The only difference is, that in one case the re-creative activity is exercised by thinking through symbols, while in the other case it is employed without the use of a book. This concentration on the reality brings about the proper relation of reading to literature. It frees literature from the slavery to reading which it has been made to serve, yet it makes literature contribute more effectively toward good reading than it has done in the past.

(2) **The instinct of inquiry.** No more predominating trait proclaims itself in the child than the instinct of inquiry. Every grown-up realizes his habit of asking questions, which trait Kipling has idealized delightfully in *The Elephant's Child.* We know also that the folk-tale in its earliest beginnings was the result of

primitive man's curiosity toward the actual physical world about him, its sun and sky, its mountain and its sea. The folk-tale therefore is the living embodiment of the child's instinct of inquiry permanently recorded in the adventures and surprises of the folk-tale characters. And because the folk-tale is so pervaded with this quest of the ages in search of truth, and because the child by nature is so deeply imitative, the folk-tale inherently possesses an educational value to stir and feed original impulses of investigation and experiment. This is a value which is above and beyond its more apparent uses.

In the creative reaction to be expected from the child's use of fairy tales the expression of this instinct of investigation unites with the instinct of conversation, the instinct of construction, and the instinct of artistic expression. In fact, it is the essence of creative reaction in any form, whether in the domain of the Industrial Shop, the Domestic Science Kitchen, the Household Arts' Sewing-Room, or the Fine Arts' Studio. To do things and then see what happens, is both the expression of this instinct and the basis of any creative return the child makes through his handling of the fairy tale. In the formation of a little play such as is given on page 149, the instinct of conversation is expressed in the talk of the Trees to the little Bird. But this talk of the Trees also expresses *doing things to see what happens;* each happening to the Bird, each reply of a Tree to the Bird, influences each successive doing of the Bird. After the Story of *Medio Pollito* all the child's efforts of making Little Half-Chick into a weathervane and of fixing the directions to his upright shaft, will be expressions of the search for the unknown, of the instinct of experiment. After the story of *The Little Elves*, the dance of the Elves to the accompaniment of music will represent an expression of the artistic instinct; but it also represents expression of the instinct for the new and the untried. After the dance is finished the child has seen himself do something he had not done before. This union of the instinct of inquiry with that of artistic expression shows itself most completely in the entire dramatization of a fairy tale.

(3) **The instinct of construction.** In his industrial work the very youngest child is daily exercising his active tendency to make things. In the kindergarten he may make the toy with which he plays, the doll-house and its furnishings, small clay dishes, etc. In the first grade he may make small toy animals, baskets, paper hats, card-board doll-furniture, little houses, book-covers, toys, etc. Self-expression, self-activity, and constructive activity would all be utilized, and the work would have more meaning to the child, if it *expressed some idea*, if after the story of *Three Bears* the child would make the Bears' kitchen, the table of wood, and the three porridge bowls of clay, or the Bears' hall with the three chairs. In the Grimm tale, *Sweet Rice Porridge*, after the story has been told and before the

re-telling, children would like to make a clay porridge-pot, which could be there before them in the re-telling. Perhaps they would make the rice porridge also, and put some in the pot, for little children are very fond of making things to eat, and domestic science has descended even into the kindergarten. After the story of *Chanticleer and Partlet*, children would enjoy making a little wagon and harnessing to it a Duck, and putting in it the Cock and the Hen, little animals they have made. In the first grade, after the story of *Sleeping Beauty*, children would naturally take great pleasure in making things needed to play the story: the paper silver and gold crowns of the maids and Princess and the Prince's sword. After the story of *Medio Pollito*, we have noted with what special interest children might make a weathervane, with Little Half-Chick upon it!

(4) **The instinct of artistic expression.** This is the instinct of drawing, painting, paper-cutting, and crayon-sketching, the instinct of song, rhythm, dance, and game, of free play and dramatization.

(*a*) One form of artistic creative reaction will be *the cutting of free silhouette pictures*. The child should attempt this with the simplest of the stories which are suited for drawing, painting, or crayon-sketching. He loves to represent the animals he sees every day; and the art work should direct this impulse and show him how to do it so that he may draw or cut out a dog, a cat, a sheep, or a goat; or simple objects, as a broom, a barrel, a box, a table, and a chair. *The Bremen Town*

Musicians, while offering a fine opportunity for dramatization, also might stimulate the child to cut out the silhouettes of the Donkey, the Dog, the Cat, and the Cock, to draw the window of the cottage and to place the animals one on top of another, looking in the window. The beautiful picture-books illustrating his fairy tales, which the child may see, will give him many ideas of drawing and sketching, and help him to arrange his silhouettes. A recent primer, *The Pantomime Primer*, will give the child new ideas in silhouettes. Recent articles in the *Kindergarten Review* will give the teacher many helpful suggestions along the line of expression. In the May number, 1915, in *Illustrated Stories*, the story of "Ludwig and Marleen," by Jane Hoxie, is shown as a child might illustrate it with paper-cutting. — A class of children were seen very pleasantly intent on cutting out of paper a basket filled with lovely tinted flowers. But how attractive that same work would have become if the basket had been Red Riding Hood's basket and they were being helped by an art-teacher to show peeping out of her basket the cake and pot of butter, with the nosegay tucked in one end. A very practical problem in paper-cutting would arise in any room when children desire to make a frieze to decorate the front wall. *The Old Woman and her Pig*, *The Country Mouse and the City Mouse*, *The Little Red Hen*, *The Story of Three Pigs*, *The Story of Three Bears*, and *Little Top-Knot*, would be admirably adapted for simple work.

(*b*) *The Straw, the Coal, and the Bean* is most likely to stir the child's impulse to *draw*. Leslie Brooke's illustration in *The House in the Wood* might aid a child who wanted to put some fun into his representation. *Birdie and Lena* or *Fundevogel*, is a story that naturally would seek illustration. Three *crayon-sketches*, one of a rosebush and a rose, a second of a church and a steeple, and a third of a pond and a duck, would be enough to suggest the tale.

(*c*) *The Story of the Wolf and Seven Kids*, if told with the proper emphasis on the climax of triumph and conclusion of joy, would lead the child to react with a *water-color sketch* of the dance of the Goat and her Kids about the well. For here you have all the elements needed for a simple picture — the sky, the full moon, the hill-top, the well, and the animals dancing in a ring. After finishing their sketches the children would enjoy comparing them with the illustration of *Der Wolf und die Sieben Geislein* in *Das Deutsche Bilderbüch*, and perhaps they might try making a second sketch. This same tale would afford the children a chance to compose a simple tune and a simple song, such as the well-taught kindergarten child to-day knows. Such are songs which express a single theme and a single mood; as, *The Muffin Man* and *To the Great Brown House;* or *There was a Small Boy with a Toot* and *Dapple Gray* in *St. Nicholas Songs*. In this tale of *The Wolf and Seven Kids*, the conclusion impresses a single mood of joy and the single theme of freedom because the Wolf is dead. The child could produce a very simple song of perhaps two lines, such as, —

> Let's sing and dance! Hurrah, hurrah!
> The Wolf is dead! Hurrah!

(*d*) It is a little difficult to get down to the simplicity of the little girl who will play her own tune upon the piano and sing to it just the number of the house in which she lives, repeating it again and again. But the child can *compose little songs* that will please him, and he can use, too, in connection with the tales, some of the songs that he knows. The first-grade child could work into *Snow White and Rose Red,* " Good morrow, little rosebush," and into *Little Two-Eyes* a lullaby such as " Sleep, baby, sleep." Later in *Hansel and Grethel* he may learn some of the simple songs that have been written for Hansel and Grethel to sing to the birds when they spend the night in the wood. In *Snow White* he may learn some of the songs written for the children's play, *Snow White.* In connection with music, the kindergarten child learns to imitate the sounds of animals, the sound of bells, whistles, the wind, etc. All this will cause him to react, so that when these occur in his stories he will want to make them.

(*e*) One of the forms of creative reaction possible to the child as a variety of expression, which has received attention most recently, has been handled by Miss Caroline Crawford in *Rhythm Plays of Childhood;* and by Miss Carol Oppenheimer in "Suggestions Concerning Rhythm Plays," in the *Kindergarten Review*, April and May, 1915. Here again the fairy tales cannot be excelled in abundant situations for rhythm plays. The sea, the wind, the clouds, the sun, the moon, the stars — all nature is rich in suggestion of rhythms. The social situations furnish the rhythm of simple housekeeping tasks. In *Snow White and Rose Red* there are the rhythms of fishing and of chasing animals. In *The Elves* we have the rhythm of shoemaking and in *The Straw Ox*, the rhythm of spinning. The story of *Thumbelina*, after its eight episodes have been re-told by the children, might very attractively be re-told in eight rhythms, each rhythm expressing a single episode. And for the oldest children, a union of the oral re-telling by individual children with the re-telling in rhythms by all the children, would give much pleasure and social exhilaration. Thumbelina in her Cradle, Thumbelina and the Toad, Thumbelina and the Swallow and Thumbelina as Queen of the Flowers — these at once suggest a cradle rhythm, a toad rhythm, the flight of birds, and a butterfly dance. Because the rhythm is a lyric form it must be remembered that the part of a story suited to a rhythm play is always a part characterized by a distinct emotional element. In the performance of rhythm plays the point is to secure the adjustment of music, motion, and idea.

(*f*) Many of the fairy tales might arouse in the child a desire *to originate a game*, especially if he were accustomed to originate games in the regular game work. A modification of the game of tag might grow from *Red Riding Hood* and a pleasant ring game easily might develop from *Sleeping Beauty.* In fact there is a traditional English game called "Sleeping Beauty." An informal ring game which would be somewhat of a joke, and would have the virtue of developing attention, might grow from *The Tin Soldier.* The Tin Soldier stands in the center while the circle is formed of Jack-in-the-boxes, with lids closed. The Tin Soldier turns round and round slowly, and when he stops looks steadily at a certain Jack-in-the-box, whereupon the Jack must bob up and retort, "Keep your eyes to yourself, Tin Soldier!" The Jack and Soldier then change places. Any Jack failing to open when looked at forfeits his place in the ring. Some games derived from folk-tales were given in the *Delineator*, November, 1914. These could not be used by the youngest without adaptation; they suggest a form of fun that so far as I know has been undeveloped.

(*g*) The artistic creative return of the child may sometimes take the form of *objectification or representation. The Steadfast Tin Soldier* is a model of the literary fairy tale which gives a stimulus to the child to represent his fairy tale objectively. As straightforward narrative it ranks high. Its very first clause is the child's point of view: "There were five and twenty tin soldiers"; for the child counts his soldiers. Certainly the theme is unique and the images clear-cut.

It makes one total impression and it has one emotional tone to which everything is made to contribute. Its message of courage and its philosophy of life, which have been mentioned previously, are not so insignificant even if the story does savor of the sentimental. Its structure is one single line of sequence, from the time this marvelous soldier was stood up on the table, until he, like many another toy, was thrown into the fire. The vivid language used gives vitality to the story, the words suit the ideas, and often the words recall a picture or suggestion; as, "The Soldier *fell headlong,*" "*trod,*" "came down in *torrents,*" "boat *bobbed,*" "*spun* round," "*clasped* his gun," "boat *shot* along," "*blinked* his eyes," etc. The method of suggestion by which an object is described through its effect on some one else, produces a very pleasing result here. You see the steadfast look of the Tin Soldier's eyes when the Jack-in-the-box says, "Keep your eyes to yourself, Tin Soldier!" The position of the Soldier in the street is given through the exclamation of the little boys who see him — "Look! there lies a Tin Soldier, let us give him a sail in the gutter!"

The setting in this story is a table in a sitting-room and the playthings on the table. The characters are two playthings. After the first telling of this story the child naturally would like to represent it. The story has made his playthings come alive and so he would like to make them appear also. This is a tale in which representation, after the first telling, will give to the child much pleasure and will give him a chance to do something with it coöperatively. He can reproduce the setting of this tale upon a table in a schoolroom. Each child could decide what is needed to represent the story and offer what he can. One child could make the yard outside the castle of green blotting-paper. Another child could furnish a mirror for the lake, another two toy green trees, one two wax swans, one a box of tin soldiers, another a jack-in-the-box, while the girls might dress a paper doll for a tinsel maid. The teacher, instructed by the class, might make a castle of heavy gray cardboard, fastening it together with heavy brass paper-fasteners and cutting out the door, windows, and tower. It is natural for children to handle playthings; and when a story like this is furnished the teacher should not be too work-a-day to enter into its play-spirit. After the representation objectively, the re-telling of the tale might be enjoyed. The child who likes to draw might tell this story also in a number of little sketches: *The Jack-in-the-box*, *The Window*, *The Boat*, *The Rat*, *The Fish*, and *The Fire*. Or a very simple little dramatic dance and song might be invented, characterized by a single mood and a single form of motion, something like this, sung to the tune of "Here we go round the mulberry bush, etc": —

Here we come marching, soldiers tin, soldiers tin, soldiers tin,
Here we come marching, soldiers tin,
On one leg steady we stand.

(Circle march on one leg).

This could easily be concluded with a game if the child who first was compelled to march on two legs had to pay some penalty, stand in the center of the ring, or march at the end of the line.

(*h*) Creative reaction as a result of listening to the telling of fairy tales, appears in its most varied form of artistic expression in *free play and dramatization*. It is here that the child finds a need for the expression of all his skill in song and dance, construction, language, and art, for here he finds a use for these things.

In free play the child represents the characters and acts out the story. His desire to play will lead to a keenness of attention to the story-telling, which is the best aid to re-experiencing, and the play will react upon his mind and give greater power to visualize. Nothing is better for the child than the freedom and initiative used in dramatization, and nothing gives more self-reliance and poise than to act, to do something. — We must remember that in the history of the child's literature it was education that freed his spirit from the deadening weight of didacticism in the days of the *New England Primer*. And we must now have a care that education never may become guilty of crushing the spirit of his freedom, spontaneity, and imagination, by a dead formalism in its teaching method. — The play develops the voice, and it gives freedom and grace to bodily movements. It fixes in the child mind the details of the story and impresses effectively many a good piece of literature; it combines intellectual, emotional, artistic, and physical action. The simplest kindergarten plays, such as *The Farmer*, *The Blacksmith*, and *Little Travelers*, naturally lead into playing a story such as *The Sheep and the Pig* or *The Gingerbread Man*. *The Mouse that Lost Her Tail* and *The Old Woman and Her Pig* are delightful simple plays given in *Chain Stories and Playlets* by Mara Chadwick and E. Gray Freeman, suited to the kindergarten to play or the first grade to read and play. Working out a complete dramatization of a folk-tale such as *Sleeping Beauty*, in the first grade, and having the children come into the kindergarten and there play it for them, will be a great incentive toward catching the spirit of imaginatively entering into a situation which you are not. This is the essential for dramatization. *Johnny Cake* is a good tale to be played in the kindergarten because it uses a great number of children. As the kindergarten room generally is large, it enables the children who represent the man, the woman, the little boy, etc., to station themselves at some distance.

There are some dangers in dramatization which are to be avoided: —

(1) *Dramatization often is in very poor form.* The result is not the important thing, but the process. And sometimes teachers have understood this to mean, "Hands off!" and left the children to their crude impulses, unaided and unimproved. When the child shows *what* he is trying to do the teacher may show him *how* he can do what he wants to do. By suggestion

and criticism she may get him to improve his first effort, provided she permits him to be absolutely free when he acts. — The place of this absolute freedom in the child's growth has been emblazoned to the kindergarten by the Montessori System. — Also by participating in the play as one of the characters, the teacher may help to a better form. Literature will be less distorted by dramatization when teachers are better trained to see the possibilities of the material, when through training they appreciate the tale as one of the higher forms of literature, and respect it accordingly. Also it will be less distorted by dramatization when the tales selected for use are those containing the little child's interests, when he will have something to express which he really knows about. Moreover, as children gain greater skill in expression in construction, in the game, in song, in dance, and in speech, the parts these contribute to the play will show a more perfected form. Each expression by the child grows new impressions, gives him new sensory experiences. Perhaps if the high school would realize the possibilities in a fairy tale such as *Beauty and the Beast*, work it up into really good artistic form, and play it for the little children, much would be gained not only towards good form in dramatics, in both the elementary school and the high school, but towards unifying the entire course of literature from the kindergarten to the university. Using Crane's picture-book as a help, they might bring into the play the beauty of costume and scenery, the court-jester, and Beauty's pages. Into the Rose-Garden they might bring a dance of Moon Fairies, Dawn Fairies, Noon, and Night who, in their symbolic gauzy attire, dance to persuade Beauty to remain in the Beast's castle. There might be singing fairies who decorate the bushes with fairy roses, and others who set the table with fairy dishes, singing as they work: —

> See the trees with roses gay,
> Fairy roses, fairy roses, etc.

Elves and Goblins might surround the Beast when dying. The change of scene from the simple home of Beauty to the rich castle of the Beast, and the change of costume, would furnish ample opportunity for original artistic work from older students. For the little child it is good to see the familiar dignified with art and beauty; and for the older student the imagination works more freely when dealing with rather simple and familiar elements such as the folk-tale offers. *Cinderella*, like *Beauty and the Beast*, offers abundant opportunity to the high school student for a play or pantomime which it would be good for the little people to see. The stately minuet and folk-dances of different peoples may be worked into the ball-scene. And here, too, the beautiful picture-books will suggest features of costume and scenery.

(2) *Dramatization may develop boldness in a child.* The tendency is to use children with good dramatic ability continually for leading parts, even when the

children choose the parts. This fault may be counteracted by distinguishing between work for growth and one or two rather carefully prepared plays to be given on special occasions. It is also counteracted by looking well to the social aspect of the play, by introducing features such as the song, dance, or game, where all have a part, or by adding attractive touches to less important parts, so that while a character may still be leading it will have no reason to feel over-important. This danger is not prominent until after the first grade.

(3) *Dramatization may spoil some selections.* Beautiful descriptions which make a tale poetic are not to be represented, and without them a tale is cheapened. Such is the case with *The King of the Golden River* and *The Ugly Duckling*. Care should be exercised to choose for dramatization only what is essentially dramatic and what is of a grade suited to the child. Tales suited to the little child are largely suited for dramatization.

(4) *Dramatization has omitted to preserve a sequence in the selections used from year to year.* A sequence in dramatization will follow naturally as the tales offered from year to year show a sequence in the variety of interests they present and the opportunities for growth and activity they offer. Plays most suited to the kindergarten are those which do not require a complete re-telling of the story in the acting, so that the child need not say so much. Such are stories like *The Old Woman and Her Pig*, *Henny Penny*, *The Foolish Timid Rabbit*, *Little Tuppen*, *Three Billy-Goats*,

Johnny Cake, and *Billy Bobtail*. When the course of literature in the elementary school gets its content organized, the sequence of dramatization will take care of itself.

Dramatization has one rather unusual virtue: —

(1) *Dramatization may be used to establish a good habit.* An indolent child may be given the part of the industrious child in the play. At first the incongruity will amuse him, then it will support his self-respect or please his vanity, then it will prove to him the pleasure of being industrious, and finally stimulate the desire to be that which before he was not. It may build a habit and, if repeated, fortify one. This is the true "Direct Moral Method." The so-called "Direct Moral Method," advocated by Dr. Gould, an English educator, which in telling a story separates the moral from the tale to emphasize it and talk about it, leaves the child a passive listener with only a chance to say "Yes" or "No" or a single word in answer to the moral questions. It is unnatural because it directs the child's attention away from the situation, action, and people which interest him. It does not parallel life in which morals are tied up with conduct. One must ask, "According to this method what will the child recall if his mind reverts to the story — courage, or the variety of images from the number of short-stories told to impress the abstract moral idea of courage?" Dramatization like life represents character in the making and therefore helps to make character.

Illustrations of creative return. Let us look now at a few tales illustrating the creative return possible to the child. *The Country Mouse and the City Mouse* is an animal tale that offers to the kindergarten child a chance to prove how intensely he enters into the situation by the number of details he will improvise and put into his dramatization in representing life in the country and life in the city. The good feast atmosphere in this tale pleases little children and suits it to their powers. It is a fine tale to *unite the language expression and dramatization.* It is especially suited to call forth reaction from the child also in the form of *drawing or crayon sketching.* Here it is best for the child to attempt typical bits. Complete representation tires him and it is not the method of art, which is selective. The field of corn and two mice may be shown in the country scene; and a table with cheese, some plates filled with dainties, and two mice in the city scene. Here again this return relates itself to the presentation of the tale as literature. For if the story has been presented so as to make the characters, the plot, and the setting stand out, the child naturally will select these to portray in a sketch. In his expression the child will represent what he chooses, but the teacher by selecting from among the results the one which is of most value, leads him to a better result in a following attempt. It is the *teacher's selection among the results of activity* that brings about development. Freedom with guidance is no less free, but it is freedom under that stimulation which helps the child to make more of himself than he knew was possible. — The kindergarten would proclaim to the Montessori System the place of *guidance of freedom* in the child's growth.

The Elves and the Shoemaker offers to a first grade a pleasing opportunity for the *fairy tale to unite with the dramatic game.* One child may act as narrator, standing to tell the story from the beginning to the end of the evening's conversation, "I should like to sit up to-night and see who it is that makes the shoes." At this point, noiselessly a dozen or more Elves may troop in, and seating themselves sing and act the first part of the *Dramatic Game of Little Elves*, one form of which is given by Miss Crawford. After they have stitched, rapped, and tapped quickly, and the shoes are made, they depart hurriedly. The narrator now continues the story, telling how the Shoemaker and his wife made little clothes for the Elves, ending with what happened on Christmas Eve, when they put the gay jackets and caps on the table and hid in the corner to watch. At this point the Elves come in a second time, donning their new clothes; and sing and dance the second part of the dramatic game. As they dance out of sight the narrator concludes the story. If the primary children made these clothes or if the kindergarten children bought them at Christmas time to give to the poor, the play[1] would take on a real human value.

[1] *Little Two-Eyes* and *Snow White* are tales also suited to the first grade for dramatization. See *Appendix*.

Sleeping Beauty, another tale suited to the first grade, is admirably adapted for dramatization. — In all this work the children do the planning but the teacher directs their impulses, criticizes their plans, and shows them what they have done. She leads them to see the tale in the correct acts and scenes, to put together what belongs together. *Sleeping Beauty* naturally outlines itself into the ten main incidents we have noted before. If the story has been presented according to the standards given here, the children will see the story in those main incidents. In the dramatization they might work together narration of the story and the dramatic game, *Dörnroschen*. A wide circle of children might be the chorus while the players take their places in the center of the circle. The narrator, one of the circle, stands apart from it as he narrates. The version here used is the McLoughlin one, illustrated by Johann and Leinweber.

Sleeping Beauty

Place: Castle. King, Queen, and courtiers take their places within the circle. The circle moves to waltz step, singing stanza 1, of the dramatic game: —

The Princess was so beautiful, beautiful, beautiful, etc.

At the conclusion of stanza 1, the circle stops, the narrator steps forth and tells the story to the end of the words, "one had to stay at home."

Scene i. The Feast. Twelve fairies enter, each presenting her gift and making a speech. The wicked thirteenth comes in and pronounces her curse, and the twelfth fairy softens it to sleep. The King proclaims his decree, that all spindles in the land be destroyed.

Scene ii. The Attic. Princess goes to the attic. Old lady sits spinning. Princess pricks herself and falls asleep. Narration begins with "The King and Queen who had just come in fell asleep," and ends with "not a leaf rustled on the trees around the castle." At the close of the narration, the circle moves, singing stanza 5 of the dramatic game: —

A great hedge grew up giant high, giant high, giant high, etc.

Scene iii. The Castle Grounds. The Prince talks to an old Man outside the castle. The Prince comes to the hedge, which parts, and he enters. The Prince wakens the Princess and the rest of the castle. The narrator then closes with "By and by the wedding of the Prince . . . to the end of their lives they lived happy and contented." The courtiers then form into couples, and the circle, in couples, follow the courtiers. The Prince and Princess lead in a slow waltz while all sing stanza 10 of the dramatic game: —

And all the people made merry then, merry then, merry then, etc.

Here we do not have complete dramatization, narration, or dramatic game. Only three short parts are narrated, only three leading scenes are represented, and only three high points of narrative are depicted in the dramatic game. The music, which the specialist in physical education can furnish, might be: —

Galloping........... Wild Horseman.
Fairy Run.......... Chalef Book, p. 18.
Climbing to Tower... Chaly, p. 10.
Guy Walk Music.
Phyllis.............. Seymour Smith.
Bleking............. Folk-Dance Book.

In connection with the *dramatic game*, there is only one tale in Grimm which contains a folk-game. This tale is somewhat incomplete as it stands in Grimm. It could become a tale suited for dramatization in the first grade, beginning the play with the folk-game. An original, amplified version of this tale, *The Little Lamb and the Little Fish* is given in the *Appendix*.

An original little play similar to one which the kindergarten children could work out is given below. This play is based on the *pourquois* tale, *Why the Evergreen Trees Never Lose Their Leaves.*[1] It affords much play of originality because familiar trees may be used; and the talk of the Trees to the Bird may have some relation to the characteristics of the Trees. It could be used by children of six, seven, or eight years of age. It could serve as a Christmas play because of its spirit of kindness. North Wind might wear a wig and the Frost King wear a crown and carry a wand. Little Bird could have wings, one of which is broken, or simply carry one arm sleeveless.

The play might open with a rhythmic flight of the birds to the music of "The Swallow's Flight," in *Kindergarten Review*, May, 1915. The rhythm play of the birds would be especially pleasing because different birds would be represented by different children. The play would furnish a fine opportunity also for a rhythmic dance of the wind, which could form a distinct interlude later on in the play. In connection with the wind the beautiful picture-book, *Windschen*, by Elsa

[1] A similar tale is told by Miss Holbrook in *The Book of Nature Myths*. Also by Mary McDowell as "The Three Little Christmas Trees." A simple version of this tale, "The Three Little Christmas Trees that Grew on the Hill," is given in *The Story-Teller's Book* by Alice O'Grady and Frances Throop.

Beskow, might be referred to. Here the wind is personified as the playmate of Hans Georg. Its refined art, lovely color, and imaginative illustration, would stimulate the child's artistic representation of the wind.

The Bird and the Trees: A Play

Time......Daytime, in late autumn.
Place......The Forest.
Characters: Poplar, Oak, Maple, Willow, Spruce, Pine, Juniper, the Bird, North Wind, and the Frost King.

Trees of the forest. "See that great crowd of birds flying away! They must be going South where the air is warm, and where they can find berries to eat. There is one left behind. Why, he is coming this way. What can he want?"

The Bird. "Oh, I can fly no farther! My wing hurts and I cannot hold it up. I am tired and cold and hungry. I must rest in this forest. Maybe some good kind tree will help me. Dear friend Poplar, my wing is broken and my friends have all gone South. Will you let me live in your branches until they come back again?"

Poplar. "I am sorry but do you not see how my leaves are all a-tremble at the thought of taking in a strange bird? Ask some other tree!"

The Bird. "It might not be very warm there at any rate. And the wind might blow me off the branches. I will try the Oak, he is so big and mighty. Dear old Oak-tree, you are so big and strong, will you let me rest in your branches tonight among your thick warm leaves? I am a poor little Bird with a broken wing and I cannot fly!"

Oak. "Oh, you must not ask me, little Bird, for all day long my little friends, the squirrels, have been jumping across my branches, gathering nuts and seeking holes to store their acorns in. I have no room for a stranger."

The Bird. "Ah! I did not think the Oak could be so cruel. Perhaps Maple will help me, she always seemed kind like a Mother. Dear, beautiful Maple, I am tired. May I rest among your lovely red leaves until my broken wing is mended and my friends come back to me?"

Maple. "Oh, no, I could not think of it! I have just dressed my leaves all in red and you might spoil their lovely clothes. Do go away. There are other trees in the forest not so gay as I."

The Bird. "What should I do? No one wants to help me. Can I not find one kind tree? Dear kind Willow, your branches bend almost to the ground. Could I live in them until the spring-time?"

Willow. "Really, little Bird with the broken wing, you are a stranger. You should have gone with the other birds. Maybe some other tree can help you but we willows are particular."

The Bird. "I do not know where to go and I 'm so cold! I wonder if the other birds have reached the beautiful warm South."

Spruce. "Little Bird, little Bird, where are you going?"

The Bird. "I do not know. I am very cold."

Spruce. "Come, make a big hop and rest in this snug corner of my branches. You can stay with me all winter if you like."

The Bird. "You are so good, dear Spruce-tree. Will you really let me?"

Spruce. "If your friends the birds have left you, your other friends, the trees, will surely help you. Ho, Pine-tree, you would help a little Bird with a broken wing, would n't you?"

Pine. "Oh, yes, dear Bird! My branches are not wide but I am tall and thick, and I will keep the cold North Wind from you."

Juniper. "And maybe I can help. Are you hungry, little Bird? You can eat my nice little berries whenever you like."

The Bird. "Thank you, kind friends! I will go to sleep now on this nice branch of the Spruce-tree. Good-night, dear Trees."

Spruce, Pine, and Juniper. "Good-night, little Bird."

North Wind. "*Oo, — Oo!* — Now I must run in and out among all the trees of the forest. — But who comes here?"

Frost King. " Stop, North Wind! I have just gone before you, as King Winter said, and touched the trees of the forest. But the trees that have been kind to the Bird with the broken wing, those I did not touch. They shall keep their leaves. Do not you harm them! "

North Wind. " Very well, King Frost. Good-bye! *Oo!* — *Oo!* — (The Wind frolics among the Trees, bending branches, careering wildly, shaking leaves.) " Little Spruce-tree, you have been kind to the Bird, I will not blow on you! Dear Pine-tree, you are tall and keep the Bird warm, I will not blow on you! Little Juniper, you gave the Bird your berries, I will not blow on you! "

(*The following morning.*)

The Bird. " Good-morning, dear Spruce-tree, your branch was warm and safe. — Why, what has happened to the other Trees? Look at the big Oak and the lovely Maple and all the rest! See how bare their branches are; and on the ground their shining leaves lie in red and yellow and brown heaps! O, how glad I am that your leaves have not fallen; they are bright and green! And so are Pine-tree's and Juniper's. I will call you my Evergreen Trees, and I will stay with you until the Spring! "

The English fairy tale, *The Magpie's Nest*, told by Joseph Jacobs, might be dramatized by first-grade children. This tale might offer the problem of observing how different birds make their nests and how they vary their calls. It also might offer the language problem of making suitable rhymes. An original dramatization of the *pourquois* tale is given in the *Appendix*.

Andersen's *Fir Tree* would offer a fine opportunity for a first grade at Christmas time. The fir tree has become vitally interesting through nature study at this time of the year. The children love to make things to decorate a tree. They have a short list of stories they can tell by this time. All this can be utilized in a Christmas tree play. — For the play use the original story, not a weakened version. — A pleasant Christmas play could end most happily with the story-telling under the tree. For the play an actual small fir tree may be in the room placed so that it may be moved easily. A child standing closely behind it may represent it and speak for it through its branches. The air and the sun, ordinarily not to be represented, in this case may be, as they come up to the Tree and talk to it. Much freedom of originality may be displayed through the children's entering into the character of the Fir Tree and improvising speeches.

The Fir Tree

Time.......Spring.
Place......Forest.
Characters: Sun, Air, Hare, Woodmen, Swallow, Stork, Sparrows, Children, Servants, and Fir Tree.

Act I, Scene i. A Fir Tree in the forest.
Sun and Air talk to it.
Children sit under its branches.
A Hare comes and jumps over it.
Woodcutters come.
A Swallow comes and talks to it.
A Stork comes and talks to it.
Sparrows talk to it.

(Have the Tree removed. Apparently from a cart outside the door, a larger Christmas Tree may be brought in and planted in a sand-box by two servants, students from grammar grades. The same child now grown older, represents the Tree.)

Act II, Scene i. The Fir Tree brought into the room.
The decorating of the Tree by the Children and Teacher.
Talk of the Children about the Tree when decorating it.

Singing of Christmas carols; dancing of folk-dances; or recitation of Christmas poems, after the decoration of the Tree.

The distribution of gifts by the Children. An audience to whom the Children wanted to give presents, could be invited.

The Story-telling under the Tree.

The presence of visiting children would create an audience for the story-telling. The selection of the story-teller and the story or stories might be the result of a previous story contest. The contest and the story-telling under the Tree would be ideal drill situations. The entire play would serve as a fine unification of the child's work in nature, in construction, in physical education, in music, in composition, and in literature. Everything he does in the play will be full of vital interest to him; and his daily tasks will seem of more worth to him when he sees how he can use them with so much pleasure to himself and to others. This play is an example of the organizing of ideas which a good tale may exercise in the mind of the child and the part the tale as an organized experience may play in his development.

The creative return desired by the teacher, as well as the choice of tales for particular purposes, will depend largely on the controlling ideas in the program. It must be remembered that the child of to-day is not bookish nor especially literary; and he has increasing life interests. In the ordinary school year, work naturally divides itself into the main season festivals. While story work is here presented in its separate elements, any teacher realizes the possibility of making the story work lead up to and culminate in the Thanksgiving, Christmas, Easter, or May Festival. Because the good story bears a close relation to nature and to human life, any good course of stories will offer to the teacher ample freedom of choice for any natural school purpose. The good tale always gains by being placed in a situation where it assists in carrying out a larger idea. When the tale is one unit of a festival program it appeals to the child as a unit in his everyday life, it becomes socially organized for him.

REFERENCES

English

Baker, F. T.; Carpenter, G. R.; and Scott, F. N.: *The Teaching of English.* Longmans.

Chubb, Percival: *The Teaching of English.* Macmillan.

Story-Telling

Bailey, Carolyn: *For the Story Teller.* Bradley.

Bryant, Sara C.: *How to Tell Stories to Children.* Houghton.

Ibid.: *Stories to Tell.* Houghton.

Buckland, Anna: *Use of Stories in the Kindergarten.* Steiger.

Coe, F. E.: *First Book of Stories for the Story-teller.* Houghton.

Hotchkiss, Mary T.: "Story-telling in the Kindergarten." *N. E. A. Report,* 1893.

Keyes, Angela: *Stories and Story-Telling.* Appleton.

Lyman, Edna: *Story-Telling.* McClurg.

McMurry, Charles: *Special Method in Primary Reading.* Macmillan.

O'Grady, Alice (Moulton), and Throop, Frances: *The Story-Teller's Book.* Rand.

Olcott, F. J.: " Story-Telling as a Means of Teaching Literature." *N.Y. Libraries;* vol. 4, pp. 38–43. Feb., 1914.

Olcott, Frances, and Pendleton, Amena: *The Jolly Book for Boys and Girls.* Houghton.

Partridge, E. N., and Partridge, G. E.: *Story-Telling in School and Home.* Sturgis.

St. John, Edward: *Stories and Story-Telling.* Westminster Press, Phila.

Shedlock, Marie: *Art of the Story Teller.* Appleton.

Speare, Georgina: " Story-Telling as an Art." *Kindergarten Review,* Dec., 1913, to May, 1914.

The Storyteller's Company: *The Storyteller's Magazine.* New York.

The Voice

Corson, Hiram: *Voice and Spiritual Education.* Macmillan.

Curry, Samuel S.: *Foundations of Expression.* Expression Co.

Ibid.: *Province of Expression:* Expression Co.

Rush, James: *The Philosophy of the Human Voice.* Lippincott.

Quintilian, Marcus F.: *Institutes of Oratory.* Macmillan.

Gesture and Phonetics

Chamberlain, W. B., and Clark, S. H.: *Principles of Vocal Expression.* Scott.

Jespersen, Otto: *Growth and Structure of the English Language.* Stechert.

Jones, Daniel: *Pronunciation of English; Phonetics and Phonetic Transcriptions.* Putnam.

Ibid.: *Chart of English Speech Sounds.* Oxford.

Rippman, Walter: *Elements of Phonetics, English, French, and German.* Dent.

Ibid.: *The Sounds of Spoken English.* Dent.

Sweet, Henry: *Primer of Phonetics.* Oxford.

The Kindergarten

Blow, Susan; Hill, Patty; and Harrison, Elizabeth: *The Kindergarten.* Houghton.

Blow, Susan: "The Kindergarten and the Primary Grade." *Kindergarten Review*, June, 1915.

Crawford, Caroline: "The Teaching of Dramatic Arts in the Kindergarten and the Elementary School." *Teachers College Record*, Sept., 1915.

McMurry, Frank M.: "Principles Underlying the Making of School Curricula." *Teachers College Record*, Sept., 1915.

Palmer, Luella: "Montessori Suggestions for Kindergartners." *Kindergarten Review*, Feb. 1915.

Ibid.: "Problems vs. Subject Matter as a Basis for Kindergarten Curriculum." *Kindergarten Review*, Nov., 1914.

Teachers College Record: "Experimental Studies in Kindergarten Education." *Teachers College Record*, Jan., 1914.

Thorndike, Edward L.: "Foundations of Educational Achievement." *N. E. A. Report*, 1914.

The Return

Archer, William: *Play-Making.* Small.

Bailey, Carolyn: "Toy Stories." "The Story of the Woolly Dog." *Kindergarten Review*, Feb., 1915.

Baker, Franklin T., and Thorndike, Ashley H.: *Everyday English. Book One.* Macmillan.

Barnes, Earl: *Studies in Education.* Drawing. Barnes.

Buffum, Katherine: *Silhouettes to Cut in School.* Bradley.

Crawford, Caroline: *Dramatic Games and Dances.* Barnes.
Folk Dances and Games. Barnes.
The Rhythms of Childhood. Barnes.

Curry, S. S.: *Imagination and the Dramatic Instinct.* Expression Co.

Dewey, John: *The Child and the Curriculum.* University of Chicago.

Ibid.: "Imagination and Expression." *Kindergarten Magazine*, Sept., 1896.

Dow, Arthur: " Color in the Kindergarten." *Kindergarten Review*, June, 1914.
Ibid.: *Composition.* Doubleday.

Harvey, Nellie: " Japanese Art in the Kindergarten." *Kindergarten Review*, Dec., 1914.

Hervey, Walter: *Picture Work.* Revell.

Laurie, S. S.: *Lectures on Language and Linguistic Method in the School.* Macmillan.

MacIntosh, C.: " Toys Made by Little Children." *Kindergarten Review*, Jan., and Feb., 1914.

Maxwell, W. H.; Johnston, E. L.; and Barnum, M.: *Speaking and Writing.* American Book Co.

Oppenheimer, Carol: Drawing. *Kindergarten Review*, March, 1914.
Ibid.: " Scissors and Paper." *Kindergarten Review*, Jan., 1914.
Ibid.: Suggestions Concerning Rhythm Plays." *Kindergarten Review*, April and May, 1915.
Ibid.: "The Use of the Song Exercise." *Kindergarten Review*, May, 1914.

Parker School: *Francis W. Parker Year-Book*, vol. III, June, 1914. (" Expression as a Means of Developing Motives.") Francis Parker School, Chicago.

Psychological Review: Monograph — " Development of Imagination in School Children." *Suppl. Psych. Review*, vol. XI, no. 1, 1909.

Wagner, Carrie: " Furniture for the Doll House." *Kindergarten Review*, Dec., 1914.

Worst, E. F.; Barber, H.; and Seymour, M.: *Constructive Work.* Mumford.

Zook, Mabel; and Maloy, Regina: " Illustrated Stories." *Kindergarten Review*, May, 1915.

CHAPTER IV

THE HISTORY OF FAIRY TALES

The gods of ancient mythology were changed into the demi-gods and heroes of ancient poetry, and these demi-gods again became, at a later age, the principal characters of our nursery tales. — MAX MÜLLER.

Stories originally told about the characters of savage tales, were finally attracted into the legends of the gods of ancient mythology, or were attributed to demi-gods and heroes. — ANDREW LANG.

I. THE ORIGIN OF FAIRY TALES

Now that we have indicated the worth of fairy tales, have observed those principles which should guide the teacher in choosing and in interpreting a tale, and have stated those rules which should govern the story-teller in the telling of the tale, we may well ask a few further questions concerning the nature of these fairy tales. What is a fairy tale and whence did it come, and how are we to find its beginning? Having found it, how are we to follow it down through the ages? How shall it be classed, what are the available types which seek to include it and show its nature? And lastly, what are the books which are to be the main practical sources of fairy tales for the teacher of little children? The remaining pages attempt to give some help to the teacher who wishes to increase her resources with an intelligent knowledge of the material she is handling.

Many times the question, "What is a fairy tale?" has been asked. One has said: "The fairy tale is a poetic presentation of a spiritual truth." George MacDonald has answered: "*Undine* is a fairy tale." Mr. G. K. Chesterton has said: "A fairy tale is a tale told in a morbid age to the only remaining sane person, a child. A legend is a fairy tale told to men when men were sane." Some, scorning to reply, have treated the question as one similar to, "What poem do you consider best in the English language?" As there are many tales included here which do not contain a fairy, fairy tales here are taken to include tales which contain something fairy or extraordinary, the magic or the marvelous — fairies, elves, or trolls, speaking animals, trees, or a talkative Tin Soldier. The Myth proper and the Fable are both excluded here, while the *pourquois* tale, a myth development, and the Beast tale, a short-story fable development, are both included.

The origin of the word "fairy," as given by Thomas Keightley in his *Fairy Mythology*, and later in the Appendix of his *Tales and Popular Fictions*, is the Latin *fatum*, "to enchant." The word was derived directly from the French form of the root. The various forms of the root were: —

Latin. . . . .*fatum*, "to enchant."
French. . . . . . .*fee, feerie*, "illusion."
Italian. . . . . . .*fata*.
Provençal. . . .*fada*.

In old French romance, *fee* was a "woman skilled in magic." "All those women were called Fays who had to do with enchantment and charms and knew the power and virtue of words, of stones, and of herbs, by which they were kept in youth and in great beauty and in great riches." This was true also of the Italian *fata*.

The word "fairy" was used in four senses. *Fairy* represented: —

(1) Illusion, or enchantment.
(2) Abode of the Faes, the country of the Fays.
(3) Inhabitants collectively, the people of Fairyland.
(4) The individual in Fairyland, the fairy Knight, or Elf.

The word was used in the fourth sense before the time of Chaucer. After the appearance of Spenser's *Faerie Queene* distinctions became confused, and the name of the real fairies was transferred to "the little beings who made the green, sour ringlets whereof the ewe not bites." The change adopted by the poets gained currency among the people. Fairies were identified with nymphs and elves. Shakespeare was the principal means of effecting this revolution, and in his *Midsummer Night's Dream* he has incorporated most of the fairy lore known in England at his time. But the tales are older than their name.

The origin of fairy tales is a question which has kept many very able scholars busy and which has not yet been settled to the satisfaction of many. What has been discovered resolves itself mainly into four different origins of fairy tales: —

I. Fairy tales are detritus of myth, surviving echoes of gods and heroes

Against this theory it may be said that, when popular tales have incidents similar to Greek heroic myths, the tales are not detritus of myth, but both have a more ancient tale as their original source. There was: —

(1) A popular tale which reflected the condition of a rude people, a tale full of the monstrous and the miraculous.

(2) The same tale, a series of incidents and plot, with the monstrous element modified, which survived in the oral traditions of illiterate peasantry.

(3) The same plot and incidents, as they existed in heroic epics of cultivated people. A local and historical character was given by the introduction of known places and native heroes. Tone and manners were refined by literary workmanship, in the *Rig Veda*, the Persian *King-book*, the *Homeric Epics*, etc.

The Grimms noted that the evolution of the tale was from a strongly marked, even ugly, but highly expressive form of its earlier stages, to that which possessed external beauty of mold. The origin is in the fancy of a primitive people, the survival is through *Märchen* of peasantry, and the transfiguration into epics is by literary artists. Therefore, one and the same tale may be the source of Perrault's *Sleeping Beauty*, also of a *Greek myth*, and also of an *old tale of illiterate peasantry*. This was the opinion held by Lang, who said, "For the roots of stories, we must look, not in the clouds but upon the earth, not in the various aspects of nature but in the daily occurrences and surroundings, in the current opinions and ideas of savage life."

In the savage *Märchen* of to-day, the ideas and incidents are the inevitable result of the mental habits and beliefs of savages. We gain an idea of the savage mind through Leviticus, in the Bible, through Herodotus, Greek and Roman geographers, Aristotle, Plutarch, Pliny, etc., through voyagers, missionaries, and travelers, and through present savage peoples. Savage existence is based on two great institutions: —

(*a*) The division of society into clans. — Marriage laws depend on the conception that these clans descend from certain plants, animals, or inorganic objects. There was the belief in human descent from animals and kinship and personal intercourse with them.

(*b*) Belief in magic and medicine-men, which resulted in powers of metamorphosis, the effect of incantation, and communion with the dead. — To the savage all nature was animated, all things were persons. The leading ideas of savage peoples have already been referred to in the list of motifs which appear in the different fairy tales, as given by Lang, mentioned under the "Preparation of the Teacher," in *The Telling of the Tale.*

II. Fairy tales are myths of Sun, Dawn, Thunder, Rain, etc.

This is sometimes called the Sun-Myth Theory or the Aryan Theory, and it is the one advocated by Max Müller and by Grimm.

The fairy tales were primitive man's experience with nature in days when he could not distinguish between nature and his own personality, when there was no supernatural because everything was endowed with a personal life. They were the poetic fancies of light and dark, cloud and rain, day and night; and underneath them were the same fanciful meanings. These became changed by time, circumstances in different countries, and the fancy of the tellers, so that they became sunny and many-colored in the South, sterner and wilder in the North, and more home-like in the Middle and West. To the Bushmen the wind was a bird, and to the Egyptian fire was a living beast. Even *The Song of Six-Pence* has been explained as a nature-myth, the pie being the earth and sky, the birds the twenty-four hours, the king the sun, the queen the moon, and the opening of the pie, day-break.

Every word or phrase became a new story as soon as the first meaning of the original name was lost. Andrew Lang tells how Kephalos the sun loved Prokris the dew, and slew her by his arrows. Then when the first meaning of the names for sun, dew, and rays was lost, Kephalos, a shepherd, loved Prokris, a nymph, and we have a second tale which, by a folk-etymology, became the *Story of Apollo, the Wolf.* Tales were told of the sun under his frog name; later people forgot that *frog* meant " sun," and the result was the popular tale, *A Frog, He Would A-Wooing Go.*

In regard to this theory, " It is well to remember," says Tylor in his *Primitive Culture,* " that rash inferences which, on the strength of mere resemblances, derive episodes of myth from episodes of nature, must be regarded with utter distrust; for the student who has no more stringent criterion than this for his myths of sun and sky and dawn will find them wherever it pleases him to seek them." There is a danger of being carried away by false analogies. But all scholars agree that some tales are evidently myths of sun and dawn. If we examine the natural history of savages, we do find summer feasts, winter feasts, rituals of sorrow for the going of summer and of rejoicing for its return, anxious interest in the sun, interest in the motion of the heavenly bodies, the custom of naming men and women from the phenomena of nature, and interest in making love, making war, making fun, and making dinner.

III. Fairy tales all arose in India, they are part of the common Aryan heritage and are to be traced by the remains of their language

They were first written in the *Vedas*, the sacred Sanskrit books of Buddhism. This theory is somewhat allied to the Sun-Myth Theory. This theory was followed by Max Müller and by Sir George Cox.

The theory of a common source in India will not answer entirely for the origin of tales because many similar tales have existed in non-Aryan countries. Old tales were current in Egypt, 2000 B.C., and were brought from there by Crusaders, Mongol missionaries, the Hebrews, and Gypsies.

The idea of connecting a number of disconnected stories, as we find in *Arabian Nights*, *The Canterbury Tales*, and the *Decameron*, is traced to the idea of making Buddha the central figure in the folk-literature of India. And Jacobs says that at least one-third of all the stories common to the children of Europe are derived from India, and by far the majority of the drolls. He also says that generally, so far as incidents are marvelous and of true fairy-like character, India is the probable source, because of the vitality of animism and transformation in India in all time. Moreover, as a people, the Hindus had spread among their numbers enough literary training and mental grip to invent plots.

And again, there is an accepted connection in myth

and language between all Aryan languages and Sanskrit. According to Sir George Dasent, "The whole human race has sprung from one stock planted in the East, which has stretched its boughs and branches laden with the fruit of language and bright with the bloom of song and story, by successive offshoots to the utmost parts of the earth." Dasent tells how the Aryans who went west, who went out to *do*, were distinguished from the nations of the world by their common sense, by their power of adapting themselves to circumstances, by making the best of their position, by being ready to receive impressions, and by being able to develop impressions. They became the Greeks, the Latins, the Teutons, the Celts, and the Slavonians. The Aryans who stayed at home, remained to *reflect*, and were distinguished by their power of thought. They became a nation of philosophers and gave to the world the Sanskrit language as the basis of comparative philology. Dasent shows how legends, such as the *Story of William Tell* and *Dog Gellert*, which have appeared in many Aryan peoples were common in germ to the Aryan tribes before migration. Joseph Jacobs has more recently settled the travels of *Gellert*, tracing its literary route from the Indian *Vinaya Pitaka*, through the *Fables of Bidpai*, *Sindibad*, *Seven Sages of Rome*, *Gesta Romanorum*, and the Welsh *Fables of Cottwg*, until the legend became localized in Wales.

IV. Fairy tales owe their origin to the identity of early fancy

Just as an individual, after thinking along certain lines, is surprised to come upon the exact sequence of his thought in a book he had never seen, so primitive peoples in remote parts of the world, up against similar situations, would express experience in tales containing similar motifs. A limited set of experiences was presented to the inventive faculty, and the limited combinations possible would result in similar combinations. The Aryan Jackal, the Mediæval Reynard, the Southern Brer Rabbit, and the Weasel of Africa, are near relations. Dasent said, "In all mythology and tradition there are natural resemblances, parallelisms, suggested to the senses of each race by natural objects and everyday events; and these might spring up spontaneously all over the earth as home-growths, neither derived by imitation from other tribes, nor from the tradition of a common stock."

It is probable that all four theories of the origin of fairy tales are correct and that fairy tales owe their origin not to any one cause but to all four.

to many

II. THE TRANSMISSION OF FAIRY TALES

Oral transmission. The tale, having originated, may have been transmitted in many ways: by women compelled to marry into alien tribes; by slaves from Africa to America; by soldiers returning from the

Crusades; by pilgrims returning from the Holy Land or from Mecca; by knights gathering at tournaments; by sailors and travelers; and by commercial exchange between southern Europe and the East — Venice trading with Egypt and Spain with Syria. Ancient tales of Persia spread along the Mediterranean shores. In this way the Moors of Spain learned many a tale which they transmitted to the French. *Jack the Giant-Killer* and *Thomas Thumb*, according to Sir Walter Scott, landed in England from the very same keels and warships which conveyed Hengist and Horsa and Ebba the Saxon. A recent report of the Bureau of Ethnology of the Smithsonian Institution of the United States expressed the opinion that the *Uncle Remus Tales* have an Indian origin. Slaves had associated with Indian tribes such as the Cherokees, and had heard the story of the Rabbit who was so clever that no one could fool him. Gradually the Southern negroes had adopted the Indian tales and changed them. Joseph Jacobs claims to have found the original of the " Tar Baby " in the *Jataka Tales.* A tale, once having originated, could travel as easily as the wind. Certainly a good type when once hit upon was diffused widely. Sir Walter Scott has said: " A work of great interest might be compiled from the origin of popular fiction and the transmission of similar tales from age to age and from country to country. The mythology of one period would then appear to pass into the romance of the next century, and that into the nursery tales of subsequent ages. Such an investigation would show that these fictions, however wild and childish, possess such charms for the populace as to enable them to penetrate into countries unconnected by manners and language, and having no apparent intercourse to afford the means of transmission."

Thomas Keightley, in *Tales and Popular Fictions*, has given interesting examples of the transmission of tales. Selecting *Jack the Giant-Killer*, he has shown that it is the same tale as Grimm's *The Brave Tailor*, and *Thor's Journey to Utgard* in the Scandinavian *Edda*. Similar motifs occur also in a Persian tale, *Ameen of Isfahan and the Ghool*, and in the *Goat and the Lion*, a tale from the *Panchatantra*. Selecting the *Story of Dick Whittington* he has shown that in England it was current in the reign of Elizabeth; that two similar tales, Danish legends, were told by Thiele; that a similar Italian tale existed at the time of Amerigo Vespucci, which was a legend told by Arlotto in 1396–1483; that another similar Italian tale was connected with the origin of Venice, in 1175; and that a similar tale existed in Persia in 1300, before 1360, when Whittington of England was born. He also pointed out that the *Odyssey* must have traveled east as well as west, from Greece, for Sindbad's adventure with the Black Giant is similar to that of Ulysses with the Cyclops.

Another interesting set of parallels shown by him is connected with the *Pentamerone* tale, *Peruonto*. This is the Straparola *Peter the Fool,* the Russian *Emelyan the Fool,* the Esthonian tale by Laboulaye, *The Fairy Craw-Fish,* and the Grimm *The Fisherman and his Wife.* The theme of a peasant being rewarded by the fish he had thrown back into the water takes on a delightful varied form in the tale of different countries. The magic words of Emelyan, "Up and away! At the pike's command, and at my request, go home, sledge!" in each variant take an interesting new form.

Literary transmission. The travels of a tale through oral tradition are to be attempted with great difficulty and by only the most careful scholarship. One may follow the transmission of tales through literary collections with somewhat greater ease and exactness. Popular tales have a literature of their own. The following list seeks to mention the most noteworthy collections: —

No date. *Vedas.* Sanskrit.

No date. *Zend Avesta.* Persian.

Fifth century, B.C. *Jatakas.* Probably the oldest literature. It was written at Ceylon and has been translated into 38 languages, in 112 editions. Recently the Cambridge edition has been translated from the Pali, edited by E. B. Cowell, published by Putnam, New York, 1895–1907.

4000 B.C. *Tales of Ancient Egypt.* These were the tales of magicians, recorded on papyrus.

600 B.C. (about). *Homeric Legends.*

200 B.C. (about). *Book of Esther.*

Second century, A.D. *The Golden Ass, Metamorphoses of Apuleius.*

550 A.D. *Panchatantra*, the *Five Books.* This was a Sanskrit collection of fables, the probable source of the *Fables of Bidpai.*

Second century, A.D. *The Hitopadesa*, or *Wholesome Instruction.* A selection from the *Panchatantra*, first edited by Carey, in 1804; by Max Müller, in 1844.

550 A.D. *Panchatantra.* Pehlevi version.

Tenth century, A.D. *Panchatantra.* Arabic version.

Eleventh century, A.D. *Panchatantra.* Greek version.

Twelfth century, A.D. *Panchatantra.* Persian version.

1200 A.D. *Sanskrit Tales.* These tales were collected by Somadeva Bhatta, of Cashmere, and were published to amuse the Queen of Cashmere. They have been translated by Brockhaus, 1844. Somadeva's *Ocean of the Streams of Story* has been translated by Mr. Tawney, of Calcutta, 1880.

Tales of the West came from the East in two sources: —

1262–78. (1) *Directorium Humanæ Vitæ*, of John of Capua. This was translated from the *Hebrew*, from the *Arabic* of the eighth century, from the *Pehlevi* of Persia of the sixth century, from the *Panchatantra*, from the *Sanskrit original.* This is the same as the famous Persian version, *The Book of Calila and Dimna*, attributed to Bidpai, of India. There was a late Persian version, in 1494, and one in Paris in 1644, which was the source of La Fontaine.

Thirteenth century. (2) *The Story of the Seven Sages of Rome*, or *The Book of Sindibad.* This appeared in Europe as the Latin *History of the Seven Sages of Rome*, by Dame Jehans, a monk in the Abbey of Haute Selve. There is a Hebrew, an Arabic, and a Persian version. It is believed the Persian version came from Sanskrit but the Sanskrit original has not yet been found.

Tenth century. *Reynard the Fox.* This was first found as a Latin product of the monks, in a cloister by the banks of the Mosel and Mass. *Reynard the Fox* shares with *Æsop's Fables* the distinction of being folk-lore raised into literature. It is a series of short stories of adventure forming a romance. These versions are known: —

1180. German-*Reinhart*, an epic of twelve adventures by Heinrich Glichesäre.

1230. French-*Roman de Renard*, with its twenty-seven branches.

1250. Flemish-*Reinaert*, part of which was composed by Willem, near Ghent.

1148. *Ysengrimus*, a Latin poem written at Ghent.

Thirteenth century. *Of the Vox and of the Wolf*, an English poem.

Later date. *Rainardo*, Italian.

Later date. Greek *mediæval version.*

Reynard the Fox [1] was first printed in England by Caxton in

[1] Joseph Jacobs, in his Introduction to the Cranford edition, and Ashton, in *Chap-Books of the Eighteenth Century*, furnish most of the facts mentioned here.

1481, translated from a Dutch copy. A copy of Caxton's book is in the British Museum. Caxton's edition was adapted by "Felix Summerley"; and Felix Summerley's edition, with slight changes, was used by Joseph Jacobs in his Cranford edition.

A Dutch prose romance, *Historie von Reynaert de Vos* was published in 1485. A German copy, written in Lower Saxony was published in 1498. A chap-book, somewhat condensed, but giving a very good account of the romance, was published in London in 1780, printed and sold in Aldermary Churchyard, Bow Lane. This chap-book is very much finer in language than many of the others in Ashton's collection. Its structure is good, arranged in nine chapters. It shows itself a real classic and would be read with pleasure to-day. Goethe's poem, *Reineke Fuchs,* was published in 1794. This version was more refined than previous ones but it lost in simplicity. Monographs have been written on *Reynard* by Grimm, Voigt, Martin, and Sudre.

Raginhard was a man's name, meaning "strong in counsel," and was common in Germany which bordered on France. This name naturally was given to the beast who lived by his wits. Grimm considered *Reynard* the result of a Teutonic Beast Epic of primitive origin. Later research has exploded this theory and has decided that all versions are descended from an original French one existing between 1150 and 1170. Modern editions have come from the Flemish version. The literary artist who compiled *Reynard* took a nucleus of fables and added to it folk-tales which are known to have existed in the eleventh and twelfth centuries and which exist to-day as tradition among some folk. The folk-tales included in *Reynard* are: *Reynard and Dame Wolf; The Iced Wolf's Tail; The Fishes in the Car; The Bear in the Cleft; The Wolf as Bell-Ringer;* and *The Dyed Fox.* The method of giving individual names to the animals such as Reynard, Bruin, and Tibert, was current among the Folk before a literary form was given to *Reynard.* As this was the custom in the province of Lorraine it is supposed that the origin of these names was in Lorraine. Other names, such as Chanticleer, the Cock, and Noble, the Lion, were given because of a quality, and indicate a tendency to allegory. These names increase in the later development of the romance. In the beginning when the beasts had only personal adventures, these were told by the Folk to raise a laugh. Later there was a meaning underneath the laugh and the Beast Epic Comedy of the Folk grew into the world Beast Satire of the literary artist.

Reynard exhibits the bare struggle for existence which was generally characteristic of Feudal life. Cunning opposes force and triumphs over it. The adventurous hero appeals because of his faculty of *adjustment*, his power to adapt himself to circumstances and to master them. He also appeals because of his small size when compared with the other animals. In the Middle Ages *Reynard* appealed because it was a satire upon the monks. Of *Reynard* Carlyle has said, " It comes before us with a character such as can belong only to very few; that of being a true World's Book which through centuries was everywhere at home, the spirit of which diffused itself into all languages and all minds."

About one tenth of European folk-lore is traced to collections used in the Middle Ages: *Fables of Bidpai*, *Seven Wise Masters*, *Gesta Romanorum*, and *Barlaam and Josophat*. These tales became diffused through the *Exempla* of the monks, used in their sermons, through the *Novelle* of Italy, the *Decameron* of Boccaccio, the *Tales of Chaucer*, Painter's *Palace of Pleasure*, and the *Elizabethan Drama* of England. One half of La Fontaine's *Fables* are of Indian sources.

1326. The *Gesta Romanorum*, written in Latin. This was a compilation, by the monks, of stories with a moral appended to each. It was the most popular story-book before the invention of printing. In England it was printed by Wynkyn de Worde, of which edition the only known copy is at St. John's College, Cambridge. The earliest manuscript of the collection is dated 1326. Between 1600 and 1703 fifteen editions of the book prove its popularity. One English version is by Sir Frederick Madden, who lived 1801–73. The author of the *Gesta Romanorum* is unknown, but was likely a German. The stories included are miscellaneous and vary in different editions. Among its stories are Oriental tales, tales of the deeds of Roman Emperors, an early form of *Guy of Warwick*, the casket episode of *The Merchant of Venice*, a story of the Jew's bond, a tale of the Emperor Theodosius, being a version of *King Lear*, the story of the Hermit, and a tale of Aglas, the daughter of the Roman Emperor Pompey, being a version of *Atalanta and her Race*.

1000 A.D. (about). *Shah-Nameh*, or *King-book of Persia*, by Ferdousee, born about 940 A.D. This book is the pride and glory of Persian literature. It was written by the Persian poet at the command of the king, who wished to have preserved the old traditions and heroic glories of Persians before the Arabian conquest. Ferdousee declared that he invented none of his material, but took it from the *Bostan-Nameh* or *Old-Book*.

The *King-Book* is very ancient, it is the Persian Homer. It was the labor of thirty years. It consisted of 56,000 distichs or couplets, for every thousand of which the Sultan had promised the poet one thousand pieces of gold. Instead of the elephant-load of gold promised, the Sultan sent in payment 60,000 small silver coins. This so enraged the poet that he gave away one third to the man who brought them, one third to a seller of refreshments, and one third to the keeper of the bath where the messenger found him. After the poet's death the insult was retrieved by proper payment. This was refused by his one daughter, but accepted by the other and used to erect a public dike the poet had always desired to build to protect his native town from the river. The fine character of the tales of the *King-Book* is shown in the tale of *Roostem and Soohrab*, taken from this book, which Keightley has translated in *Tales and Popular Fictions*. Keightley considered it superior to any Greek or Latin tale. Modern literature knows this tale through Matthew Arnold's poem.

1548 (not later than). *The Thousand and One Nights*, Arabian. 12 volumes. Galland's French translation appeared in 1704. This was supplemented by Chavis and Cazotte, and by Caussin de Percival. Monsieur Galland was Professor of Arabic in the Royal College of Paris. He was a master of French and a fairly good scholar of Arabic. He brought his manuscript, dated 1548, to Paris from Constantinople. He severely abbreviated the original, cutting out poetical extracts and improving the somewhat slovenly style. In his translation he gave to English the new words, *genie*, *ogre*, and *vizier*. His work was very popular.

Boulak and Calcutta texts are better than the Galland. They contain about two hundred and fifty stories. The Cairo edition has been admirably translated by Edward W. Lane, in 3 volumes (1839–41) published in London. This is probably the best edition. It also omits many poetical quotations. A recent edition using Lane's translation is by Frances

Olcott, published by Holt in 1913. Editions which attempt to be complete versions are by John Payne (13 volumes, 1882–84), and by Sir Richard Burton (16 volumes, 1885–88). Lane and Burton give copious notes of value. The recent edition by Wiggin and Smith used the editions of Scott and Lane.

The stories in *Arabian Nights* are Indian, Egyptian, Arabian, and Persian. Scenes are laid principally in Bagdad and Cairo. Lane considered that the one hundred and fifteen stories, which are common to all manuscripts, are based on the Pehlevi original. The idea of the frame of the story came from India. This was the birth of the serial story. There is authority for considering the final collection to have been made in Egypt. Cairo is described most minutely and the customs are of Egypt of the thirteenth century and later. The stories must have been popular in Egypt as they were mentioned by an historian, 1400–70. Lane considered that the final Arabic collection bears to Persian tales the same relation that the *Æneid* does to the *Odyssey.* Life depicted is Arabic, and there is an absence of the great Persian heroes. Internal evidence assists in dating the work. Coffee is mentioned only three times. As its use became popular in the East in the fourteenth century this indicates the date of the work to be earlier than the very common use of coffee. Cannon, which are mentioned, were known in Egypt in 1383. Additions to the original were probably made as late as the sixteenth century. *The Arabian Nights* has been the model for many literary attempts to produce the Oriental tale, of which the tales of George Meredith are notable examples.

Thomas Keightley, in *Tales and Popular Fictions,* considered Persia the original country of *The Thousand and One Nights,* and *The Voyages of Sinbad,* originally a separate work. He showed how some of these tales bear marks of Persian extraction and how some had made their way to Europe through oral transmission before the time of Galland's translation. He selected the tale, " Cleomedes and Claremond," and proved that it must have been learned by a certain Princess Blanche, of Castile, and transmitted by her to France about 1275. This romance must have traveled to Spain from the East. It is the same as "The Enchanted Horse" in *The Thousand and One Nights*, and through Keightley's proof, is originally Persian. Keightley also selected the Straparola tale, *The Dancing Water, the Singing Apple, and the Beautiful Green Bird*, and proved it to be the same as Grimm's *Three Little Birds*, as a Persian *Arabian Night's* tale, and also as *La Princesse Belle Etoile*, of D'Aulnoy. But as Galland's translation appeared only the year after Madame D'Aulnoy's death, Madame D'Aulnoy must have obtained the tale elsewhere than from the first printed version of *Arabian Nights*.

No date. *The Thousand and One Days*. This is a Persian collection containing the "History of Calaf."

1550. *Straparola's Nights*, by Straparola. This collection of jests, riddles, and twenty-one stories was published in Venice. The stories were taken from oral tradition, from the lips of ten young women. Some were agreeable, some unfit, so that the book was forbidden in Rome, in 1605, and an abridged edition prepared. There was a complete Venetian edition in 1573, a German translation in 1679, a French one in 1611, and a good German one with valuable notes, by Schmidt, in 1817. Straparola's *Nights* contained stories similar to the German *The Master Thief*, *The Little Peasant*, *Hans and the Hedge-Hog*, *Iron Hans*, *The Four Brothers*, *The Two Brothers*, and *Dr. Know-all*.

1637. *The Pentamerone*, by Basile. Basile spent his early youth in Candia or Crete, which was owned by Venice. He traveled much in Italy, following his sister, who was a noted singer, to Mantua. He probably died in 1637. There may have been an earlier edition of *The Pentamerone*, which sold out. It was republished in Naples in 1645, 1674, 1714, 1722, 1728, 1749, 1788, and in Rome in 1679. This was the best collection of tales formed by a nation for a long time. The traditions were complete, and the author had a special talent for collecting them, and an intimate knowledge of dialect. This collection of fifty stories may be looked upon as the basis of many others. Basile wrote independently of Straparola, though a few tales are common to both. He was very careful not to alter the tale as he took it down from the people. He told his stories with allusions to manners and customs, to old stories and mythology. He abounds in picturesque, proverbial expressions, with turns and many similes, and displays a delightful exuberance of fancy. A valuable translation, with notes, was written by Felix Liebrecht, in 1842, and an English one by John Edward Taylor, in 1848. Keightley, in *Fairy Mythology*, has translated three of these tales and in *Tales and Popular Fictions*, two tales. Keightley's were the first translations of these tales into any language other than Italian. Among the stories of Basile are the German *Cinderella, How Six got on in the World, Rapunzel, Snow White, Dame Holle, Briar Rose,* and *Hansel and Grethel.*

1697. *The Tales of Mother Goose*, by Charles Perrault. In France the collecting of fairy tales began in the seventeenth century. French, German, and Italian tales were all derived independently by oral tradition. In 1696, in *Recueil*, a magazine published by Moetjens, at The Hague, appeared *The Story of Sleeping Beauty*, by Perrault. In 1697 appeared seven other tales by Perrault. Eight stories were published in 12mo, under a title borrowed from a *fabliau*, *Contes de ma Mère l'Oye*. In a later edition three stories were added, *The Ass's Skin*, *The Clever Princess*, and *The Foolish Wishes*. The tales of Perrault were: —

1. The Fairies.
2. The Sleeping Beauty in the Wood.
3. Bluebeard.
4. Little Red Riding Hood.
5. Puss-in-Boots.
6. Cinderella.
7. Rique with the Tuft.
8. Little Thumb.
9. The Ass's Skin.
10. The Clever Princess.
11. The Foolish Wishes.

Immediately afterwards the tales appeared published at Paris in a volume entitled, *Histoires ou Contes du Temps Passe, avec des Moralites — Contes de ma Mère l'Oye*. The earliest translation into English was in a book containing French and English, *Tales of Passed Times, by Mother Goose, with Morals. Written in French by M. Charles Perrault and Englished by R. S., Gent.* An English translation by Mr. Samber was advertised in the English *Monthly Chronicle*, March, 1729. Andrew Lang, with an introduction, has edited these tales from the original edition, published by the Clarendon Press, Oxford, 1888. These tales made their way slowly in England, but gradually eclipsed the native English tales and legends which had been discouraged by Puritan influence. In Perrault's time, when this influence was beginning to decline, they superseded the English tales, crowding out all but *Jack the Giant-Killer, Tom Hickathrift, Jack and the Beanstalk, Tom Thumb,* and *Childe Rowland.*

1650–1705. *Fairy Tales,* by Madame D'Aulnoy. In France there were many followers of Perrault. The most important of these was Madame D'Aulnoy. She did not copy Perrault. She was a brilliant, witty countess, and brought into her tales, entitled *Contes de Fées,* the graces of the court. She adhered less strictly to tradition than Perrault, and handled her material freely, making additions, amplifications, and moral reflections, to the original tale. Her weaving together of incidents is artistic and her style graceful and not unpleasing. It is marked by ornamentation, sumptuousness, and French sentimentality. It shows a lack of naïveté resulting from the palace setting given to her tales, making them adapted only to children of high rank. Often her tale is founded on a beautiful tradition. *The Blue-Bird,* one of the finest of her tales, was found in the poems of Marie de France, in the thirteenth century. Three of her tales were borrowed from Straparola. Among her tales the most important are: —

Graciosa and Percinet. (Basile.)

The Blue-Bird. (Contains a motif similar to one in *The Singing, Soaring Lark.*)

The White Cat. (Similar to *Three Feathers* and *The Miller's Boy and the Cat.*)

The Hind in the Wood. (Similar to *Rumpelstiltskin.*)
The Good Little Mouse. (Basile.)
The Fair One with the Golden Locks. (*Ferdinand the Faithful.*)
The Yellow Dwarf.
Princess Belle Etoile. (Straparola.)

The careful translation of Madame D'Aulnoy's tales by Mr. Planché faithfully preserves the spirit of the original.

There were many imitators of Countess D'Aulnoy, in France, in the eighteenth century. Their work was on a much lower level and became published in the *Cabinet des Fées*, a collection of stories including in its forty volumes the work of many authors, of which the greater part is of little value. Of those following D'Aulnoy three deserve mention: —

1711–1780. *Moral Tales*, by Madame de Beaumont. These were collected while the author was in England. Of these we use *Prince Cherry*. Madame de Beaumont wrote a children's book in which is found a tale similar to *The Singing, Soaring Lark*, entitled *The Maiden and the Beast*. She also wrote 69 volumes of romance.

1765. *Tales*, by Madame Villeneuve. Of these we use *Beauty and the Beast*.

1692–1765. *Tales*, by Comte de Caylus. The author was an antiquarian and scholar. Of his tales we use *Sylvain and Yocosa*.

Very little attempt has been made in modern times to include in our children's literature the best of foreign literature for children, for there has been very little study of foreign books for children. Certainly the field of children's literature would be enriched to receive translations of any books worthy of the name classic. A partial list of French fairy tales is here given, indicating to children's librarians how little has been done to open up this field, and inviting their labor: —

Bibliothèque Rose, a collection. (What should be included?)

Bibliothèque des Petits Enfants, a collection. (What should be included?)

1799–1874. *Fairy Tales from the French*, by Madame de Ségur. These tales are published by Winston. We also use her *Story of a Donkey*, written in 1860 and published by Heath in 1901.

1866. *Fairy Tales of all Nations*, by Edouard Laboulaye.

1902. *Last Fairy Tales*, also by Laboulaye.

Tales, by Zenaide Fleuriot. (What should be included?)

1910. *Chantecler*, by Edmund Rostand. Translated by Gertrude Hall, published by Duffield.

1911. *The Honey Bee*, by Anatole France; translated by Mrs. Lane; published by Lane.

1911. *The Blue-Bird*, by Maurice Maeterlinck; published by Dodd.

In Great Britain many old tales taken from tradition were included in the Welsh Mabinogion, Irish sagas, and Cornish Mabinogion. Legends of Brittany were made known by the poems of Marie de France, who lived in the thirteenth century. These were published in Paris, in 1820. In fact, most of the early publications of fairy tales were taken from the French.

Celtic tales have been collected in modern times in a greater number than those of any nation. This has been due largely to the work of J. F. Campbell. Celtic tales are unusual in that they have been collected while the custom of story-telling is yet flourishing among the Folk. They are therefore of great literary and imaginative interest. They are especially valuable as the oldest of the European tales. The Irish tale of *Connla and the Fairy Maiden* has been traced to a date earlier than the fifth century and therefore ranks as the oldest tale of modern Europe. The principal Celtic collections are: —

Iolo M.S., published by the Welsh M.S. Society.

Mabinogion, translated by Lady Guest. (Contains tales that trace back to the twelfth century.)

Y Cymrodor, by Professor Rhys.

1825. *Fairy Legends and Traditions of the South of Ireland*, by T. Crofton Croker.

1842. *Popular Rhymes of Scotland.* Chambers.

1860–62. *Popular Tales of the West Highlands*, by J. F. Campbell.

Tales, collected and published with notes, by Mr. Alfred Nutt.

1866. By Patrick Kennedy, the Irish Grimm. *Legendary Fictions of the Irish Celts; Fireside Stories of Ireland* (1870); and *Bardic Stories of Ireland* (1871).

In England the publication of fairy tales may be followed more readily because the language proves no hindrance and the literature gives assistance. In England the principal publications of fairy tales were: —

1604. *Pasquil's Jests.* Contained a tale similar to one of Grimm's.

1635. *A Tract, A Descryption of the Kynge and Quene of Fairies, their habit, fare, abode, pomp, and state.*

Eighteenth century (early). *Madame D'Aulnoy's Tales*, a translation.

1667–1745. *Gulliver's Travels*, by Dean Swift. (One modern edition, with introduction by W. D. Howells, and more than one hundred illustrations by Louis Rhead, is published by Harpers. Another edition, illustrated by Arthur Rackham, is published by Dutton.)

1700–1800. *Chap-Books.* Very many of these books, especially the best ones, were published by William and Cluer Dicey, in Aldermary Church Yard, Bow Lane, London. Rival publishers, whose editions were rougher in engraving, type, and paper, labored in Newcastle.

The chap-books were little paper books hawked by chapmen, or traveling peddlers, who went from village to village with "Almanacks, Bookes of Newes, or other trifling wares." These little books were usually from sixteen to twenty-four pages in bulk and in size from two and one half inches by three and one half inches to five and one half inches by four and one quarter inches. They sold for a penny or sixpence and became the very popular literature of the middle and lower classes of their time. After the nineteenth century they became widely published, deteriorated, and gradually were crowded out by the *Penny Magazine* and *Chambers's Penny Tracts and Miscellanies.* For many years before the Victorian period, folk-lore was left to the peasants and kept out of reach of the children of the higher classes. This was the reign of the moral tale, of Thomas Bewick's *Looking Glass of the Mind* and Mrs. Sherwood's *Henry and His Bearer.* Among the chap-books published by William and Cluer Dicey, may be mentioned: *The Pleasant and Delightful History of Jack and the Giants* (part second was printed and sold by J. White); *Guy, Earl of Warwick; Bevis of Hampton; The History of Reynard the Fox*, dated 1780; *The History of Fortunatus*, condensed from an edition of 1682; *The Fryer and the Boy; A True Tale of Robin Hood* (Robin Hood Garland Blocks, from 1680, were used in the London Bridge Chap-Book edition); *The Famous History of Thomas Thumb; The History of Sir Richard Whittington;* and *The Life and Death of St. George. Tom Hickathrift* was printed by and for M. Angus and Son, at Newcastle-in-the-Side: *Valentine and Orson* was printed at Lyons, France, in 1489; and in England by Wynkyn de Worde. Among the chap-books many tales not fairy tales were included. With the popularity of *Goody Two Shoes* and the fifty little books issued by Newbery, the realistic tale of modern times made a sturdy beginning. Of these realistic chap-books one of the most popular was *The History of Little Tom Trip*, probably by Goldsmith, engraved by the famous Thomas Bewick, published by T. Saint, of Newcastle. This was reprinted by Ed. Pearson in 1867.

Of *Jack the Giant-Killer*, in Skinner's *Folk-Lore*, David Masson has said: " Our *Jack the Giant-Killer* is clearly the last modern transmutation of the old British legend, told in Geoffrey of Monmouth, of Corineüs the Trojan, the companion of the Trojan Brutus when he first settled in Britain; which Corineüs, being a very strong man, and particularly good-humored, is satisfied with being King of Cornwall, and killing out all the aboriginal giants there, leaving to Brutus all the rest of the island, and only stipulating that, whenever there is a peculiarly difficult giant in any part of Brutus' dominions, he shall be sent for to finish the fellow."

Tom Hickathrift, whose history is given in an old number of *Fraser's Magazine*, is described by Thackeray as one of the publisher Cundall's books, bound in blue and gold, illustrated by Frederick Taylor in 1847. According to Thackeray this chap-book tale was written by Fielding. Speaking of the passage, " The giant roared hideously but Tom had no more mercy on him than a bear upon a dog," he said: " No one but Fielding could have described battle so." Of the passage, " Having increased his strength by good living and improved his courage by drinking strong ale," he remarked: " No one but Fielding could have given such an expression." The quality of the English of this chap-book is apparent in the following sentence, taken from Ashton's version: " So Tom stepped to a gate and took a rail for a staff."

In regard to their literary merit the chap-books vary greatly. Some evidently are works of scholars who omitted to sign their names. In the collection by Ashton those deserving mention for their literary merit are: *Patient Grissel*, by Boccaccio; *Fortunatus; Valentine and Orson; Joseph and His Brethren; The Friar and the Boy; Reynard the Fox*, from

Caxton's translation; *Tom Hickathrift*, probably by Fielding; and *The Foreign Travels of Sir John Mandeville.*

1708–90. Chap-Books. Printed by J. White, of York, established at Newcastle, 1708. These included: *Tom Hickathrift; Jack the Giant-Killer;* and *Cock Robin.*

1750. *A New Collection of Fairy Tales.* 2 vols.

1760. *Mother Goose's Melodies.* A collection of many nursery rhymes, songs, and a few old ballads and tales, published by John Newbery. The editor is unknown, but most likely was Oliver Goldsmith. The title of the collection may have been borrowed from Perrault's *Contes de ma Mère l'Oye*, of which an English version appeared in 1729. The title itself has an interesting history dating hundreds of years before Perrault's time. By 1777 *Mother Goose's Melodies* had passed the seventh edition. In 1780 they were published by Carnan, Newbery's stepson, under the title *Sonnets for the Cradle.* In 1810 *Gammer Gurton's Garland*, a collection, was edited by Joseph Ritson, an English scholar. In 1842 J. O. Halliwell issued, for the Percy Society, *The Nursery Rhymes of England.* The standard modern text should consist of Newbery's book with such additions from Ritson and Halliwell as bear internal evidence of antiquity and are true nursery rhymes.

1770. *Queen Mab, A Collection of Entertaining Tales of Fairies.*

1783. *The Lilliputian Magazine.* Illustrated by Thomas Bewick, published by Carnan.

1788. *The Pleasing Companion, A Collection of Fairy Tales.*

1788. *Fairy Tales Selected from the Best Authors*, 2 vols.

1770–91. Books published by John Evans, of Long Lane. Printed on coarse sugar paper. They included: *Cock Robin*, 1791; *Mother Hubbard; Cinderella;* and *The Tragical Death of an Apple Pye.*

1809. *A Collection of Popular Stories for the Nursery*, translated from French, Italian, and Old English, by Benjamin Tabart, in 4 volumes.

1810 (about). *Lilliputian Library*, by J. G. Rusher, of Bridge St., Banbury. The Halfpenny Series included:

Mother Hubbard and Her Dog; Jack The Giant-Killer; Dick Whittington and His Cat; The History of Tom Thumb (Middlesex); *Death and Burial of Cock Robin; and Cinderella and Her Glass Slipper.* The Penny Series included: *History of a Banbury Cake, and Jack the Giant-Killer,* designed by Craig, engraved by Lee. Of Rusher's books those engraved by the Bewick School were: *Cock Robin; The History of Tom Thumb;* and *Children in the Wood.* Rusher's books also included: *Mother Hubbard and Her Dog, Cinderella and Her Glass Slipper,* and *Dick Whittington and His Cat,* all designed by Cruikshank, engraved by Branstone.

1818. *Fairy Tales, or the Lilliputian Cabinet,* collected by Benj. Tabart, London. This was a new edition of the collection of 1809, and contained twenty-four stories. A full review of it may be seen in the *Quarterly Review,* 1819, No. 41, pp. 91–112. The tales included translations from Perrault, Madame D'Aulnoy, Madame de Beaumont, tales from *The Thousand and One Nights,* and from *Robin Hood;* and the single tales of *Jack the Giant-Killer, Tom Thumb,* and *Jack and the Bean-Stalk.*

1824, 1826. *German Popular Stories,* translated by Edgar Taylor, with illustrations by Cruikshank, published by Charles Tilt, London. A new edition, introduction by Ruskin, was published by Chatto & Windus, 1880.

The above are the main collections of fairy tales in England. Many individual publications show the gradual development of fairy tale illustration in England:[1] —

1713–1767. John Newbery's *Books for Children.* Among these were *Beauty and the Beast,* by Charles Lamb, 1765, and *Sinbad the Sailor,* 1798.

1778. *Fabulous Histories of the Robins.* Mrs. Sarah Trim-

[1] This list has been compiled largely from " Children's Books and Their Illustrators," by Gleeson White, in *The International Studio,* Special Winter Number, 1897–98.

mer. Cuts designed by Thomas Bewick, engraved by John Thompson, Whittingham's Chiswick Press.

1755–1836. *Life and Perambulations of a Mouse;* and *Adventures of a Pin-Cushion.* Dorothy Kilner.

1785. Baron Munchausen's *Narratives of His Famous Travels and Campaigns in Russia.* Rudolf Raspe.

1788. *Little Thumb and the Ogre.* Illustrated by William Blake; published by R. Dutton.

1790. *The Death and Burial of Cock Robin.* Illustrated by Thomas Bewick. Catnach.

1807. *Tales from Shakespeare.* Charles and Mary Lamb. W. J. Godwin and Co. William Blake illustrated an edition of these tales, probably the original edition.

1813. Reprints of forgotten books, by Andrew Tuer: *Dame Wiggins of Lee; The Gaping Wide-Mouthed Waddling Frog: The House that Jack Built. Dame Wiggins of Lee* was first printed by A. K. Newman and Co., Minerva Press. Original cuts by R. Stennet or Sinnet. Reprinted by Allen, 1885, with illustrations added by Kate Greenaway.

1841. *King of the Golden River.* John Ruskin. Illustrated by Richard Doyle, 1884.

1844. *Home Treasury,* by "Felix Summerley" (Sir Henry Cole). "Felix Summerley" was a reformer in children's books. He secured the assistance of many of the first artists of his time: Mulready, Cope, Horsley, Redgrave, Webster, all of the Royal Academy, Linnell and his three sons, Townsend, and others. These little books were published by Joseph Cundall and have become celebrated through Thackeray's mention of them. They aimed to cultivate the affections, fancy, imagination, and taste of children, they were a distinct contrast to the Peter Parley books. They were new books, new combinations of old materials, and reprints, purified but not weakened. Their literature possessed brightness. The books were printed in the best style of the Chiswick Press, with bindings and end papers especially designed. They included these tales: *Puck's Reports to Oberon; Four New Fairy Tales; The Sisters; Golden Locks; Grumble and Cherry; Little Red Riding Hood,* with four colored illustrations by Webster; *Beauty and the Beast,* with four colored illustrations by Horsley; *Jack and the Bean-Stalk*, with four colored illustrations by Cope; *Jack the Giant-Killer*, also illustrated by Cope; and *The Pleasant History of Reynard, the Fox*, with forty of the fifty-seven etchings made by Everdingen, in 1752.

1824–1883. Publications by Richard Doyle. These included *The Fairy Ring*, 1845; *Snow White and Rosy Red*, 1871; *Jack the Giant-Killer*, 1888, etc.

1846. *Undine*, by De La Motte Fouqué, illustrated by John Tenniel, published by James Burns.

1846. *The Good-Natured Bear*, by Richard Hengist Horne, the English critic. This was illustrated by Frederick Taylor, published probably by Cundall. The book is now out of print, but deserves to be reprinted.

1847–1864. *Cruikshank Fairy Library*. A series of small books in paper wrappers. Not equal to the German popular stories in illustration. It included *Tom Thumb*, 1830; *John Gilpin*, 1828 (realistic); and *The Brownies*, 1870.

1847. *Bob and Dog Quiz*. Author unknown. Revived by E. V. Lucas in *Old-fashioned Tales*. Illustrated by F. D. Bedford; published by Stokes, 1905.

1850. *The Child's Own Book*. Published in London. There was an earlier edition, not before 1830. The introduction, which in the 1850 edition was copied from the original, indicates by its style that the book was written early in the nineteenth century. The book was the delight of generations of children. It was a collection containing tales from *Arabian Nights*, Perrault's tales of *Cinderella, Puss-in-Boots, Hop-o'-my-Thumb, Bluebeard*, etc., D'Aulnoy's *Valentine and Orson*, chap-book stories of *Dick Whittington, Fortunatus, Griselda, Robinson Crusoe, The Children in the Wood, Little Jack*, and others. A recent edition of this book is in the *Young Folks' library*, vol. 1, published by Hall & Locke, Boston, 1901.

1850 (about). *The Three Bears*. Illustrated by Absalon and Harrison Weir. Addy and Co.

1824–1889. Work by Mrs. Mary Whateley. She had a Moslem school in Cairo and exerted a fairy tale influence.

1826–1887. *The Little Lame Prince; Adventures of a*

Brownie; and *The Fairy Book.* Produced by Mrs. Dinah Muloch Craik.

1854. *The Rose and the Ring,* by William M. Thackeray. A modern edition contains the original illustrations with additions by Monsell. Crowell.

1855. *Granny's Story Box.* A collection. Illustrated by J. Knight; published by Piper, Stephenson, and Spence.

1856. *Granny's Wonderful Chair,* containing *Prince Fairy-foot.* Written by Frances Browne, a blind Irish poetess.

1863. *Water Babies.* Charles Kingsley. Sir Noel Patton. The Macmillan Company.

1865. *Stories Told to a Child, including Fairy Tales; Mopsa the Fairy,* 1869. By Jean Ingelow.

1865. *Alice's Adventures in Wonderland,* by Lewis Carroll (Charles Dodgson), with 42 illustrations by John Tenniel, published by Macmillan Company, Oxford. First edition recalled. Later editions were published by Richard Clay, London.

1869. *At the Back of the North Wind; The Princess and the Goblin,* 1871. By George MacDonald. Arthur Hughes. Strahan. Reprinted by Blackie.

1870. *The Brownies;* 1882, *Old-fashioned Fairy Tales.* By Juliana Ewing.

1873. *A Series of Toy-Books for Children,* by Walter Crane (1845–1914). Published by Routledge and printed in colors by Edmund Evans. Twenty-seven of these stories in nine volumes are published by John Lane, Bodley Head. *Princess Fioromonde,* 1880, *Grimm's Household Stories,* 1882, and *The Cuckoo Clock,* 1887, all by Mrs. Molesworth, were also illustrated by Crane.

1878–. *Picture-Books,* by Randolph Caldecott (1846–1886). These were sixteen in number. They are published by F. Warne.

1875–. *Stories from the Eddas; Dame Wiggins of Lee* (Allen); and *The Pied Piper of Hamelin.* These delightful books by Kate Greenaway (1846–1901) were published by Routledge and engraved by Edmund Evans. They are now published by F. Warne.

This brings the English side of the subject down to the present time. Present editions of fairy tales are given in Chapter VI.

In Germany there were also many translations from the French of Perrault and D'Aulnoy. There were editions in 1764, 1770, etc. Most of those before the *Grimms' Tales* were not important. One might mention: —

1782. *Popular German Stories*, by Musäus.

1818. *Fables, Stories, and Tales for Children*, by Caroline Stahl.

1819. *Bohemian Folk-Tales*, by Wolfgang Gerle.

1812–1814. *Kinder und Haus-Märchen*, by Jacob and William Grimm. The second edition was published in 3 volumes in Berlin, by Reiner, in 1822. This latter work formed an era in popular literature and has been adopted as a model by all true collectors since.

Concerning the modern German fairy tale, the Germans have paid such special attention to the selection and grading of children's literature that their library lists are to be recommended. Wolgast, the author of *Vom Kinderbuch*, is an authority on the child's book. The fairy tale received a high estimate in Germany and no nation has attained a higher achievement in the art of the fairy tale book. The partial list simply indicates the slight knowledge of available material and would suggest an inviting field to librarians. A great stimulus to children's literature would be given by a knowledge of what the Germans have already accomplished in this particular. In Germany a child's book, before it enters the market, must first be accepted by a committee who test the book according to a standard of excellence. Any book not coming up to the standard is rejected. A few of the German editions in use are given: —

Bilderbücher, by Löwensohn.
Bilderbücher, by Scholz.
Liebe Märchen. One form of the above, giving three tales in one volume.
Märchen, by W. Hauff, published by Löwe. One edition, illustrated by Arthur Rackham, is published by Dutton. *The Caravan Tales* is an edition published by Stokes.
Märchen, by Musäus, published by Von K. A. Müller.
1777–1843. *Undine*, by La Motte Fouqué. A recent edition, illustrated by Rackham, is published by Doubleday.
1817–77. *Books* by Otillie Wildermuth. (What of hers should be translated and included?)
Hanschen im Blaubeerenwald; Hanschens Skifart Märchen, both by Elsa Beskow, published by Carl.
Windchen; and *Wurzelkindern*, both by Sybille von Olfers, published by Schreiber.
Das Märchen von den Sandmannlein, by Riemann, published by Schreiber.
Der Froschkönig, by Liebermann, published by Scholz.
Weisst du wieviel Sternlein stehen, by Lewinski, published by Schreiber.

In Sweden there appeared translations of Perrault and D'Aulnoy. *The Blue-Bird* was oftenest printed as a chap-book. Folk-tales were collected in: —

Swedish Tales, a collection. H. R. Von Schroter.
1844. *Folk-Tales.* George Stevens and Hylten Cavallius.

Sweden has given us the modern fairy tale, *The Wonderful Adventures of Nils* (2 volumes). This delightful tale by Selma Lagerlöf, born 1858, and a winner of the Nobel prize, has established itself as a child's classic. It has been translated by V. S. Howard, published by Doubleday, 1907.

In Norway we have: —

1851. *Norske Folkeeventyr,* collected by Asbjörnsen and Moe.

1862. *Norse Tales.* The above tales translated by Sir George W. Dasent.

In Denmark we have: —

Sagas of Bodvar Biarke.

Danske Folkeeventyr, by M. Winther, Copenhagen, 1823.

1843–60. *Danmarks Folkesagn,* 3 vols., by J. M. Thiele.

1805–1875. *Fairy Tales,* by Hans Christian Andersen. These tales are important as marking the beginning of the modern fairy tale. They are important also as literary fairy tales and have not been equaled in modern times.

In Slavonia we have: —

Wochentliche Nachrichten, by Busching, published by Schottky.

In Hungary we have: —

1822. *Märchen der Magyaren,* by George von Gaal.

In Greece and Russia no popular tales were collected before the time of the Grimms.

In Italy the two great collections of the world of fairy tales have been mentioned. Italy has also given the modern fairy tale which has been accepted as a classic: *Pinocchio,* by C. Collodi (Carlo Lorenzini). This has been illustrated by Copeland, published by

Ginn; and illustrated by Folkhard, published by Dutton.

In America the publication of fairy tales was at first a reprinting of English editions. In colonial times, previous to the revolution, booksellers imported largely from England. After the revolution a new home-growth in literature gradually developed. At first this was largely in imitation of literature in England. After the time of Washington Irving a distinct American adult literature established itself. The little child's toy-book followed in the wake of the grown-up's fiction. The following list[1] shows the growth of the American fairy tale, previous to 1870. Recent editions are given in Chapter VI.

1747–1840. *Forgotten Books of the American Nursery, A History of the Development of the American Story-Book.* Halsey, Rosalie V. Boston, C. E. Goodspeed & Co., 1911. 244 pp.

1785–1788. *Isaiah Thomas, Printer, Writer, and Collector. Nichols, Charles L.* A paper read April 12, 1911, before the Club of Odd Volumes. . . . Boston. Printed for the Club of Odd Volumes, 1912. 144 pp. List of juveniles 1787–88: pp. 132–33.

1785. *Mother Goose.* The original Mother Goose's melody, as first issued by John Newbery, of London, about A.D. 1760. Reproduced in facsimile from the edition as reprinted by Isaiah Thomas, of Worcester, Mass., A.D. 1785 (about) . . . Albany, J. Munsell's Sons, 1889. 28 pp.

1787. *Banbury Chap-Books and Nursery Toy-Book Litera-*

---

[1] The following list, compiled by Mr. H. H. B. Meyer, the chief bibliographer of the Library of Congress, has been furnished through the courtesy of the United States Bureau of Education. A few additional books were inserted by the author. The books at the head of the list give information on the subject.

ture (of the eighteenth and early nineteenth centuries) . . . Pearson, Edwin. With very much that is interesting and valuable appertaining to the early typography of children's books relating to Great Britain and America. . . . London, A. Reader, 1890: 116 pp. Impressions from wood-cut blocks by T. and J. Bewick, Cruikshank, Craig, Lee, Austin, and others.

1789. *The Olden Time Series.* Gleanings chiefly from old newspapers of Boston and Salem, Mass. Brooks, Henry M., *comp.* Boston, Ticknor & Co., 1886. 6 vols. *The Books that Children Read in 1798* . . . by T. C. Cushing: vol. 6, pp. 62–63.

1800–1825. Goodrich, S. G. *Recollections of a Lifetime.* New York, Miller, Orton, and Mulligan, 1856. 2 vols. Children's books (1800–1825): vol. 1, pp. 164–74.

1686. *The History of Tom Thumb.* John Dunton, Boston.

1728. *Chap-Books.* Benjamin Franklin, Philadelphia.

1730. *Small Histories.* Andrew Bradford, Philadelphia. These included *Tom Thumb, Tom Hickathrift,* and *Dick Whittington.*

1744. *The Child's New Plaything.* Draper & Edwards, Boston. Reprint. Contained alphabet in rhyme, proverbs, fables, and stories: *St. George and the Dragon; Fortunatus; Guy of Warwick; Brother and Sister; Reynard the Fox;* and *The Wolf and the Kids.*

1750. John Newbery's books. Advertised in Philadelphia *Gazette.* The *Pretty Book for Children* probably included *Cinderella, Tom Thumb,* etc.

1760. All juvenile publications for sale in England. Imported and sold by Hugh Gaine, New York.

1766. *Children's books.* Imported and sold by John Mein, a London bookseller who had a shop in Boston. Included *The Famous Tommy Thumb's Story Book; Leo the Great Giant; Urax, or the Fair Wanderer;* and *The Cruel Giant, Barbarico.*

1787. All Newbery's publications. Reprinted by Isaiah Thomas, Worcester, Mass.

1794. *Arabian Nights. The Arabian Nights Entertain-*

ments. . . . The first American edition. . . . Philadelphia, H. & P. Rice; Baltimore, J. Rice & Co., 1794. 2 vols.

1804. *Blue Beard. A New History of Blue Beard, written by Gaffer Black Beard, for the Amusement of Little Jack Black and his Pretty Sisters.* Philadelphia, J. Adams, 1804. 31 pp.

1819. *Rip Van Winkle.* A legend included in the works of Washington Irving, published in London, 1819.

1823. *A Visit from St. Nicholas.* Clement Clark Moore, in Troy *Sentinel,* Dec. 23, 1823. Written the year before for his own family. The first really good American juvenile story, though in verse.

1825. *Babes in the Wood.* The history of the children of the wood. . . . To which is added an interesting account of the Captive Boy. New York, N. B. Holmes. 36 pp. Plates.

1833. *Mother Goose.* The only true Mother Goose Melodies; an exact reproduction of the text and illustrations of the original edition, published and copyrighted in Boston in 1833 by Munroe & Francis. . . . Boston, Lee & Shepard, 1905. 103 pp.

1836. *The Fairy Book.* With eighty-one engravings on wood, by Joseph A. Adams. New York, Harper & Bros. 1836. 301 pp. Introduction by "John Smith." Edited by C. G. Verplanck, probably.

1844. *Fairy Land, and Other Sketches for Youths,* by the author of *Peter Parley's Tales* (Samuel G. Goodrich). Boston, J. Munroe & Co. 167 pp. Plates, Cromo. Lith. of Bouvé & Sharp, Boston.

1848. *Rainbows for Children,* by L. Maria Child, *ed.* New York, C. S. Francis & Co. 170 pp. 28 original sketches . . . by S. Wallin. . . . B. F. Childs, wood engraver: p. 8. Advertising pages: New books published by C. S. Francis & Co., N.Y. . . . *The Fairy Gift and the Fairy Gem.* Four volumes of choice fairy tales. Each illustrated with 200 fine engravings by French artists: p. 2.

1851. *Wonder Book,* by Nathaniel Hawthorne. Illustrated by W. Crane, 60 designs, published by Houghton, 1910.

1852. *Legends of the Flowers,* by Susan Pindar. New York, D. Appleton & Co., 178 pp.

1853. *Fairy Tales and Legends of Many Nations,* by

Charles B. Burkhardt. New York, Chas. Scribner. 277 pp. Illustrated by W. Walcutt and J. H. Cafferty.

1854. *The Little Glass Shoe, and Other Stories for Children.* Philadelphia, Charles H. Davis. 128 pp. Advertising pages: A description of illustrated juvenile books, published by Charles H. Davis: 16 pp. *A Book of Fairy Stories:* p. 9.

1854. *The History of Whittington and His Cat.* Miss Corner and Alfred Crowquill. *Dick Whittington* is said to have been the best seller among juvenile publications for five hundred years.

1855. *Flower Fables,* by Louisa May Alcott. Boston, G. W. Briggs & Co. 182 pp.

1855. *The Song of Hiawatha,* by Henry Wadsworth Longfellow. Published now by Houghton, illustrated by Frederick Remington.

1864. *Seaside and Fireside Fairies,* by George Blum. Translated from the German of Georg Blum and Louis Wahl. By A. L. Wister. Philadelphia, Ashmead & Evans, 292 pp.

1867. *Grimm's Goblins,* selected from the *Household Stories* of the Brothers Grimm. Jacob L. K. Grimm. Boston, Ticknor & Fields. 111 pp.

1867. *Fairy Book. Fairy Tales of All Nations,* by Edouard Laboulaye. Translated by Mary Booth. New York, Harper & Bros., 363 pp. Engravings.

1867. *The Wonderful Stories of Fuz-buz the Fly and Mother Grabem the Spider.* By S. Weir Mitchell. Philadelphia, J. B. Lippincott & Co. 79 pp.

1868. *Folks and Fairies.* Stories for little children. Lucy R. Comfort. New York, Harpers, 259 pp. Engravings. Advertising pages: Six fairy tales published by Harper & Bros.

1870. *Cinderella, or The Little Glass Slipper.* Boston, Fields, Osgood & Co. 1871. 8 pp. Colored plates by Alfred Fredericks.

1873. *Mother Goose.* Illustrations of Mother Goose's Melodies. By Alexander Anderson. New York. Privately printed by C. L. Moreau (Analectic Press), 1873, 36 l. 10 numb. l. (Designed and engraved on wood.)

1870. *Beauty and the Beast,* by Albert Smith. New York,

Manhattan Pub. Co., 1870. 64 pp. With illustrations by Alfred Crowquill.

This brings the American child's fairy tale up to recent publications of the present day which are given in the chapter, "Sources of Material." An attempt has been made here to give a glimpse of folk and fairy tales up to the time of the Grimms, and a view of modern publications in France, Germany, England, and America. The Grimms started a revolution in folk-lore and in their lifetime took part in the collection of many tales of tradition and influenced many others in the same line of work. An enumeration of what was accomplished in their lifetime appears in the notes of *Grimm's Household Tales*, edited by Margaret Hunt, published by Bohn's Libraries, vol. II, pp. 531, etc.

In modern times the Folk-Lore Society of England and America has been established. Now almost every nation has its folk-lore society and folk-tales are being collected all over the world. Altogether probably Russia has collected fifteen hundred such tales, Germany twelve hundred, Italy and France each one thousand, and India seven hundred. The work of the Grimms, ended in 1859, was continued by Emanuel Cosquin, who, in his *Popular Tales of Lorraine*, has made the most important recent contribution to folk-lore, — important for the European tale and important as showing the relation of the European tale to that of India.

The principal recent collections of folk-lore are: —

Legends and Fairy Tales of Ireland. Croker. 1825.
Welsh and Manx Tales. Sir John Rhys. 1840–.
Popular Rhymes of Scotland. Chambers. 1847.
Tales of the West Highlands. Campbell. 1860.
Popular Tales from the Norse. Dasent. 1862.
Zulu Nursery Tales. Callaway. 1866.
Old Deccan Days. Frere. 1868.
Fireside Tales of Ireland. Kennedy. 1870.
Indian Fairy Tales. Miss Stokes. 1880.
Buddhist Birth Stories. Rhys Davids. 1880.
Kaffir Folk-Lore. Theal. 1882.
Folk-Tales of Bengal. Day. 1883.
Wide Awake Stories. Steel and Temple. 1884.
Italian Popular Tales. Crane. 1885.
Popular Tales of Lorraine. Cosquin. 1886.
Popular Tales and Fictions. Clouston. 1887.
Folk-Tales of Kashmir. Knowles. 1887.
Tales of Ancient Egypt. Maspero. 1889.
Tales of the Sun. Mrs. Kingscote. 1890.
Tales of the Punjab. Steel. 1894.
Jataka Tales. Cowell. 1895.
Russian Folk-Tales. Bain. 1895.
Cossack Fairy Tales. Bain. 1899.
New World Fairy Book. Kennedy. 1906.
Fairy Tales, English, Celtic, and Indian. Joseph Jacobs. 1910–11.

This brings the subject down to the present time. The present-day contributions to folk-lore are found best in the records of the Folk-lore Society, published since its founding in London, in 1878; and daily additions, in the folk-lore journals of the various countries.

REFERENCES

Adams, Oscar Fay: *The Dear Old Story-Tellers.* Lothrop.

Ashton, John: *Chap-Books of the 18th Century.* Chatto & Windus. London, 1882.

Bunce, John T.: *Fairy Tales, Origin and Meaning.* Macmillan, 1878.

Chamberlain, A. F.: *The Child and Childhood in Folk-Thought.* Macmillan.

Clouston, W. A.: *Popular Tales and Fictions.* Edinburgh, Blackwoods, 1887.

Cyclopædia: "Mythology." *Encyclopædia Britannica.*

Cox, Miss Roalfe: *Cinderella.* Introduction by Lang. Nutt, 1892.

Dasent, George W.: *Popular Tales from the Norse.* Introduction. Routledge.

Fiske, John: *Myth and Myth-Makers.* Houghton.

Field, Mrs. E. M.: *The Child and His Book.* Gardner, Darton & Co.

Frazer, J. G.: *The Golden Bough.* (Spring ceremonies and primitive view of the soul.) Macmillan.

Frere, Miss: *Old Deccan Days.* Introduction. McDonough.

Godfrey, Elizabeth: *English Children in the Olden Time.* Dutton, 1907.

Grimm, William and Jacob: *Household Tales.* Edited with valuable notes, by Margaret Hunt. Introduction by Lang. Bell & Sons, Bohn's Libraries.

Guerber, Hélène A.: *Legends of the Middle Ages.* (Reynard the Fox) American Book Co.

Halliwell, J. O.: *Nursery Rhymes of England.*

Ibid.: Popular Rhymes and Nursery Tales. Smith, 1849.

Halsey, Rosalie: *Forgotten Books of the American Nursery.* Goodspeed, Boston, 1911.

Hartland, E. S.: *Science of Fairy Tales.* Preface. Scribner, 1891.

Ibid.: English Folk and Fairy Tales. Camelot series, Scott, London.

Hartland, Sidney: *Legend of Perseus* (origin of a tale).

Hewins, Caroline M.: *The History of Children's Books. Atlantic*, 61: 112 (Jan., 1888).

Jacobs, Joseph: *Reynard the Fox*. Cranford Series. Macmillan.

Ibid.: *Fairy Tales*. Introduction, Notes and Appendix. Putnam.

Keightley, Thomas: *Fairy Mythology*. Macmillan.

Ibid.: *Tales and Popular Fictions*. Whittaker & Co., London, 1834.

Lang, Andrew: *Custom and Myth*. Longmans, London, 1893.

Mabie, Hamilton: *Fairy Tales Every Child Should Know*. Introduction. Doubleday.

MacDonald, George: *The Light Princess*. Introduction. Putnam.

Magazine: "Myths and Fairy Tales." *Fortnightly Review*, May, 1872.

Mitchell, Donald G.: *About Old Story-Tellers*. Scribners. 1877.

Moses, Montrose: *Children's Books and Reading*. Kennerley.

Mulock, Miss: *Fairy Book*. Preface. Crowell.

Pearson, Edwin. *Banbury Chap-Books and Nursery Toy-Book Literature* (18th and early 19th centuries). London. A. Reader, 1890.

Perrault, Charles: *Popular Tales*. Edited by A. Lang. Introduction. Oxford, 1888.

Ritson, J.: *Fairy Tales*. Pearson, London, 1831.

Scott, Sir Walter: *Minstrelsy of Scottish Border*. Preface to Tamlane, "Dissertation on Fairies," p. 108.

Skinner, H. M.: *Readings in Folk-Lore*. American Book Co.

Steel, Flora A.: *Tales of the Punjab*. Introduction and Appendix. Macmillan.

Tabart, Benj.: *Fairy Tales, or the Lilliputian Cabinet*. London, 1818.

Review: *The Quarterly Review*, 1819, No. 41, pp. 91–112.

Tappan, Eva M.: *The Children's Hour*. Introduction to "Folk-Stories and Fables." Houghton.

Taylor, Edgar: *German Popular Stories*. Introduction by Ruskin. Chatto & Windus.

Tylor, E. B.: *Primitive Culture.* Holt, 1889.
Warner: *Fairy Tales. Library of the World's Best Literature,* vol. 30.
Welsh, Charles: *Fairy Tales Children Love.* Introduction. Dodge.
Ibid.: "The Early History of Children's Books in New England." *New England Magazine,* n.s. 20: 147–60 (April, 1899).
Ibid.: A Chap-Book. Facsimile Edition. 1915. World Book Co.
Ibid.: Mother Goose. Facsimile Edition. 1915. World Book Co.
White, Gleeson: "Children's Books and Their Illustrators." *International Studio,* Special Winter Number, 1897–98.

CHAPTER V

CLASSES OF FAIRY TALES

But the fact that after having been repeated for two thousand years, a story still possesses a perfectly fresh attraction for a child of to-day, does indeed prove that there is in it something of imperishable worth. — Felix Adler.

Whatever has, at any time, appealed to the best emotions and moved the heart of a people, must have for their children's children, political, historical, and cultural value. This is especially true of folk-tales and folk-songs. — P. P. Claxton, *United States Commissioner of Education.*

I. AVAILABLE TYPES OF TALES

From all this wealth of accumulated folk-material which has come down to us through the ages, we must select, for we cannot crowd the child with all the folk-stuff that folk-lore scientists are striving to preserve for scientific purposes. Moreover, naturally much of it contains the crudities, the coarseness, and the cruelties of primitive civilization; and it is not necessary that the child be burdened with this natural history of a past society. We must select from the past. In this selection of what shall be presented to the child we must be guided by two standards: First, we owe it to the child to hand on to him his literary heritage; and secondly, we must help him to make of himself the ideal man of the future. Therefore the tales we offer must contribute to these two standards. The tales selected will be those which the ages have found interesting; for the fact that they have lived proves their fitness, they have lived because there was something in them that appealed to the universal heart. And because of this fact they will be those which in the frequent re-tellings of ages have acquired a classic form and therefore have within themselves the possibility of taking upon them a perfect literary form. The tales selected will be those tales which, as we have pointed out, contain the interests of children; for only through his interests does the child rise to higher interests and finally develop to the ideal man. They will be those tales which stand also the test of a classic, the test of literature, the test of the short-story, and the test of narration and of description. The child would be handicapped in life to be ignorant of these tales.

Tales suitable for the little child may be viewed under these seven classes of available types: (1) the accumulative, or clock story; (2) the animal tale; (3) the humorous tale; (4) the realistic tale; (5) the romantic tale; (6) the old tale; and (7) the modern tale.

I. The Accumulative Tale.

The accumulative tale is the simplest form of the tale. It may be: —

(1) A tale of simple repetition.

(2) A tale of repetition with an addition, incremental iteration.

(3) A tale of repetition, with variation.

Repetition and rhythm have grown out of communal conditions. The old stories are measured utterances. At first there was the spontaneous expression of a little community, with its gesture, action, sound, and dance, and the word, the shout, to help out. There was the group which repeated, which acted as a chorus, and the leader who added his individual variation. From these developed the folk-tale with the dialogue in place of the chorus.

Of the accumulative tales, *The House that Jack Built* illustrates the first class of tales of simple repetition. This tale takes on a new interest as a remarkable study of phonics. If any one were so happy as to discover the phonic law which governs the euphony produced by the succession of vowels in the lines of Milton's poetry, he would enjoy the same law worked out in *The House that Jack Built*. The original, as given by Halliwell in his *Nursery Rhymes of England*, is said to be a Hebrew hymn, at first written in Chaldaic. To the Hebrews of the Middle Ages it was called the *Haggadah*, and was sung to a rude chant as part of the Passover service. It first appeared in print in 1590, at Prague. Later, in Leipzig, it was published by the German scholar, Liebrecht. It begins: —

> A kid, a kid, my father bought
> For two pieces of money:
> A kid, a kid,
> Then came the cat and ate the kid, etc.

Then follow the various repetitive stanzas, the last one turning back and reacting on all the others: —

Then came the Holy One, blessed be He,
And killed the angel of death,
That killed the butcher,
That slew the ox,
That drank the water,
That quenched the fire,
That burned the staff,
That beat the dog,
That bit the cat,
That ate the kid,
That my father bought
For two pieces of money:
A kid, a kid.

The remarkable similarity to *The Old Woman and Her Pig*[1] at once proclaims the origin of that tale also. The interpretation of this tale is as follows: The kid is the Hebrews; the father by whom it was purchased, is Jehovah; the two pieces of money are Aaron and Moses; the cat is the Assyrians; the dog is the Babylonians; the staff is the Persians; the fire is the Greek Empire and Alexander; the water is the Romans; the ox is the Saracens; the butcher is the Crusaders; and the angel of death is the Turkish Power. The message of this tale is that God will take vengeance over the Turks and the Hebrews will be restored to their own land.

Another tale of simple repetition, whose fairy element is the magic key, is *The Key of the Kingdom*, also found in Halliwell's *Nursery Rhymes of England*: —

[1] *The Woman and Her Kid*, a version of this tale adapted from an ancient Jewish Sacred Book, is given in *Boston Kindergarten Stories*, p. 171.

This is the key of the kingdom.
In that kingdom there is a city,
In that city there is a town,
In that town there is a street,
In that street there is a lane,
In that lane there is a yard,
In that yard there is a house,
In that house there is a room,
In that room there is a bed,
On that bed there is a basket,
In that basket there are some flowers.
Flowers in the basket, basket on the bed,
bed in the room, etc.

The Old Woman and Her Pig illustrates the second class of accumulative tale, where there is an addition, and like *Titty Mouse and Tatty Mouse,* where the end turns back on the beginning and changes all that precedes. Here there is a more marked plot. This same tale occurs in Shropshire Folk-Lore, in the *Scotch Wife and Her Bush of Berries,* in *Club-Fist,* an American folk-game described by Newell, in Cossack fairy tales, and in the Danish, Spanish, and Italian. In the Scandinavian, it is *Nanny, Who Would n't Go Home to Supper,* and in the Punjab, *The Grain of Corn,* also given in *Tales of Laughter.* I have never seen a child who did not like it or who was not pleased with himself for accomplishing its telling. It lends itself most happily to illustration. *Titty Mouse and Tatty Mouse* pleases because of the liveliness of its images, and because of the catastrophe at the end, which affects the child just as the tumble of his huge pile of blocks — the crash and general upheaval delight him. This tale has so many variants that it illustrates well the diffusion of fairy tales. It is Grimm's *The Spider and the Flea,* which as we have seen, is appealing in its simplicity; the Norse *The Cock Who Fell into the Brewing Vat;* and the Indian *The Death and Burial of Poor Hen.* The curious succession of incidents may have been invented once for all at some definite time, and from thence spread to all the world.

Johnny Cake and *The Gingerbread Man* also represent the second class of accumulative tale, but show a more definite plot; there is more story-stuff and a more decided introduction and conclusion. *How Jack Went to Seek His Fortune* also shows more plot. It contains a theme similar to that of *The Bremen Town Musicians,* which is distinctly a beast tale where the element of repetition remains to sustain the interest and to preserve unity, but where a full-fledged short-story which is structurally complete, has developed. A fine accumulative tale belonging to this second class is the Cossack *Straw Ox,* which has been described under "The Short-Story." Here we have a single line of sequence which gets wound up to a climax and then unwinds itself to the conclusion, giving the child, in the plot, something of that pleasure which he feels in winding up his toy animals to watch them perform in the unwinding.

The Three Bears illustrates the third class of repetitive story, where there is repetition and variation. Here the iteration and parallelism have interest like the refrain of a song, and the technique of the story is like that of *The Merchant of Venice.* This is the ideal fairy story for the little child. It is unique in that it is the only instance in which a tale written by an author has become a folk-tale. It was written by Southey, and appeared in *The Doctor*, in London, in 1837. Southey may have used as his source, *Scrapefoot*, which Joseph Jacobs has discovered for us, or he may have used *Snow White*, which contains the episode of the chairs. Southey has given to the world a nursery classic which should be retained in its purity of form. The manner of the Folk, in substituting for the little old woman of Southey's tale, Goldilocks, and the difference that it effects in the tale, proves the greater interest children naturally feel in the tale with a child. Similarly, in telling *The Story of Midas* to an audience of eager little people, one naturally takes the fine old myth from Ovid as Bulfinch gives it, and puts into it the Marigold of Hawthorne's creation. And after knowing Marigold, no child likes the story without her. Silver hair is another substitute for the little Old Woman in *The Three Bears.* The very little child's reception to *Three Bears* will depend largely on the previous experience with bears and on the attitude of the person telling the story. A little girl who was listening to *The Three Bears* for the first time, as she heard how the Three Bears stood looking out of their upstairs window after Goldilocks running across the wood, said, "Why did n't Goldilocks lie down beside the Baby Bear?" To her the Bear was associated with the friendly Teddy Bear she took with her to bed at night, and the story had absolutely no thrill of fear because it had been told with an emphasis on the comical rather than on the fearful. Similar in structure to *The Three Bears* is the Norse *Three Billy-Goats*, which belongs to the same class of delightful repetitive tales and in which the sequence of the tale is in the same three distinct steps.

II. The Animal Tale

The animal tale includes many of the most pleasing children's tales. Indeed some authorities would go so far as to trace all fairy tales back to some ancestor of an animal tale; and in many cases this certainly can be done just as we trace *Three Bears* back to *Scrapefoot.* The animal tale is either an old beast tale, such as *Scrapefoot* or *Old Sultan;* or a fairy tale which is an elaborated development of a fable, such as *The Country Mouse and the City Mouse* or the tales of *Reynard the Fox* or Grimm's *The King of the Birds*, and *The Sparrow and His Four Children;* or it is a purely imaginary creation, such as Kipling's *The Elephant's Child* or Andersen's *The Bronze Pig.*

The beast tale is a very old form which was a story of some successful primitive hunt or of some primitive man's experience with animals in which he looked up to the beast as a brother superior to himself in strength, courage, endurance, swiftness, keen scent, vision, or cunning. Later, in more civilized society, when men became interested in problems of conduct, animals were introduced to point the moral of the tale, and we have the fable. The fable resulted when a truth was stated in concrete story form. When this truth was in gnomic form, stated in general terms, it became compressed into the proverb. The fable was brief, intense, and concerned with the distinguishing characteristics of the animal characters, who were endowed with human traits. Such were the *Fables of Æsop*. Then followed the beast epic, such as *Reynard the Fox*, in which the personality of the animals became less prominent and the animal characters became types of humanity. Later, the beast tale took the form of narratives of hunters, where the interest centered in the excitement of the hunt and in the victory of the hunter. With the thirst for universal knowledge in the days following Bacon there gradually grew a desire to learn also about animals. Then followed animal anecdotes, the result of observation and imagination, often regarding the mental processes of animals. With the growth of the scientific spirit the interest in natural history developed. The modern animal story since 1850 has a basis of natural science, but it also seeks to search the motive back of the action, it is a psychological romance. The early modern animal tales such as *Black Beauty* show sympathy with animals, but their psychology is human. In Seton Thompson's *Krag*, which is a masterpiece, the interest centers about the personality and the mentality of the animal and his purely physical characteristics. Perhaps it is true that these physical characteristics are somewhat imaginary and overdrawn and that overmuch freedom has been used in interpreting these physical signs. In Kipling's tales we have a later evolution of the animal tale. His animals possess personality in emotion and thought. In the forest-friends of Mowgli we have humanized animals possessing human power of thinking and of expressing. In real life animal motives seem simple, one dominant motive crowds out all others. But Kipling's animals show very complex motives, they reason and judge more than our knowledge of animal life justifies. In the *Just-So Stories* Kipling has given us the animal *pourquois* tale with a basis of scientific truth. Of these delightful fairy tales, *The Elephant's Child* and *How the Camel Got His Hump* may be used in the kindergarten. Perhaps the latest evolution of the animal tale is by Charles G. D. Roberts. The animal characters in his *Kindred of the Wild* are given animal characteristics. They have become interesting as exhibiting these traits and not as typifying human motives; they show an animal psychology. The tales have a scientific basis, and the interest is centered in this and not in an exaggeration of it.

Having viewed the animal tale as a growth let us look now at a few individual tales: —

One of the most pleasing animal tales is *Henny*

Penny, or *Chicken Licken*, as it is sometimes called, told by Jacobs in *English Fairy Tales*. Here the enterprising little hen, new to the ways of the world, ventures to take a walk. Because a grain of corn falls on her top-knot, she believes the sky is falling, her walk takes direction, and thereafter she proceeds to tell the king. She takes with her all she meets, who, like her, are credulous, — Cocky Locky, Ducky Daddles, Goosey Poosey, and Turky Lurky, — until they meet Foxy Woxy, who leads them into his cave, never to come out again. This is similar to the delightful Jataka tale of *The Foolish Timid Rabbit*, which before has been outlined for telling, which has been re-told by Ellen C. Babbit. In this tale a Rabbit, asleep under a palm tree, heard a noise, and thought "the earth was all breaking up." So he ran until he met another Rabbit, and then a hundred other Rabbits, a Deer, a Fox, an Elephant, and at last a Lion. All the animals except the Lion accepted the Rabbit's news and followed. But the Lion made a stand and asked for facts. He ran to the hill in front of the animals and roared three times. He traced the tale back to the first Rabbit, and taking him on his back, ran with him to the foot of the hill where the palm tree grew. There, under the tree, lay a cocoanut. The Lion explained the sound the Rabbit had heard, then ran back and told the other animals, and they all stopped running. *Brother Rabbit Takes Some Exercise*, a tale from *Nights with Uncle Remus* is very similar to *Henny*

Penny and could be used at the same time. It is also similar to Grimm's *Wolf and Seven Kids*, the English *Story of Three Pigs*, the Irish *The End of the World*, and an Italian popular tale.

The Sheep and the Pig, adapted from the Scandinavian by Miss Bailey in *For the Children's Hour*, given also in Dasent's *Tales from the Field*, is a delightfully vivacious and humorous tale which reminds one of *Henny Penny*. A Sheep and Pig started out to find a home, to live together. They traveled until they met a Rabbit and then followed this dialogue: —

> *R.* "Where are you going?"
> *S. and P.* "We are going to build us a house."
> *R.* "May I live with you?"
> *S. and P.* "What can you do to help?"

The Rabbit scratched his leg with his left hind foot for a minute and said, "I can gnaw pegs with my sharp teeth and I can put them in with my paws." "Good," said the Sheep and the Pig, "you may come with us!" Then they met a gray Goose who could pull moss and stuff it in cracks, and a Cock who could crow early and waken all. So they all found a house and lived in it happily.

The Spanish *Medio Pollito*, or *Little Half-Chick*, is another accumulative animal tale similar to *Henny Penny*, and one which is worthy of university study. The disobedient but energetic hero who went off to Madrid is very appealing and constantly amusing, and the tale possesses unusual beauty. The interest centers in the character. The beauty lies in the setting of the adventures, as Medio Pollito came to a stream, to a large chestnut tree, to the wind, to the soldiers outside the city gates, to the King's Palace at Madrid, and to the King's cook, until in the end he reached the high point of immortalization as the weather-vane of a church steeple.

The Story of Three Pigs could contend with *The Three Bears* for the position of ideal story for little people. It suits them even better than *The Three Bears*, perhaps because they can identify themselves more easily with the hero, who is a most winning, clever individual, though a Pig. The children know nothing of the standards of the Greek drama, but they recognize a good thing; and when the actors in their story are great in interest and in liveliness, they respond with a corresponding appreciation. The dramatic element in *The Three Pigs* is strong and all children love to dramatize it. The story is the Italian *Three Goslings*, the Negro *Tiny Pig*, the Indian *Lambikin*, and the German *The Wolf and Seven Kids*. This tale is given by Andrew Lang in his *Green Fairy Book*. The most satisfactory presentation of the story is given by Leslie Brooke in his *Golden Goose Book*. The German version occurred in an old poem, *Reinhart Fuchs*, in which the Kid sees the Wolf through a chink. Originally the characters must have been Kids, for little pigs do not have hair on their "chinny chin chins."

One of the earliest modern animal tales is *The Good-Natured Bear*,[1] by Richard Hengist Horne, the English critic. This tale was written in 1846, just when men were beginning to gain a greater knowledge of animal life. It is both psychological and imaginative. It was brought to the attention of the English public in a criticism, *On Some Illustrated Christmas Books*,[2] by Thackeray, who considered it one of the "wittiest, pleasantest, and kindest of books, and an admirable story." It is now out of print, but it seems to be worthy of being preserved and reprinted. The story is the autobiography of a Bear, who first tells about his interesting experiences as a Baby Bear. He first gives to Gretchen and the children gathered about him an account of his experience when his Mother first taught him to walk alone.

III. The Humorous Tale

The humorous tale is one of the most pleasing to the little child. It pleases everybody, but it suits him especially because the essence of humor is a mixture of love and surprise, and both appeal to the child completely. Humor brings joy into the world, so does the little child, their very existence is a harmony. Humor sees contrasts, shows good sense, and feels

[1] See Appendix.

[2] William M. Thackeray, *Miscellanies*. v. Boston: James Osgood & Co., 1873. "Titmarsh among Pictures and Books"; "On Some Illustrated Christmas Books," 1846.

compassion. It stimulates curiosity. Its laughter is impersonal and has a social and spiritual effect. It acts like fresh air, it clarifies the atmosphere of the mind and it enables one to see things in a sharply defined light. It reveals character; it breaks up a situation, reconstructs it, and so views life, interprets it. It plays with life, it frees the spirit, and it invigorates the soul.

Speaking of humor, Thackeray, in "A Grumble About Christmas Books," 1847, considered that the motto for humor should be the same as the talisman worn by the Prioress in Chaucer: —

> About hire arm a broche of gold ful shene,
> On which was first ywritten a crowned *A*,
> And after, *Amor vincit omnia.*

He continued: "The works of the real humorist always have this sacred press-mark, I think. Try Shakespeare, first of all, Cervantes, Addison, poor Dick Steele, and dear Harry Fielding, the tender and delightful Jean Paul, Sterne, and Scott, — and Love is the humorist's best characteristic and gives that charming ring to their laughter in which all the good-natured world joins in chorus."

The humorous element for children appears in the repetition of phrases such as we find in *Three Bears*, *Three Pigs*, and *Three Billy-Goats;* in the contrast in the change of voice so noticeable also in these three tales; in the contrast of ideas so conspicuous in Kipling's *Elephant's Child;* and in the element of surprise so evident when Johnny Cake is eaten by the Fox, or when Little Hen eats the bread, or when Little Pig outwits the Wolf. The humorous element for children also lies in the incongruous, the exaggerated, or in the grotesque, so well displayed in Lear's *Nonsense Rhymes*, and much of the charm of *Alice in Wonderland*. The humorous element must change accordingly for older children, who become surprised less easily, and whose tales therefore, in order to surprise, must have more clever ideas and more subtle fancy.

The Musicians of Bremen is a good type of humorous tale. It shows all the elements of true humor. Its philosophy is healthy; it views life as a whole and escapes tragedy by seeing the comic situation in the midst of trouble. It is full of the social good-comradeship which is a condition of humor. It possesses a suspense that is unusual, and is a series of surprises with one grand surprise to the robbers at their feast as its climax. The Donkey is a noble hero who breathes a spirit of courage like that of the fine Homeric heroes. His achievement of a home is a mastery that pleases children. And the message of the tale, which after all, is its chief worth — that there ought to be room in the world for the aged and the worn out, and that "The guilty flee when no man pursueth" — appeals to their compassion and their good sense. The variety of noises furnished by the different characters is a pleasing repetition with variation that is a special element of humor; and the grand chorus of music leaves no doubt as to the climax. We must view life with these four who are up against the facts of life, and whose lot presents a variety of contrast. The Donkey, incapacitated because of old age, had the courage to set out on a quest. He met the Dog who could hunt no longer, stopping in the middle of the road, panting for breath; the Cat who had only stumps for teeth, sitting in the middle of the road, wearing an unhappy heart behind a face dismal as three rainy Sundays; and the Rooster who just overheard the cook say he was to be made into soup next Sunday, sitting on the top of the gate crowing his last as loud as he could crow. The Donkey, to these musicians he collected, spoke as a leader and as a true humorist.

In a simple tale like *The Bremen Town Musicians* it is surprising how much of interest can develop: the adventure in the wood; the motif of some one going to a tree-top and seeing from there a light afar off, which appears in *Hop-o'-my-Thumb* and in many other tales; the example of coöperation, where all had a unity of purpose; an example of a good complete short-story form which illustrates introduction, setting, characters and dialogue — all these proclaim this one of the fine old stories. In its most dramatic form, and to Jacobs its most impressive one, it appears in the Celtic tales as *Jack and His Comrades*. It may have been derived from *Old Sultan*, a Grimm tale which is somewhat similar to *The Wolf and the Hungry Dog*, in Steinhowel, 1487. *How Jack Sought His Fortune* is an English tale of coöperation which is similar but not nearly so pleasing. A Danish tale of coöperation, *Pleiades*, is found in Lansing's *Fairy Tales*. *How Six Traveled Through the World* is a Grimm tale which, though suited to older children, contains the same general theme.

Very many of the tales suited to kindergarten children which have been mentioned in various chapters, contain a large element of humor. The nonsense drolls are a type distinct from the humorous tale proper, yet distinctly humorous. Such are the realistic *Lazy Jack*, *Henny Penny*, and *Billy Bobtail*. Then since repetition is an element of humor, many accumulative tales rank as humorous: such as *Lambikin*, *The Old Woman and Her Pig*, *Medio Pollito*, *The Straw Ox*, *Johnny Cake*, and *Three Billy-Goats*. Among the humorous tales proper are Andersen's *Snow Man; The Cat and the Mouse in Partnership; The Rabbit Who Wanted Red Wings; The Elephant's Child;* and very many of the Uncle Remus Tales, such as *Why the Hawk Catches Chickens*, *Brother Rabbit and Brother Tiger*, and *Heyo, House!* all in *Uncle Remus and the Little Boy*. *The Story of Little Black Mingo* in *Tales of Laughter*, is a very attractive humorous tale, but it is more suited to the child of the second grade.

Drakesbill is a French humorous accumulative tale with a plot constructed similarly to that of the Cossack *Straw Ox*. Drakesbill, who was so tiny they called him Bill Drake, was a great worker and soon saved a hundred dollars in gold which he lent to the King. But as the King never offered to pay, one morning Drakesbill set out, singing as he went, "Quack, quack, quack, when shall I get my money back?" To all the objects he met and to their questions he replied, "I am going to the King to ask him to pay me what he owes me." When they begged, "Take me with you!" he was willing, but he said, "You must make yourself small, get into my mouth, and creep under my tongue!" He arrived at the palace with his companions concealed in his mouth: a Fox, a Ladder, Laughing River, and Wasp-Nest. On asking to see the King, he was not escorted with dignity but sent to the poultry-yard, to the turkeys and chickens who fought him. Then he surprised them by calling forth the Fox who killed the fowls. When he was thrown into a well, he called out the Ladder to help him. When about to be thrown into the fire, he called out the River who overwhelmed the rest and left him serenely swimming. When surrounded by the King's men and their swords he called out the Wasp-Nest who drove away all but Drakesbill, leaving him free to look for his money. But he found none as the King had spent all. So he seated himself upon the throne and became King. The element of humor here, as has been mentioned previously, is that Drakesbill, after every rebuff of fortune maintained his happy, fresh vivacity, and triumphantly repeated his one cry, "Quack, quack, quack, when shall I get my money back?" There is humor, too, in the repetition of dialogue, as on his way to the

King he met the various characters and talked to them. Humor lies also in the real lively surprises which Drakesbill so effectively gave during his visit to the King. One can see how this tale might have been a satire reflecting upon a spendthrift King.

IV. The Realistic Tale

The realistic fairy tale has a great sympathy with humble life and desires to reproduce faithfully all life worth while. The spirit of it has been expressed by Kipling —

> each in his separate star,
> Shall draw the Thing as he sees It, for the God of Things as They are.

Sometimes the realistic story has a scientific spirit and interest. A realistic tale that is good will present not only what is true but what is possible, probable, or inevitable, making its truth impressive. Very often it does not reach this ideal. A transcript of actual life may be selected, but that is a photograph and not a picture with a strong purpose to make one point, and with artistic design. The characters, though true to life, may be lifeless and colorless, and their doings and what happens to them uninteresting. For this reason, many modern writers of tales for children, respecting the worth of the realistic, neglect to comply with what the realistic demands, and produce insipid, unconvincing tales. The realistic tale should deal with the simple and the ordinary rather than with the exceptional; and the test is not how much, but how little, credulity it arouses.

Grimm's *Hans in Luck* is a perfect realistic tale, as are Grimm's *Clever Elsa* and the Norse *Three Sillies*, although these tales are suited to slightly older children. The drolls often appear among the realistic tales, as if genuine humor were more fresh when related to the things of actual life. The English *Lazy Jack* is a delightful realistic droll which contains motifs that appear frequently among the tales. The Touchstone motif of a humble individual causing nobility to laugh appears in Grimm's *Dummling and His Golden Goose*. It appears also in *Zerbino the Savage*, a most elaborated Neapolitan tale retold by Laboulaye in his *Last Fairy Tales;* a tale full of humor, wit, and satire that would delight the cultured man of the world.

In *Lazy Jack* the setting is in humble life. A poor mother lived on the common with her indolent son and managed to earn a livelihood by spinning. One day the mother lost patience and threatened to send from home this idle son if he did not get work. So he set out. Each day he returned to his mother with his day's earnings. The humor lies in what he brought, in how he brought it, and in what happened to it; in the admonition of his mother, "You should have done so and so," and Jack's one reply, "I'll do so another time"; in Jack's literal use of his mother's admonition, and the catastrophe it brought him on the following day, and on each successive day, as he brought home a piece of money, a jar of milk, a cream cheese, a tom-cat, a shoulder of mutton, and at last a donkey. The humor lies in the contrast between what Jack did and what anybody " with sense " knows he ought to have done, until when royalty beheld him carrying the donkey on his shoulders, with legs sticking up in the air, it could bear no more, and burst into laughter. This is a good realistic droll to use because it impresses the truth, that even a little child must reason and judge and use his own common sense.

The Story of the Little Red Hen is a realistic tale which presents a simple picture of humble thrift. Andersen's *Tin Soldier* is a realistic tale which gives an adventure that might happen to a real tin soldier. *The Old Woman and her Pig*, whose history has been given under *The Accumulative Tale*, is realistic. Its theme is the simple experience of an aged peasant who swept her house, who had the unusual much-coveted pleasure of finding a dime, who went to market and bought a Pig for so small a sum. But on the way home, as the Pig became contrary when reaching a stile, and refused to go, the Old Woman had to seek aid. So she asked the Dog, the Stick, the Fire, etc. She asked aid first from the nearest at hand; and each object asked, in its turn sought help from the next higher power. One great source of pleasure in this tale is that each object whose aid is sought is asked to do the thing its nature would compel it to do — the Dog to bite, the

Stick to beat, etc.; and each successive object chosen is the one which, by the law of its nature, is a master to the preceding one. The Dog, by virtue of ability to bite, has power over the Pig; the Stick has ability to master the Dog; and Water in its power to quench is master over Fire. Because of this intimate connection of cause and effect, this tale contributes in an unusual degree to the development of the child's reason and memory. He may remember the sequence of the plot or remake the tale if he forgets, by reasoning out the association between the successive objects from whom aid was asked. It is through this association that the memory is exercised.

How Two Beetles Took Lodgings, in *Tales of Laughter*, is a realistic story which has a scientific spirit and interest. Its basis of truth belongs to the realm of nature study. Its narration of how two Beetles set up housekeeping by visiting an ant-hill and helping themselves to the home and furnishings of the Ants, would be very well suited either to precede or to follow the actual study of an ant-hill by the children. The story gives a good glimpse of the home of the Ants, of their manner of living, and of the characteristics of the Ants and Beetles. It is not science mollified, but a good story full of life and humor, with a basis of scientific truth.

Many tales not realistic contain a large realistic element. The fine old romantic tales, such as *Cinderella*, *Sleeping Beauty*, and *Bremen Town Musicians*, have a large realistic element. In *The Little Elves* we have the realistic picture of a simple German home. In *Beauty and the Beast* we have a realistic glimpse of the three various ways the wealthy merchant's daughters accommodated themselves to their father's loss of fortune, which reminds us of a parallel theme in Shakespeare's *King Lear*. In *Red Riding Hood* we have the realistic starting out of a little girl to visit her grandmother. This realistic element appeals to the child because, as we have noted, it accords with his experience, and it therefore seems less strange.

In *Titty Mouse and Tatty Mouse* the setting is realistic but becomes transformed into the romantic when natural doings of everyday life take on meaning from the unusual happening in the tale. It is realistic for Titty Mouse and Tatty Mouse to live in a little house, to get some corn, to make a pudding, and to put it on to boil. But when the pot tumbled over and scalded Titty, the romantic began. The stool which was real and common and stood by the door became transformed with animation, it talked: "Titty's dead, and so I weep"; and it hopped! Then a broom caught the same animation from the same theme, and swept; a door jarred; a window creaked; an old form ran round the house; a walnut tree shed its leaves; a little bird moulted his pretty feathers; a little girl spilled her milk; a man tumbled off his ladder; and the walnut tree fell with a crash, upsetting everything and burying Titty in the ruins. They all learned to convey the same message. The common and customary became uncommon and unusual with extraordinary life, feeling, and lively movement.

Other romantic tales with a large realistic element are *The Three Bears*, *The Three Pigs*, and *The Three Billy-Goats*, animal tales which of necessity must be largely realistic, for their foundation is in the facts of the nature, habits, and traits of the animal characters they portray.

V. The Romantic Tale

The romantic tale reflects emotion and it contains adventure and the picturesque; it deals with dreams, distant places, the sea, the sky, and objects of wonder touched with beauty and strangeness. The purpose of the romantic is to arouse emotion, pity, or the sense of the heroic; and it often exaggerates character and incidents beyond the normal. The test of the romantic tale as well as of the realistic tale is in the reality it possesses. This reality it will possess, not only because it is true, but because it is also true to life. And it is to be remembered that because of the unusual setting in a romantic tale the truth it presents stands out very clearly with much impressiveness. *Red Riding Hood* is a more impressive tale than *The Three Bears*.

Cinderella is a good type of the old romantic tale. It has a never-ending attraction for children just as it has had for all peoples of the world; for this tale has as many as three hundred and forty-five variants, which have been examined by Miss Cox. In these variants there are many common incidents, such as the hearth abode, the helpful animal, the heroine disguise, the ill-treated heroine, the lost shoe, the love-sick prince, magic dresses, the magic tree, the threefold flight, the false bride, and many others. But the one incident which claims the tale as a Cinderella tale proper, is the recognition of the heroine by means of her shoe. In the Greek *Rhodope*, the slipper is carried off by an eagle and dropped into the lap of the King of Egypt, who seeks and marries the owner. In the Hindu tale the Rajah's daughter loses her slipper in the forest where it is found by the Prince. The interpretation of *Cinderella* is that the Maiden, the Dawn, is dull and gray away from the brightness of the sun. The Sisters are the Clouds that shadow the Dawn, and the Stepmother is Night. The Dawn hurries away from the pursuing Prince, the Sun, who, after a long search, overtakes her in her glorious robes of sunset.

This tale is the Hindu *Sodewa Bai*, the Zuni *Poor Turkey Girl*, and the English *Rushen Coatie*, *Cap-o'-Rushes*, and *Catskin*. *Catskin*, which Mr. Burchell told to the children of the Vicar of Wakefield, is considered by Newell as the oldest of the Cinderella types, appearing in Straparola in 1550, while *Cinderella* appeared first in Basile in 1637. *Catskin*, in ballad form as given by Halliwell, was printed in Aldermary Churchyard, England, in 1720; and the form as given by Jacobs well illustrates how the prose tale developed from the old ballad. The two most common forms of *Cinderella* are Perrault's and Grimm's, either of which is suited to the very little child. Perrault's *Cinderella* shows about twenty distinct differences from the Grimm tale: —

(1) It omits the Mother's death-bed injunction to Cinderella.
(2) It omits the wooden shoes and the cloak.
(3) The Stepmother assigns more modern tasks. It omits the pease-and-beans task.
(4) It shows Cinderella sleeping in a garret instead of on the hearth.
(5) It omits the Father.
(6) It omits the hazel bough.
(7) It omits the three wishes.
(8) It substitutes the fairy Godmother for the hazel tree and the friendly doves.
(9) It substitutes transformation for tree-shaking.
(10) It omits the episode of the pear tree and of the pigeon-house.
(11) It omits the use of pitch and axe-cutting.
(12) It omits the false bride and the two doves.
(13) It substitutes two nights at the ball for three nights.
(14) It makes C. forgiving and generous at the end. The Sisters are not punished.
(15) It contains slippers of glass instead of slippers of gold.
(16) It simplifies the narrative, improves the structure, and puts in the condition, which is a keystone to the structure.
(17) It has no poetical refrain.
(18) It is more direct and dramatic.
(19) It draws the characters more clearly.
(20) Is it not more artificial and conventional?

This contrast shows the Grimm tale to be the more poetical, while it is the more complex, and contains more barbarous and gruesome elements unsuited to the child of to-day. Of the two forms, the Grimm tale seems the superior tale, however, and if rewritten in a literary form suited to the child, might become even preferable.

Sleeping Beauty, which is another romantic tale that might claim to be the most popular fairy tale, has for its theme the long sleep of winter and the awakening of spring. The Earth goddess, pricked by winter's dart, falls into a deep sleep from which she is awakened by the Sun who searches far for her. This tale is similar to the Norse *Balder* and the Greek *Persephone*. Some of its incidents appear also in *The Two Brothers*, an Egyptian tale of the Nineteenth Dynasty of Seti II, in which the Hathors who pronounce the fate of the Prince correspond to the wicked old Fairy. The spindle whose prick caused slumber is the arrow that wounded Achilles, the thorn which pricked Siegfried, the mistletoe which wounded Balder, and the poisoned nail of the demon in *Surya Bai*. In the northern form of the story we find the ivy, which is the one plant that can endure winter's touch. The theme of the long sleep occurs in the mediæval legend of *The Seven Sleepers of Ephesus*, in the English *The King of England and His Three Sons*, poetically as Tennyson has given it in his *Day-Dream*, and in the *Story of Brunhilde*, in *Siegfried*. Here a hedge of flames encircles Brunhilde who is awakened at the touch of Siegfried's magic sword, just as Sleeping Beauty is awakened by the

Prince's kiss. The kiss may be a survival of an ancient form of worship of some local goddess. In the Hindu *Panch-Rhul Ranee*, seven ditches surmounted by seven hedges of spears, surround the heroine. Of the Perrault and Grimm versions of *Sleeping Beauty*, the Perrault version is long and complex because it contains the minor tale of the cruel stepmother added to the main tale, while the Grimm *Briar Rose* is a model of structure easily separated into ten leading episodes. *Sleeping Beauty* appeared in Basile's *Pentamerone* where there is given the beautiful incident of the baby sucking the spike of flax out of its sleeping mother's fingers. The Perrault version agrees with that of Basile in naming the twins, who are Sun and Moon in the *Pentamerone*, Day and Dawn.

Red Riding Hood is another romantic tale [1] that could claim to be the one most popular fairy tale of all fairy tales. Similar tales occur in the story of the Greek Kronos swallowing his children, in the Algonquin legend repeated in *Hiawatha*, and in an Aryan story of a Dragon swallowing the sun and being killed by the sun-god, Indra. *Red Riding Hood* appeals to a child's sense of fear, it gives a thrill which if not too intense, is distinctly pleasing. But it pleases less noticeably perhaps because of its atmosphere of love and service, and because it presents a picture of a dear

[1] A few romantic tales for the first grade are treated in the Appendix: *Puss-in-Boots, Lord Peter, Tom Thumb, Little Thumb,* and *Snow White and Rose Red.*

little maid. The Grandmother's gift of love to the child, the bright red hood, the mother's parting injunction, the Wolf's change of aspect and voice to suit the child — all these directly and indirectly emphasize love, tenderness, and appreciation of simple childhood. The child's errand of gratitude and love, the play in the wood, the faith in the woodcutter's presence — all are characteristic of a typical little maid and one to be loved. There is in the tale too, the beauty of the wood — flowers, birds, and the freshness of the open air. The ending of the tale is varied. In Perrault the Wolf ate Grandmother and then ate Red Riding Hood. In Grimm one version gives it that the Hunter, hearing snoring, went to see what the old lady needed. He cut open the Wolf, and Grandmother and Red Riding Hood became alive. He filled the Wolf with stones. When the Wolf awoke, he tried to run, and died. All three were happy; the Hunter took the skin, Grandmother had her cake and wine, and Red Riding Hood was safe and had her little girl's lesson of obedience. Another Grimm ending is that Little Red-Cap reached the Grandmother before the Wolf, and after telling her that she had met him, they both locked the door. Then they filled a trough with water in which the sausages had been boiled. When the Wolf tried to get in and got up on the roof, he was enticed by the odor, and fell into the trough. A great deal of freedom has been used in re-telling the ending of this tale, usually with the purpose of preventing the Wolf from eating Red Riding Hood. In regard to the conclusion of *Red Riding Hood,* Thackeray said: "I am reconciled to the Wolf eating Red Riding Hood because I have given up believing this is a moral tale altogether and am content to receive it as a wild, odd, surprising, and not unkindly fairy story."

The interpretation of *Red Riding Hood* —which the children need not know — is that the evening Sun goes to see her Grandmother, the Earth, who is the first to be swallowed up by the Wolf of Night and Darkness. The red cloak is the twilight glow. The Hunter may be the rising Sun that rescues all from Night. *Red Riding Hood* has been charmingly elaborated in Tieck's *Romantic Poems,* and a similar story appears in a Swedish popular song, *Jungfrun i'Blaskagen,* in *Folkviser* 3; 68, 69.

VI, VII. The Old Tale and the Modern Tale

The old fairy tale is to be distinguished from the modern fairy tale. Most of the tales selected have been old tales because they possess the characteristics suited to the little child. The modern fairy tale may be said to begin with Andersen's *Fairy Tales.* — Since Andersen has been referred to frequently and as a study of *The Tin Soldier* has already been given, Andersen's work can receive no more detailed treatment here. — The modern fairy tale, since the time of Andersen, has yet to learn simplicity and sincerity. It often is long and involved and presents a multiplicity of images that is confusing. It lacks the great art qualities of the old tale, the central unity and harmony of character and plot. The *idea* must be the soul of the narrative, and the problem is to make happen to the characters things that are expressive of the idea. The story must hold by its interest, and must be sincere and inevitable to be convincing. It must understand that the method of expression must be the method of suggestion and not that of detail. The old tale set no boundaries to its suggestion. It used concrete artistry; but because the symbol expressed less it implied more. The modern tale is more definitely intentional and it often sets boundaries to its suggestion because the symbol expresses so much. Frequently it emphasizes the satiric and critical element, and its humor often is heavy and clumsy. To be literature, as has been pointed out, besides characters, plot, setting, and dialogue, a classic must present truth; it must have emotion and imagination molded with beauty into the form of language; and it must have the power of a classic to bestow upon the mind a permanent enrichment. Any examination of the modern fairy tale very frequently shows a failure to meet these requirements.

The modern tale is not so poor, however, when we mention such tales as Lewis Carroll's *Alice in Wonderland,* Oscar Wilde's *Happy Prince,* Alice Brown's *Gradual Fairy,* Frances Browne's *Prince Fairyfoot,* Miss Mulock's *Little Lame Prince,* Barrie's *Peter Pan,*

Jean Ingelow's *Mopsa, the Fairy* and *The Ouphe in the Wood*, Field's *The Story of Claus*, Stockton's *Old Pipes and the Dryad*, Kingsley's *Water Babies*, Ruskin's *King of the Golden River*, Collodi's *Pinocchio*, Maeterlinck's *Blue-Bird*, Kipling's *Just-So Stories* and the tales of the *Jungle Books*, Selma Lagerlöf's *Wonderful Adventures of Nils*, the *Uncle Remus Tales* of Harris, etc. But these classics are, with a few exceptions, the richness of the primary and elementary literature. The modern fairy tale suited to the kindergarten child, is at a disadvantage, for most likely it is hidden away in some magazine, waiting for appreciation to bring some attention to it. And in these complex modern days it is difficult to secure a tale whose simplicity suits the little child.

Among the best tales for little people are Miss Harrison's *Hans and the Four Giants* and *Little Beta and the Lame Giant.* In *Little Beta and the Lame Giant* a natural child is placed in unusual surroundings, where the gentleness of the giant and the strength of love in the little girl present strong contrasts that please and satisfy. *The Sea Fairy and the Land Fairy* in *Some Fairies I have Met*, by Mrs. Stawell, though possessing much charm and beauty, is too complicated for the little people. It is a quarrel of a Sea Fairy and a Land Fairy. It is marked by good structure, it presents a problem in the introduction, has light fancy suited to its characters, piquant dialogue, good description, visualized expressions, and it presents distinct pictures. Its method is direct and it gets immediately into the story. Its method of personification, which in this, perhaps the best story of the collection, is rather delightful, in some of the others is less happy and is open to question. *How Double Darling's Old Shoes Became Lady Slippers*, by Candace Wheeler, in *St. Nicholas*, is a really delightful modern fairy story suited to be read to the little child. It is the experience of a little girl with new shoes and her dream about her old shoes. But the story lacks in structure, there is not the steady rise to one great action, the episode of the Santa Claus tree is somewhat foreign and unnecessary, and the conclusion falls flat because the end seems to continue after the problem has been worked out.

In *The Dwarf's Tailor*, by Underhill, there is much conversation about things and an indirect use of language, such as "arouse them to reply" and "continued to question," which is tedious. The humor is at times heavy, quoting proverbs, such as "The pitcher that goes too often to the well is broken at last." The climax is without interest. The scene of the Dwarfs around the fire — in which the chief element of humor seems to be that the Tailor gives the Dwarf a slap — is rather foolish than funny. The details are trite and the transformation misses being pleasing. Again there is not much plot and the story does not hold by its interest. In *The Golden Egg and the Cock of Gold*, by Scudder, the conversation is not always to the point, is somewhat on the gossipy order, is trite, and the suspense is not held because the climax is told beforehand. Mrs. Burton Harrison's *Old Fashioned Fairy Book* is very pleasing, but it was written for her two sons, who were older children. It has the fault of presenting too great a variety of images and it lacks simplicity of structure. Its *Juliet*, or *The Little White Mouse*, which seems to be a re-telling of D'Aulnoy's *Good Little Mouse*, contains a good description of the old-time fairy dress. *Deep Sea Violets*, perhaps the best-written story in the book, gives a good picture of a maiden taken to a Merman's realm. *Rosy's Stay-at-Home Parties* has delightful imagination similar to that of Andersen.

Five Little Pigs, by Katherine Pyle, is a delightful little modern story, which could be used with interest by the child who knows *The Story of Three Little Pigs*. *The Little Rooster*, by Southey, is a very pleasing realistic tale of utmost simplicity which, because of its talking animals, might be included here. A criticism of this tale, together with a list of realistic stories containing some realistic fairy tales suited to the kindergarten, may be read in *Educational Foundations*, October, 1914. *The Hen That Hatched Ducks*, by Harriet Beecher Stowe, is a pleasing and sprightly humorous tale of Madam Feathertop and her surprising family of eight ducks, and of Master Gray Cock, Dame Scratchard and Dr. Peppercorn. A modern tale that is very acceptable to the children is *The Cock, the Mouse, and the Little Red Hen*, by Félicité Lefèvre, which is a re-telling of the *Story of the Little Red Hen* combined with the story of *The Little Rid Hin.* In this tale the two old classic stories are preserved but re-experienced, with such details improvised as a clever child would himself naturally make. These additional details appeal to his imagination and give life-likeness and freshness to the tale, but they do not detract from the impression of the original or confuse the identity of the characters in the old tales.

One must not forget *Peter Rabbit* — that captivating, realistic fairy tale by Beatrix Potter — and his companions, *Benjamin Bunny, Pigling Bland, Tom Kitten,* and the rest, of which children never tire. *Peter Rabbit* undoubtedly holds a place as a kindergarten classic. In somewhat the same class of merry animal tales is *Tommy and the Wishing Stone,* a series of tales by Thornton Burgess, in *St. Nicholas,* 1915. Here the child enjoys the novel transformation of becoming a Musk-rat, a Ruffed Grouse, a Toad, Honker the Goose, and other interesting personages. A modern fairy tale which is received gladly by children is *Ludwig and Marleen,* by Jane Hoxie. Here we have the friendly Fox who grants to Ludwig the wishes he asks for Marleen. The theme parallels for the little people the charm of *The Fisherman and His Wife,* a Grimm tale suited to the second grade. Among modern animal tales *The Elephant's Child,*[1] one of the *Just-So Stories* by Rudyard Kipling, ranks high as a fairy tale produced for little children by one of the great literary masters of the short-story.

[1] See *Appendix.*

A modern tale that is a bit of pure imagination and seems an attempt to follow Grimm and Andersen, is *A Quick-Running Squash,* in Aspinwall's *Short Stories for Short People.* It uses the little boy's interest in a garden — his garden. — Interest centers about the fairy, the magic seed, the wonderful ride, and the happy ending. It uses the simple, everyday life and puts into it the unusual and the wonderful where nothing is impossible. It blends the realistic and the romantic in a way that is most pleasing. *The Rich Goose,* by Leora Robinson, in the *Outlook,* is an accumulative tale with an interesting ending and surprise. *Why the Morning Glory Climbs,* by Elizabeth McCracken, in Miss Bryant's *How to Tell Stories,* is a simple fanciful tale. *The Discontented Pendulum,* by Jane Taylor, in Poulssen's *In the Child's World,* is a good illustration of the modern purely fanciful tale. *What Bunch and Joker saw in the Moon,* in *Wide-Awake Chatterbox,* about 1887, is a most delightful modern fanciful tale, although it is best suited to the child of nine or ten. *Greencap,* by Ruth Hays, in *St. Nicholas,* June, 1915, appeals to the child through the experience of Sarah Jane, whose Mother and Father traveled to India. Sarah went to live with Aunt Jane and there met Greencap who granted the proverbial "three wishes." *Alice in Wonderland* ranks in a class by itself among modern fanciful tales but it is better suited to the child of the third and fourth grades.

A modern fairy tale which is suited to the child's

simplicity and which will stimulate his own desire to make a tale, is *The Doll Who Was Sister to a Princess,* one of the *Toy Stories* by Carolyn Bailey which have been published by the *Kindergarten Review* during 1914–15. Among modern tales selected from *Fairy Stories Re-told from St. Nicholas,* appear some interesting ones which might be read to the little child, or told in the primary grades. Among these might be mentioned: —

The Ballad of the Blacksmith's Sons, a modern tale in verse by Mary E. Wilkins.

Casperl, by H. C. Bunner, a modern Sleeping Beauty tale. This tale has the virtue of not being complex and elaborate. It has the underlying idea that "People who are helping others have a strength beyond their own."

Ten Little Dwarfs, by Sophie Dorsey, from the French of Emile Souvestre. It tells of the ten little Dwarfs who lived in the Good-wife's fingers.

Wondering Tom, by Mary Mapes Dodge. This is a bright story of a boy who Hamlet-like, hesitated to act. Tom was always wondering. The story contains a fairy, Kumtoo-thepoynt, who sat on a toadstool and looked profound. It is realistic and romantic and has fine touches of humor. It tells how Wondering Tom became transformed into a Royal Ship-Builder.

How An Elf Set Up Housekeeping, by Anne Cleve. This is a good tale of fancy. An Elf set up housekeeping in a lily and obtained a curtain from a spider, down from a thistle, a stool from a toad who lived in a green house in the wood, etc.

The Wish-Ring, translated from the German by Anne Eichberg. This is a tale with the implied message that "The best way to secure one's best wish is to work for it."

The Hop-About Man, by Agnes Herbertson, in

Little Folks Magazine, is a very pleasing modern romantic fairy tale for little children. Wee Wun was a gnome who lived in the Bye-Bye meadow in a fine new house which he loved. As he flew across the Meadow he had his pockets full of blue blow-away seeds. In the Meadow he found a pair of shoes, of blue and silver, and of course he took them home to his new house. But first he scattered the blue blow-away seeds over the garden wall in the Stir-About-Wife's garden where golden dandelions grew. And the seeds grew and crowded out the dandelions. Next day Wee Wun found a large blue seed which he planted outside his house; and on the following morning a great blue blow-away which had grown in a night, made his house dark. So he went to the Green Ogre to get him to take it away. When he came home he found, sitting in his chair, the Hop-About-Man, who had come to live with him. He had been forewarned of this coming by the little blue shoes when they hopped round the room singing: —

> Ring-a-ding-dill, ring-a-ding-dill,
> The Hop-About-Man comes over the hill.
> Why is he coming, and what will he see?
> Rickety, rackety, — one, two, three.

The story then describes Wee Wun's troubles with the Hop-About-Man, who remained an unwelcome inhabitant of the house where Wee Wun liked to sit all alone. The Hop-About-Man made everything keep hopping about until Wee Wun would put all careless things straight, and until he would give back to him his blue-and-silver shoes. One day, Wee Wun became a careful housekeeper and weeded out of the dandelion garden all the blue blow-away plants that grew from the seeds he had scattered there in the Stir-About-Wife's garden, and when he came home his troubles were over, and the Hop-About-Man was gone.

Perhaps one reason for the frequent failure of the modern fairy tale is that it fails to keep in harmony with the times. Just as the modern novel has progressed from the romanticism of Hawthorne, the realism of Thackeray, through the psychology of George Eliot, and the philosophy of George Meredith, so the little child's story—which like the adult story is an expression of the spirit of the times—must recognize these modern tendencies. It must learn, from *Alice in Wonderland* and from *A Child's Garden of Verses*, that the modern fairy tale is not a *Cinderella* or *Sleeping Beauty*, but the modern fairy tale is the child's mind. The real fairy world is the strangeness and beauty of the child mind's point of view. It is the duty and privilege of the modern fairy tale to interpret the child's psychology and to present the child's philosophy of life.

REFERENCES

Century Co.: *St. Nicholas Magazine*, 1915; *St. Nicholas Fairy Stories Re-told.*

Gates, Josephine: "And Piped Those Children Back Again," (Pied Piper) *St. Nicholas*, Nov., 1914.

Hays, Ruth: "Greencap," *St. Nicholas*, June, 1915.

Hazlitt, William; *Essays.* ("Wit and Humor.") Camelot Series. Scott.

Hooker, B.: "Narrative and the Fairy Tale," *Bookman*, 33: June and July, 1911, pp. 389–93, pp. 501–05.

Ibid: "Types of Fairy Tales," *Forum*, 40: Oct., 1908, pp. 375–84.

Martin, John: *John Martin's Book* (Magazine), 1915

Meredith, George: *The Comic Spirit.* Scribners.

Moulton, Alice O'Grady, and Literature Committee: "Humorous Tales" *Kindergarten Review*, Dec., 1914.

Perry, Bliss: *A Study of Prose Fiction.* ("The Romantic" and "The Realistic.") Houghton.

CHAPTER VI

SOURCES OF MATERIAL FOR FAIRY TALES: A LIST OF FAIRY TALES, PICTURES, PICTURE-BOOKS, POEMS, AND BOOKS

Shall we permit our children, without scruple, to hear any fables composed by any authors indifferently, and so to receive into their minds opinions generally the reverse of those which, when they are grown to manhood, we shall think they ought to entertain?—Plato, in *The Republic.*

Any list of fairy tales for little children must be selected from those books which, as we have noted, contain the best collections of folk-lore, and from books which contain tales that rank as classics. An examination of the tales of Perrault, of Grimm, of Dasent, of Andersen, of Jacobs, of Harris, and of miscellaneous tales, to see what are suited to the little child, would result in the following lists of tales. Those most worthy of study for the kindergarten are marked with an asterisk and those suited to the first grade are marked "1." No attempt has been made to mention all the varied sources of a tale or its best version. The Boston Public Library issues a *Finding List of Fairy Tales and Folk Stories,* which may be procured easily, and the Carnegie Library at Pittsburg issues in its monthly bulletin for December, 1913, vol. 18, no. 10, a *List of Folk-Tales,* and other stories which may be dramatized. The Baker, Taylor Company, in 1914, issued a *Graded Guide to Supplementary Reading*, which contains a list of many of the best editions of folk and fairy tales suited to primary grades. A list of school editions is included in this book. But one cannot fail to be impressed with the general low literary standard of many school editions of fairy tales when judged by the standards here applied to the tales themselves.

I. A LIST OF FAIRY TALES AND FOLK TALES

Tales of Perrault:

* Cinderella.
1 Little Thumb.
1 Puss-in-Boots.
* Red Riding Hood.
1 Sleeping Beauty.
1 The Three Wishes.

Tales of the Grimms:

1 Birdie and Lena.
1 Briar Rose.
* The Cat and the Mouse in Partnership.
1 Chanticleer and Partlet.
    1. How they Went to the Hills to Eat Nuts.
    2. The Visit to Mr. Korbes.
    3. The Death of Partlet.
* Cinderella.
* The Elves and the Shoemaker.
The Fox and the Geese.
1 The Hare and the Hedgehog.
1 The House in the Wood.
* The King of the Birds.
1 Little Brother and Sister.
1 The Little Lamb and the Little Fish.
* Little Red-Cap.
1 Little Snow White.

1 Little Two-Eyes.
Mother Holle.
1 The Nose.
1 Snow White and Rose Red.
* The Sparrow and His Four Children.
Star Dollars.
* The Spider and the Flea.
* The Straw, the Coal, and the Bean.
* The Town Musicians of Bremen.
The Willow Wren and the Bear.
* The Wolf and the Seven Kids.
* The Wonderful Porridge Pot.

Norse Tales:

Cock and Hen.
The Cock and Hen A-Nutting.
The Cock and Hen That Went to the Dovrefell.
Cock, Cuckoo, and Black Cock.
* Doll i' the Grass.
1 Gertrude's Bird.
1 Katie Woodencloak (read).
1 The Lad Who Went to the North Wind.
1 Lord Peter (read).
One's Own Children Are Always Prettiest.
* Three Billy Goats.
1 Thumbikin (read).
* Why the Bear is Stumpy-tailed (pourquois).

English Tales, by Jacobs:

* The Cat and the Mouse.
* Henny Penny.
1 The History of Tom Thumb.
* How Jack Went to Seek His Fortune.
1 Jack and the Bean-Stalk.
* Johnny Cake.
* Lazy Jack.
* The Magpie's Nest.
1 Master of all Masters.
* Mr. Miacca.

1 Mr. Vinegar.
* The Old Woman and Her Pig.
* Puddock, Mousie, and Ratton.
1 Scrapefoot. More English Fairy Tales.
* The Story of Three Bears.
* The Story of Three Little Pigs.
* Teeny Tiny.
* Titty Mouse and Tatty Mouse.

Modern Fairy Tales, by Andersen:

* The Fir Tree.
* Five Peas in a Pod.
1 The Happy Family (retold in *Tales of Laughter*).
Little Ida's Flowers (read).
* Ole-Luk-Oie (read to end of Thursday).
  Thursday, Wedding of a Mouse.
* The Princess and the Pea.
* The Snow Man.
1 The Steadfast Tin Soldier.
The Top and the Ball.
* Thumbelina.
What the Moon Saw:
  * Little Girl and Chickens.
  * The New Frock (realistic).
  * Little Chimney Sweep.
  * Bear Who Played "Soldiers."
  * Bread and Butter.

Uncle Remus Tales, by Harris, in *Nights with Uncle Remus:*

* Brer Rabbit and the Little Tar Baby.
* Brother Rabbit and the Little Girl.
* Brother Rabbit Takes a Walk.
* Brother Rabbit Takes Some Exercise.
* Cutta cord-la (similar to Wolf and Seven Kids).
* How Brother Rabbit Broke Up a Party.
* How Brother Rabbit Frightens His Neighbors.
* How Mr. Rooster Lost His Dinner (read).
* In Some Lady's Garden.
* Mr. Benjamin Ram (Brother Rabbit's Riddle).

* The Moon in the Mill-Pond (pourquois).
* Why Brother Bear Has No Tail (pourquois).
* Why Mr. Dog Runs After Brother Rabbit.
* Why Guinea Fowls Are Speckled (pourquois).

Uncle Remus Tales, by Harris, in *Uncle Remus and the Little Boy:*

* Brother Billy Goat's Dinner.
  Brother Fox Smells Smoke.
* Brother Rabbit and Brother Tiger.
* Brother Rabbit and Brother Lion (similar to *The Dog and His Shadow*).
* Brother Mud-Turtle's Trickery.
* Brother Rabbit's Money Mint.
1 Brother Wolf Says Grace.
1 The Fire Test (Use with *Three Pigs*).
  Fun at the Ferry.
* Heyo, House.
  The Little Rabbits.
  Mrs. Partridge Has a Fit.
  Why Brother Fox's Legs are Black.
* Why the Hawk Catches Chickens.

Tale, by Harris, in *Little Mr. Thimblefinger:*

* Why Billy-Goat's Tail Is Short.

Miscellaneous Tales:

* The Adventures of Little Field Mouse, *Stories to Tell*, Bryant.
* Beta and the Lame Giant, Miss Harrison, *In Storyland.*
* Billy Bobtail, Jane Hoxie, *Kindergarten Stories; Child-Lore Dramatic Reader*, Scribners.
* Blunder and the Wishing Gate, Louise Chollet, in *Child Life in Prose*, Whittier.
* The Boy and the Goat, or The Goat in the Turnip Field (Norwegian), *Primer*, Free and Treadwell; *Child-Lore Dramatic Reader*, Scribners.
* The Cap that Mother Made or Ander's New Cap (Swedish), *Swedish Fairy Tales*, McClurg; *For the Story-Teller*, Bailey.

1 THE CAT AND THE PARROT OR THE GREEDY CAT, *How to Tell Stories*, Bryant; *Tales of Laughter*, Wiggin and Smith.

1 THE CAT THAT WAITED, *Classics in Dramatic Form*, vol. I, Stevenson.

* THE CAT, THE COCK, AND THE FOX, *Tales of Laughter*, Wiggin and Smith.

1 CLYTIE, *Nature Myths*, Flora Cooke.

1 THE COCK, THE MOUSE, AND THE LITTLE RED HEN, Félicité Lefèvre, Jacobs.

* THE COUNTRY MOUSE AND THE CITY MOUSE, *Æsop's Fables*, Joseph Jacobs.

* DAME WIGGINS AND HER CATS, Mrs. Sharp, in *Six Nursery Classics*, Heath.

* THE DISCONTENTED PENDULUM, Jane Taylor, in *In the Child's World*, Poulsson.

* THE DOLL WHO WAS SISTER TO A PRINCESS, THE TOY STORIES, Carolyn Bailey, *Kindergarten Review*, Dec., 1914.

* DRAKESBILL, *The Story-Teller's Book*, O'Grady and Throop; *The Fairy Ring*, Wiggin and Smith; *Fire-light Stories*, Bailey.

* THE ELEPHANT'S CHILD, *Just-So Stories*, Kipling.

1 THE FIRST CHRISTMAS TREE, *A Little Book of Profitable Tales*, Eugene Field.

1 THE FIVE LITTLE PIGS, Katherine Pyle, in *Wide Awake Second Reader*, Little.

* THE FOOLISH TIMID RABBIT, *Jataka Tales Retold*, Babbit.

THE GOLDEN COCK, *That's Why Stories*, Bryce.

1 GOLDEN ROD AND ASTER, *Nature Myths*, Cooke.

THE GRAIN OF CORN (*Old Woman and Her Pig*), *Tales of the Punjab*, Steel.

1 GREENCAP, Ruth Hays, in *St. Nicholas*, June, 1915.

1 HANS AND THE FOUR BIG GIANTS, Miss Harrison, *In Storyland*.

1 THE HEN THAT HATCHED DUCKS, Harriet Beecher Stowe, in *Child Life in Prose*, Whittier.

* THE HOP-ABOUT-MAN, Agnes Herbertson, in *The Story-*

Teller's Book, O'Grady and Throop; in *Little Folks' Magazine.*

* THE HOUSE THAT JACK BUILT, *Six Nursery Classics*, D. C. Heath.

1 HOW BROTHER RABBIT FOOLED THE WHALE, *Stories to Tell*, Bryant.

* HOW THE CAMEL GOT HIS HUMP, *Just-So Stories*, Kipling.

1 HOW THE CHIPMUNK GOT THE STRIPES ON ITS BACK, *Nature Myths*, Cooke.

* HOW DOUBLE DARLING'S OLD SHOES BECAME LADY SLIPPERS, Candace Wheeler, in *St. Nicholas*, March, 1887; vol. 14, pp. 342–47.

* HOW FIRE WAS BROUGHT TO THE INDIANS, *The Book of Nature Myths*, Holbrook.

* HOW SUN, MOON, AND WEST WIND WENT OUT TO DINNER, *Old Deccan Days*, Frère.

1 THE JACKAL AND THE ALLIGATOR, *Stories to Tell*, Bryant.

1 THE JACKALS AND THE LION, *Stories to Tell*, Bryant.

1 KING SOLOMON AND THE ANTS, *Nature Myths*, Cooke.

* THE LAMBIKIN, *Tales of the Punjab*, Steel; *Indian Tales*, Jacobs.

* LITTLE JACK ROLLAROUND, *Stories to Tell*, Bryant.

* THE LITTLE RABBIT WHO WANTED RED WINGS, *For the Story-Teller*, Bailey.

* THE LITTLE RED HEN, *Stories to Tell*, Bryant.

* THE LITTLE RID HIN (Irish dialect verse), *Stories to Tell*, Bryant.

* THE LITTLE ROOSTER, Robert Southey, in *Boston Collection of Kindergarten Stories*, Hammett & Co.

* LITTLE SPIDER'S FIRST WEB, *Primer*, Free and Treadwell.

* LITTLE TOP-KNOT (Swedish), *First Reader*, Free and Treadwell.

* LITTLE TUPPEN, *Fairy Stories and Fables*, Baldwin; *Primer*, Free and Treadwell.

* LUDWIG AND MARLEEN, Jane Hoxie, in *Kindergarten Review*, vol. XI, no. 5.

* Medio Pollito, or Little Half-Chick (Spanish), *The Green Fairy Book*, Lang.
* Mezumi, the Beautiful, or The Rat Princess (Japanese), *Birch-Tree Fairy Book*, Johnson; *Tales of Laughter*, Wiggin and Smith.

1 Mr. Elephant and Mr. Frog, *Firelight Stories*, Bailey.
1 The Moon's Silver Cloak, *Classics in Dramatic Form*, Stevenson, vol. i.
1 The Mouse and the Sausage, *Stories and Story-Telling*, Angela Keyes.

* Oeyvind and Marit, from *The Happy Boy*, Björnstjerne Björnson, in *The Story-Teller's Book*, O'Grady and Throop; in *Child-Life in Prose*, Whittier.
* Peter Rabbit, *Peter Rabbit*, Beatrix Potter.

1 The Pigs and the Giant, Pyle, in *Child-Lore Dramatic Reader*, Scribners.

* The Quick-Running Squash, *Short Stories for Short People*, Aspinwall.

1 The Red-Headed Woodpecker, *Nature Myths*, Cooke.

* The Rich Goose, Leora Robinson, in *The Outlook*.
* The Robin's Christmas Song, *Birch-Tree Fairy Book*, Johnson.
* (Wee) Robin's Yule Song. *Tales of Laughter*, Wiggin and Smith.
* The Sheep and the Pig (Scandinavian), *For the Children's Hour*, Bailey.
* The Sparrow and the Crow, *Tales of the Punjab*, Steel; *Birch-Tree Fairy Book*, Johnson.
* The Straw Ox, *Cossack Fairy Tales*, Bain.
* Story of the Morning-Glory Seed, M. Eytinge, *Boston Kindergarten Stories*.

1 The Tale of a Black Cat, *Oak-Tree Fairy Book*, Johnson.
1 Tommy and the Wishing-Stone, a series, by T. Burgess, in *St. Nicholas*, 1915.
1 Travels of a Fox, *Oak-Tree Fairy Book*, Johnson.
1 The Turtle Who Could n't Stop Talking, *Jataka Tales Retold*, Babbit.

* The Unhappy Pine Tree, *Classic Stories*, McMurry.

1 WHAT BUNCH AND JOKER SAW IN THE MOON, *Wide Awake Chatterbox*, about 1887.

1 THE WHITE CAT, *Fairy Tales*, D'Aulnoy; *Fairy Tales*, vol. II, Lansing.

* WHY THE EVERGREEN TREES NEVER LOSE THEIR LEAVES, *The Book of Nature Myths*, Holbrook.

* WHY THE JUNIPER HAS BERRIES, *The Book of Nature Myths*, Holbrook.

* WHY THE MORNING GLORY CLIMBS, *How to Tell Stories*, Bryant.

1 THE WISH BIRD, *Classics in Dramatic Form*, vol. II, Stevenson.

II. BIBLIOGRAPHY OF FAIRY TALES

Baker, Franklin T.: *Bibliography of Children's Reading.* Introduction and lists. Teachers College, Columbia University.

Baker Taylor Company, The: *Graded Guide to Supplementary Reading.* 1914.

Boston Public Library: *Finding List of Fairy Tales.*

Carnegie Library, Pittsburgh. *List of Folk Tales.* Bulletin, Dec., 1913, vol. 18, no. 10.

Ibid.: *Illustrated Editions of Children's Books.* 1915.

Harron, Julia; Bacon, Corinne; and Dana, John: *American Library Economy.* Newark Free Library, Newark, New Jersey.

Haight, Rachel Webb: "Fairy Tales." *Bulletin of Bibliography*, 1912. Boston Book Co.

Hewins, Caroline: *A. L. A. List. Books for Boys and Girls.* Third Edition, 1913. A. L. A. Pub. Board, Chicago.

Kready, Laura F.: "Picture-Books for Little Children." *Kindergarten Review*, Sept., 1914.

Moulton, Alice O'Grady, and Literature Com. of I. K. U.: "Humorous Stories for Children." *Kindergarten Review*, Dec., 1914.

Salisbury, G. E., and Beckwith, M. E.: *Index to Short Stories.*

St. Louis Public Library. *Lists of Stories and Programs for Story Hours.* Give best versions.

Widdemer, Margaret: "A Bibliography of Books and Articles Relating to Children's Reading. Part I, Children's Reading in general. Part II, History of Children's Literature, etc. Part III, Guidance of Children's Reading." *Bulletin of Bibliography*, July, 1911, Oct., 1911, and Jan., 1912. Boston Book Co.

III. A LIST OF PICTURE-BOOKS [1]

Beskow, Elsa: *Hanschen im Blaubeerenwald.* Stuttgart.

Brooke, Leslie: *The Golden Goose Book.* F. Warne.

Ibid.: The *House in the Wood.* F. Warne.

Ibid.: *The Truth About Old King Cole.* F. Warne.

Browning, Robert: *The Pied Piper*, Kate Greenaway, F. Warne; Hope Dunlap, Rand; T. Butler Stoney, Dutton.

Caldecott, Randolph: *Picture-Books:*

2. *The House that Jack Built.* F. Warne.
3. *Hey Diddle Diddle Book.* F. Warne.

Coussens, P. W.: *A Child's Book of Stories.* Jessie W. Smith. Duffield.

Crane, Walter: *Picture-Books:*

Cinderella. John Lane.

Mother Hubbard. John Lane.

Red Riding Hood. John Lane.

This Little Pig. John Lane.

Grimm, Jacob and William: *Cruikshank Fairy Book.* Cruikshank, Putnam.

Ibid.: *Das Deutsche Bilderbuch.* Jos. Scholz.

1. *Dörnroschen.*
2. *Aschenputtel.*
7. *Frau Holle.*
10. *Der Wolf und Sieben Geislein.*

Ibid.: *Liebe Märchen.* 10, 11, 12. Jos. Scholz.

Ibid.: *Cherry Blossom.* Helen Stratton. Blackie and Sons.

Jerrold, Walter: *The Big Book of Fairy Tales.* Robinson. Blackie.

---

[1] Laura F. Kready, "Picture-Books for Little Children," *Kindergarten Review*, Sept., 1914.

Olfers, Sibylle: *Windschen.* J. F. Schreiber.
Ibid.: *Wurzelkindern.* J. F. Schreiber.
Sharp, Mrs.: *Dame Wiggins of Lee.* Introduction by Ruskin. Kate Greenaway. George Allen.

IV. A LIST OF PICTURES

Cinderella. 227, Meinhold. Dresden.
724, Meinhold. Dresden.
366, Teubner. Leipzig.
Canadian Magazine, Dec., 1911, by Val Prinsep, R.A.
Elves. Arthur Rackham. *St. Nicholas,* Nov., 1914.
Ibid.: *Book of Pictures.* Century.
Hop-o'-my-Thumb. *A Child's Own Book of Fairy Tales.* Dore. H. Pisan, engraver.
Elizabeth S. Forbes. *Canadian Magazine,* Dec., 1911.
Little Brother and Sister. Tempera Painting, Marianna Stokes. *Illustrated London News,* Dec., 1907.
Perrault's Tales. Kay Nielsen. *Illustrated London News,* Dec., 1913.
Red Riding Hood. Poster, Mary Stokes. *Ladies' Home Journal.*
230, Meinhold. Dresden.
77, Teubner. Leipzig and Berlin.
G. Ferrier. Engraved for *St. Nicholas,* Braun, Clement, & Co.
Supplement to *American Primary Teacher,* May, 1908.
Picture, 2 ft. by 1 ft., New Specialty Shop, Phila., Pa.
Sleeping Beauty. Mouat, London. *Canadian Magazine,* Dec., 1911. *Illustrated London News,* Dec., 1907.
Snow White. A series. Maxfield Parrish.
Picture by Elizabeth Shippen Green.
Two Series. Five pictures in each. Jessie Willcox Smith. P. F. Collier & Sons.

V. A LIST OF FAIRY POEMS

Allingham, William: *The Fairy Folk.* The Posy Ring.
Bangs, John Kendrick: *The Little Elf.* The Posy Ring.

Bird, Robert: *The Fairy Folk.* A Child's Book of Old Verses.
Dodsley, R.: *Red Caps of Fairies. Fuimus Troes,* Old Plays.
Drayton, Michael: *Nymphal III,* Poets' Elysium.
Herford, Oliver: *The Elf and the Dormouse.* The Posy Ring.
Hood, Thomas: *A Plain Direction.* Heart of Oak Books, III.
Ibid.: *Queen Mab.* A Child's Book of Old Verses.
Howitt, Mary: *The Fairies of the Caldon-Low.* The Posy Ring.
Ibid.: *Mabel on Midsummer Day.* The Story-Teller's Book, O'Grady and Throop.
Lyly, John: *The Urchin's Dance and Song. Song of the First Fairy. Song of the Second Fairy.* Maydes Metamorphosis.
McDermot, Jessie: *A Fairy Tale.* Fairy Tales. Rolfe. Amer. Book Co.
Noyes, Alfred: *The Magic Casement.* An anthology of fairy poetry, with an introduction. Dutton.
Percy, Bishop: *The Fairy Queen.* Reliques of Ancient Poetry; from The Mysteries of Love and Eloquence, London, 1658.
Shakespeare, William: *Ariel's Song; A Fairy Song; "I know a bank"; The Song of the Fairies.* Shakespeare's Dramas.
Stevenson, Robert L. *Fairy Bread; The Little Land.* A Child's Garden of Verses.
Unknown Author: *The Fairy. "Oh, who is so merry."* A Child's Book of Old Verses. Duffield.
Wilkins, Mary E.: *The Ballad of the Blacksmith's Sons.* Fairy Stories Retold from *St. Nicholas.* Century.

VI. MAIN STANDARD FAIRY TALE BOOKS

Andersen, Hans Christian: *Fairy Tales.* 2 vols. Pedersen & Stone. Houghton.
Ibid.: *Fairy Tales.* Edited by W. A. and J. K. Craigie. Oxford University Press.
Ibid.: *Fairy Stories for Youngest Children.* Lucas. Stratton. Blackie. (English edition.)
Ibid.: *Fairy Tales.* Mrs. Lucas. T. C. and W. Robinson. Dutton.
Ibid.: *Fairy Tales.* Mrs. Lucas. Helen Stratton. Dodge.
Ibid.: *Fairy Tales.* Maria L. Kirk. Lippincott.

Andersen, Hans Christian: *Fairy Tales.* Edmund Dulac. Hodder & Stoughton.
Ibid.: *Fairy Tales.* W. H. Robinson. Holt.
Ibid.: *Fairy Tales.* Braekstad. Tegner. Introd. by Gosse. Century.
Asbjörnsen, P. C.: *Fairy Tales from the Far North.* Burt.
Ibid.: *Round the Yule Log.* Introd. by Gosse. Braekstad. Lippincott.
Dasent, Sir George W.: *Popular Tales from the North.* Routledge. Dutton.
Ibid.: *Popular Tales from the North.* Putnam.
Ibid.: *Tales from the Field.* Putnam.
Grimm, Jacob and William: *Household Tales.* Margaret Hunt. Bohn's Libraries, Bell & Co.
Ibid.: *Household Tales.* Lucy Crane. Walter Crane. Macmillan.
Ibid.: *Fairy Tales.* Helen Stratton. Dodge.
Ibid.: *German Popular Stories.* Tr. Edgar Taylor. Introd. by Ruskin. 22 illustrations by Cruikshank. Chatto & Windus.
Ibid.: *Fairy Tales.* Johann & Leinweber. McLoughlin.
Ibid.: *Fairy Tales.* Arthur Rackham. Doubleday.
Ibid.: *Fairy Tales.* Hope Dunlap. Rand.
Harris, Joel Chandler: *Uncle Remus, His Songs and Sayings.* Appleton.
Ibid.: *Nights With Uncle Remus.* Church. Houghton.
Ibid.: *Uncle Remus and His Friends.* Frost. Houghton.
Ibid.: *Uncle Remus and the Little Boy.* J. M. Comte. Small.
Jacobs, Joseph: *English Fairy Tales.* 2 vols. Batten. Putnam.
Ibid.: *Celtic Fairy Tales.* 2 vols. Batten. Putnam.
Ibid.: *Indian Fairy Tales.* Batten. Putnam.
Ibid.: *The Most Delectable History of Reynard the Fox.* Frank Calderon. Macmillan.
Ibid.: *Europa's Fairy Tales.* Batten. Putnam.
O'Shea, M. V.: *Old World Wonder Stories.* Heath.
Perrault, Charles: *Tales of Mother Goose.* Welsh. Heath.
Ibid.: *Fairy Tales.* Appleton. Estes.

Perrault, Charles: *Tales of Passed Times*. Temple Classics. C. Robinson. Dutton.

Ibid.: *Popular Tales*. Edited by Andrew Lang. French; and English translation of original edition. Oxford, Clarendon Press.

VII. FAIRY TALES OF ALL NATIONS

Celtic. Jacobs. 1911. Putnam.
Chinese. Pitnam. 1910. Crowell.
Cossack. Bain. 1899. Burt.
Danish. Bay. 1899. Harper.
Donegal. McManus. 1900. Doubleday.
English. Jacobs. 1904. Putnam.
Ibid.: Folk and Fairy Stories. Hartland, born 1848. Camelot series.
French. DeSegur. 1799–1874. Winston.
German. Grimm. 1812, 1822. Bohn's Libraries.
Hungarian. Pogany. 1914. Stokes.
Indian. *Old Deccan Days*. Frère. 1868. McDonough.
Ibid.: *Tales of the Sun*. Mrs. Kingscote. 1890. W. H. Allen.
Ibid.: *Buddhist Birth Stories*. Rhys Davids. 1880. Trubner.
Ibid.: *Fairy Tales*. Stokes. 1880. Ellis & White.
Ibid.: *Folk Tales of Bengal*. Day. 1883. Macmillan.
Ibid.: *Wide Awake Stories*. Steel and Temple. 1884. Trubner.
Ibid.: *Folk-Tales of Kashmir*. Knowles. 1887. Trubner.
Ibid.: *Tales of the Punjab*. Steel. 1894. Macmillan.
Irish. Yeats. 1902. Burt.
Italian. Macdonell. 1911. Stokes.
Ibid.: Crane. 1885. Macmillan.
Japanese. Ozaki. 1909. Dutton.
Manx. Morrison. 1899. Nutt.
New World. Kennedy. 1904. Dutton.
Norse. Dasent. 1820–1896. Lippincott.
Ibid.: Mabie. 1846–. Dodd.
Papuan. Kerr. 1910. Macmillan.

Persian. Stephen. 1892. Dutton.
Ibid.: Clouston. 1907. Stokes.
Russian. Dole. 1907. Crowell.
Ibid.: Bain. Bilibin. 1914. Century.
Scottish. Grierson. 1910. Stokes.
South African. Honey. 1910. Baker & Taylor.
Welsh. Thomas. 1908. Stokes.

VIII. MISCELLANEOUS EDITIONS OF FAIRY TALES

D'Aulnoy, Madame: *Fairy Tales.* Trans. by Planché. Gordon Browne. McKay.
Ibid.: *Fairy Tales.* Introd. by Anne T. Ritchie. Scribners.
Austin, M. H.: *Basket Woman.* Houghton.
Babbit, Ellen: *Jataka Tales Retold.* Century.
Bailey, Carolyn: *Firelight Stories.* Bradley.
Bailey and Lewis: *For the Children's Hour.* Bradley.
Baldwin, James: *Fairy Stories and Fables.* Amer. Book Co.
Barrie, J. M.: *Peter Pan in Kensington Gardens.* Rackham. Scribners.
Baumbach, Rudolf: *Tales from Wonderland.* Simmons.
Bertelli, Luigi: *The Prince and His Ants.* Holt.
Bryant, Sara C.: *Best Stories to Tell to Children.* Houghton.
Burgess, Thornton: *Old Mother West Wind.* Little.
Ibid.: *The Adventures of Reddy Fox.* Little.
Ibid.: *The Adventures of Johnny Chuck.* Little.
Ibid.: *Tommy and the Wishing-stone.* Animal Tales. *St. Nicholas,* 1915.
Chapin, Anna: *The Now-a-Days Fairy Book.* Jessie W. Smith. Dodd.
Chisholm, Louey: *In Fairyland.* Katherine Cameron. Putnam.
Ibid.: *Little Red Riding Hood*; *Cinderella*; (I Read Them Myself series). Dodge.
Collection: *Half a Hundred Stories for Little People.* Bradley.
Cooke, Flora J.: *Nature Myths and Stories.* Flanagan.

Cowell, E. B.: *The Jatakas or Stories of the Buddha's Former Births*. Tr. from the Pali. 6 vols. Cambridge University Press. Putnam. 1895–1907.

Crothers, Samuel McChord: *Miss Muffet's Christmas Party*. Houghton.

Emerson, Ellen: *Indian Myths*. Houghton.

Everyman Series: *157; 365; and 541*. Dutton.

France, Anatole: *The Honey Bee*. John Lane.

Grover, Eulalie O., editor: *Mother Goose*. F. Richardson. Volland.

Harris, Joel C.: *Little Mr. Thimblefinger*. Houghton.

Harrison, Miss: In Storyland. Central Pub. Co., Chicago.

Holbrook, Florence: *The Book of Nature Myths*. Houghton.

James, Grace: *The Green Willow:* Japanese. Goble. Macmillan.

Jerrold, Walter: *The Reign of King Oberon*. Robinson. Dent. Little.

Johnson, Clifton: *Fairy Books: Oak-Tree; Birch-Tree; and Elm-Tree*. Little.

Ibid.: *Book of Fairy Tale Bears*. Houghton.

Ibid.: *Book of Fairy Tale Foxes*. Houghton.

Kingsley, Charles: *Water-Babies*. Warwick Goble. Macmillan.

Ibid.: *Water-Babies*. Introd. by Rose Kingsley. Margaret Tarrant. Dutton.

Kipling, Rudyard: *Jungle Books*. 2 vols. Original edition. Century.

Ibid.: *Jungle Books*. M. and E. Detmold. Century.

Ibid.: *Jungle Books*. A. Rackham. Doubleday.

Ibid.: *Just-So Stories*. Doubleday.

Ibid.: *Puck of Pook's Hill*. Doubleday.

Ibid.: *Rewards and Fairies*. Doubleday.

Laboulaye, Edouard: *Fairy Book*. Harper.

Ibid.: *Last Fairy Tales*. Harper.

Lang, Andrew: *Fairy Books: Red; Orange; Yellow; Green; Blue; Violet; Gray; Crimson; Brown; Pink*. Longmans.

Lansing, Marion: *Rhymes and Stories*. Ginn.

Ibid.: *Fairy Tales*. 2 vols. Ginn.

Leamy, Edward: Golden Spears. FitzGerald.

Lefèvre, Felicité: *The Cock, the Mouse, and the Little Red Hen.* Tony Sarg. Jacobs, Phila.

Lindsay, Maud: *Mother Stories; More Mother Stories.* Bradley.

Maeterlinck, Madam: *The Children's Bluebird.* Dodd.

Molesworth, Mary Louise: *The Cuckoo Clock.* Maria Kirk. Lippincott.

Mulock, Miss: *The Fairy Book.* Boyd Smith. Crowell.

Ibid.: *Fairy Book.* 32 illus. by W. Goble. Macmillan.

Ibid.: *Little Lame Prince.* Hope Dunlap. Rand.

Musset, Paul de: *Mr. Wind and Madam Rain.* Bennett. Putnam.

Nyblom, Helena: *Jolly Cable and other Swedish Fairy Tales.* Folknin. Dutton.

Olcott, Frances J.: *Arabian Nights.* Tr. by Lane. Cairo text. Selections. Holt.

Perrault, Charles: *The Story of Bluebeard.* Stone & Kimball, Chicago.

Poulsson, E.: *In the Child's World.* Bradley.

Pyle, Howard: *The Garden Behind the Moon.* Scribners.

Ibid.: *Wonder-Clock.* Harper.

Pyle, Katherine: *Fairy Tales from Many Lands.* Dutton.

Rackham, Arthur: *Mother Goose.* Century.

Ramé, Louise de la (Ouida): *Nürnberg Stove: Bimbi Stories for Children.* Page.

Rhys, Ernest: *Fairy Gold.* Herbert Cole. Dutton.

Rolfe, William: *Fairy Tales in Prose and Verse.* Amer. Book Co.

Shakespeare, William: *Midsummer Night's Dream.* With forty illustrations in color by Arthur Rackham. Doubleday.

Shedlock, Marie: *A Collection of Eastern Stories and Legends.* Foreword by T. Rhys Davids. Dutton.

Smith, Jessie Willcox: *Mother Goose.* Dodd.

Stephen, A.: *Fairy Tales of a Parrot.* Ellis. Nister. Dutton.

Stockton, F.: *The Queen's Museum.* F. Richardson. Scribners.

Tappan, Eva March: *The Children's Hour: Folk Stories and Fables.* Houghton.

Thorne-Thomson: *East o' the Sun and West o' the Moon.* Row.

Underhill, Zoe D.: *The Dwarf's Tailor.* Harper.

Valentine, Mrs. Laura: *Old, Old Fairy Tales.* F. Warne.

Welsh, Charles: *Fairy Tales Children Love.* Dodge.

Wheeler, W. A.: *Mother Goose Melodies.* Houghton.

Wiggin, Kate; and Smith, Nora: *The Fairy Ring: Tales of Laughter: Magic Casements:* and *Tales of Wonder.* Doubleday.

IX. SCHOOL EDITIONS OF FAIRY TALES

Alderman, E. A.: *Classics Old and New.* Amer. Book Co.

Alexander, G.: *Child Classics.* Bobbs.

Baker, F. T., and Carpenter, G. R.: *Language Readers.* Macmillan.

Baldwin, James: *The Fairy Reader,* I and II. Amer. Book Co.

Blaisdell, Etta (MacDonald): *Child Life in Tale and Fable.* Macmillan.

Blumenthal, Verra: *Fairy Tales from the Russian.* Rand.

Brooks, Dorothy: *Stories of Red Children.* Educational.

Bryce, Catherine: *Child-Lore Dramatic Reader.* Scribners.

Burchill, Ettinger: *Progressive Road to Reading,* Readers. Silver.

Chadwick, Mara P.: *Three Bears Story Primer.* Educational.

Chadwick, M. P. and Freeman, E. G.: *Chain Stories and Playlets: The Cat That Was Lonesome: The Mouse That Lost Her Tail;* and *The Woman and Her Pig.* World Book Co.

Coe and Christie: *Story Hour Readers.* Amer. Book Co.

Craik, Georgiana: *So Fat and Mew Mew.* Heath.

Davis, M. H. and Leung, Chow: *Chinese Fables and Folk Stories.* Amer. Book. Co.

Dole, C. F.: *Crib and Fly.* Heath.

Free and Treadwell: *Reading Literature Series.* Row, Peterson.

Grover, Eulalie O.: *Folk Lore Primer.* Atkinson.

Hale, E. E.: *Arabian Nights.* Selections. Ginn.

Heath, D, C.: *Dramatic Reader.* Heath.

Henderson, Alice: *Andersen's Best Fairy Tales.* Rand.
Hix, Melvin: *Once Upon a Time Stories.* Longmans.
Holbrook, Florence: *Dramatic Reader for the Lower Grades.* Amer. Book Co.
Howard, F. W.: *The Banbury Cross Stories: The Fairy Gift and Tom Hickathrift.* Merrill.
Johnston, E.; and Barnum, M.: *Book of Plays for Little Actors.* Amer. Book. Co.
Kennerley: *The Kipling Reader.* 2 vols. Appleton.
Ketchum and Rice: *Our First Story Reader.* Scribners.
Lang, Andrew: *Fairy Readers.* Longmans.
Lansing, M.: *Tales of Old England.* Ginn.
Mabie, H.: *Fairy Tales Every Child Should Know.* Doubleday.
McMahon, H., M., and A.: *Rhyme and Story Primer.* Heath.
McMurry, Mrs. Lida B.: *Classic Stories.* Public School Pub. Co.
Norton, Charles E.: *Heart of Oak Books.* Heath.
Norvell, F. T., and Haliburton, M. W.: *Graded Classics.* Johnson.
Perkins, F. O.: *The Bluebird Arranged for Schools.* Silver.
Pratt, Mara L.: *Legends of Red Children.* Amer. Book Co.
Roulet, Mary Nixon: *Japanese Folk-Stories and Fairy Tales.* Amer. Book Co.
Scudder, H.: *Andersen's Fairy Tales: Grimm's Fairy Tales; Fables and Folk Stories; The Children's Book.* Houghton.
Smythe, Louise: *Reynard the Fox.* Amer. Book Co.
Spaulding and Bryce: *Aldine Readers.* Newson.
Stevenson, Augusta: *Children's Classics in Dramatic Form.* 5 vols. Houghton.
Stickney, J. H.: *Andersen's Fairy Tales.* 2 series. Ginn.
Summers, Maud: *The Summers Readers.* Beattys.
Turpin, E. H.: *Andersen's Fairy Tales.* Merrill.
Underwood, Kate: *Fairy Tale Plays* (For Infants and Juniors). Macmillan.
University Pub. Co.: *Fairy Tales.* Standard Literature Series; Hans Andersen's Best Stories; Grimm's Best Stories. Newson and Co.
Van Sickle, J. H., etc.: *The Riverside Readers.* Houghton.

Varney, Alice: *Story Plays Old and New.* Amer. Book Co.
Villee: *Little Folk Dialog Reader.* Sower.
Wade, Mary H.: *Indian Fairy Tales.* Wilde.
Washburne, Mrs. M.: *Old-Fashioned Fairy Tales* (Retold from poetic versions of Thomas Hood). Rand.
White, Emma G.: *Pantomime Primer.* Amer. Book Co.
Williston, P.: *Japanese Fairy Tales.* 2 series. Rand.
Wiltse, Sara E.: *Folk Lore Stories and Proverbs.* Ginn.
Wohlfarth, J., and McMurry, Frank: *Little Folk-Tales.* 2 vols.
Zitkala-sa: *Old Indian Legends.* Ginn.

APPENDIX

ILLUSTRATIONS OF CREATIVE RETURN[1]

Tales suited for dramatization

Little Two-Eyes

Little Two-Eyes, which is suited to the first-grade child, is one of the most attractive of folk-tales and contains blended within itself the varied beauties of the tales. It is in *cante-fable* form, which gives it the poetic touch so appealing to children. It contains the magic rhymes, —

> Little kid, bleat,
> I wish to eat!
>
> Little kid, bleat,
> Clear it off, neat!

the fairy wise woman, and the friendly goat. It contains the fairy housekeeping in the forest which combines tea-party, picnic, and magic food — all of which could not fail to delight children. The lullaby to put Two-Eyes to sleep suits little children who know all there is to know about "going to sleep." The magic tree, the silver leaves, the golden fruit, the knight and his fine steed, and the climax of the tale when the golden apple rolls from under the cask — all possess unusual interest. There is exceptional beauty in the setting of this tale; and its message of the worth of goodness places it in line with *Cinderella.* It should be dramatized as two complete episodes, each of three acts: —

The Goat Episode

Place......The home and the forest.
Time......Summer.

---

[1] For *Little Two-Eyes* and *Snow White, see* note on p. 145; for *The Little Lamb and the Little Fish, see* pp. 147–48; and for *How the Birds came to have Different Nests, see* p. 151.

Act I, Scene i. A home scene showing how the Mother and Sisters despised Two-Eyes.
Scene ii. Two-Eyes and the Fairy.
Scene iii. Two-Eyes and the Goat. Evening of the first day.
Act II, Scene i. One-Eye went with Two-Eyes. Third morning.
Song . . . Feast . . . Return home.
Act III, Scene i. Three-Eyes went with Two-Eyes. Fourth morning.
Song . . . Feast . . . Return home.

The Story of Two-Eyes

Place......The forest; and the magic tree before the house.
Time......Summer.
Act I, Scene i. Two-Eyes and the Fairy.
Act II, Scene i. The magic tree. Mother and Sisters attempt to pluck the fruit.
Act III, Scene i. The Knight. Second attempt to pluck fruit.
Conclusion. The happy marriage.

Snow White

The Story of Snow White is one of the romantic fairy tales which has been re-written and staged as a play for children, and now may be procured in book form. It was produced by Winthrop Ames at the Little Theatre in New York City. The dramatization by Jessie Braham White followed closely the original tale. The entire music was composed by Edmond Rickett, who wrote melodies for a number of London Christmas pantomimes. The scenery, by Maxfield Parrish, was composed of six stage pictures, simple, harmonious, and beautiful, with tense blue skies, a dim suggestion of the forest, and the quaint architecture of the House of the Seven Dwarfs. Pictures in old nursery books were the models for the scenes. Because of the simplicity of the plot and the few characters, *Snow White* could be played very simply in four scenes, by the children of the second and third grades for the kindergarten and first grade.

Snow White

Scene i. A Festival on the occasion of Snow White's sixteenth birthday.
Scene ii. In the Forest.
Scene iii. A Room in the House of the Seven Dwarfs.
Scene iv. The Reception to Snow White as Queen, on the grounds near the young King's Palace.

The beautiful character of Snow White; the glimpse of Dwarf life — the kindly little men with their unique tasks and their novel way of living; the beauty and cheer of Snow White which her housekeeping brought into their home; their devotion to her; the adventure in the wood; the faithful Huntsman; the magic mirror; the wicked Queen; and the Prince seeking the Princess — all contribute to the charm of the tale. The songs written for the play may be learned by the children, who will love to work them into their simple play: *Snow White, as fair as a lily, as sweet as a rose;* the song of the forest fairies, *Welcome, Snow White;* and their second song which they sing as they troop about Snow White lying asleep on the Dwarf's bed, *Here you'll find a happy home, softly sleep!* or the song of Snow White to the Dwarfs, *I can brew, I can bake.*

The Little Lamb and the Little Fish

Once upon a time there lived a sister and a brother who loved each other very much. They were named Gretchen and Peterkin. One day their father who was King of the country, left them and brought home with him a new Queen who was not kind to the children. She banished them from the castle and told the King bad tales about them. So they made friends with the Cook and ate in the kitchen. Peterkin would bring water and Gretchen could carry plates and cups and saucers.

One beautiful spring day when all the children were out-of-doors playing games, Gretchen and Peterkin went to play with them, by the pond, on the meadow, beyond the castle wall. Around this pond the children would run, joining hands and singing: —

"Eneke, Beneke, let me live,
And I to you my bird will give;
The bird shall fetch of straw a bunch,
And that the cow shall have to munch;
The cow shall give me milk so sweet,
And that I'll to the baker take,
Who with it shall a small cake bake;
The cake the cat shall have to eat,
And for it catch a mouse for me,
. . . .
And this is the end of the tale."

Round and round the pond the children ran singing; and as the word "tale" fell on Peterkin he had to run away over the meadow and all the rest ran after to catch him.

But just then the wicked Queen from her window in the castle spied the happy children. She did not look pleased and she muttered words which you may be sure were not very pleasant words.

The children had been racing across the meadow after Peterkin. Now one called, "Where is Peterkin? I saw him near that tree, but now I cannot see him. Gretchen, can you see Peterkin? — Why, where 's Gretchen?"

Peterkin and Gretchen were nowhere to be seen. Suddenly a little boy said, "Where did that lamb come from over there? It must have been behind the linden tree!"

The children drew near the lamb, when what was their surprise to hear it call out to them, "Run children, run quick or the Queen will harm you! I am Gretchen! Run, and never come near the pond again!" And at the little Lamb's words the children fled.

But the little Lamb ran all about the meadow, calling, "Peterkin, Peterkin!" and would not touch a blade of grass. Sadly she walked to the edge of the pond and slowly walked round and round it calling, "Peterkin, where are you?"

Suddenly the water bubbled and a weak voice cried, "Here, Gretchen, in the pond, —

"Here Gretchen, here swim I in the pond,
Nor may I ever come near castle ground."

And the Lamb replied: —

"Ah, my brother! In the wood,
A lamb, now I must search for food."

Then Peterkin comforted Gretchen and promised early every morning to come up to the water to talk with her; and Gretchen promised to come early from the wood, before the sun was up, to be with Peterkin. And Peterkin said, "I will never forsake you, Gretchen, if you will never forsake me!" And Gretchen said, "I will never forsake you, Peterkin, if you will never forsake me!"

Then the little Lamb fled sadly to the wood to look for food and the little Fish swam round the pond. But the children did not forget their playmates. Every day they saved their goodies and secretly laid them at the edge of the wood where the Lamb could get them. And the Lamb always saved some to throw the crumbs to the little Fish in the morning.

Many days passed by. One day visitors were coming to the castle. "Now is my chance," thought the wicked Queen. So she said to the Cook, "Go, fetch me the lamb out of the meadow, for there is nothing else for the strangers!"

Now the Lamb had lingered by the pond longer than usual that morning so that the Cook easily caught her; and taking her with him tied her to the tree just outside the kitchen. But when the Cook was gone to the kitchen, the little Fish swam up from the pond into the little brook that ran by the tree and said —

"Ah, my sister, sad am I,
That so great harm to you is nigh!
And far from you I love must be,
A-swimming in the deep, deep sea!"

And the Lamb replied : —

"Ah, my brother in the pond,
Sad must I leave you, though I'm fond;
The cook has come to take my life,
Swim off to sea, — Beware!"

Just then the Cook came back and hearing the Lamb speak became frightened. Thinking it could not be a real lamb, he said, "Be still, I will not harm you. Run, hide in the wood, and when it is evening, come to the edge of the wood and I will help you!"

Then the Cook caught another lamb and dressed it for the guests. And before evening he went to a wise woman who happened to be the old Nurse who had taken care of Peterkin and Gretchen. She loved the children and she soon saw what the wicked Queen had done. She told the Cook what the Lamb and Fish must do to regain their natural forms.

As soon as it was dark the little Lamb came to the edge of the wood and the Cook said, "Little Lamb, I will tell you what you must do to be a maid again!" So the Cook whispered what the wise Woman had said. The little Lamb thanked the Cook and promised to do as he said.

Next morning very early before the break of day, the little Lamb hurried from the wood across the meadow. Not taking time to go near the pond she hastily pushed against the castle gate which the kind Cook had left unfastened for her. She ran up the path, and there under the Queen's window stood the beautiful rose-tree with only two red roses on it — just as the Cook had said. Not even glancing at the Queen's window, the little Lamb began nibbling the lowest one. And behold, there in the path stood Gretchen again! Then hastening to seize the other rose before the sun's first ray might touch it, she ran lightly down the path, away from castle ground, across the meadow to the pond. Calling little Fish to the water's edge — for he had lingered in the pond — she sprinkled over him the drops of dew in the heart of the rose. And there stood little Peterkin beside Gretchen!

Then hand in hand, Gretchen and Peterkin hurried from the pond and fled into the wood just as the sun began to show beyond the trees. There they built themselves a cottage and lived in it happily ever afterwards. The kind Cook and the wise Nurse found them and visited them. But Gretchen and Peterkin never went near castle ground until the Cook told them the Queen was no more. — *Laura F. Kready.*

How the Birds came to Have Different Nests

Time. . . .

> Once upon a time when pigs spoke rhyme,
> And monkeys chewed tobacco,
> And hens took snuff to make them tough,
> And ducks went quack, quack, quack, O!

Place. . . . Madge Magpie's Nest up in a Tree-top.
Characters: Madge Magpie, the Teacher; Thrush, Blackbird, Owl, Sparrow, Starling, and Turtle-Dove.

All the Birds. "We have come to you, Madge Magpie, to ask you to teach us how to build nests. All the Birds tell how clever you are at building nests."

Magpie. "Make a circle round about the foot of this old pear-tree. I will sit upon this limb near my nest and show you how to do it. First I take some mud and make a fine round cake with it."

Thrush. "Oh, that's how it's done, is it? I'll hurry home! Goodbye, Birds, I can't stay another minute!

Mud in a cake, mud in a cake,
To-whit, to-whee, a nest I'll make!"

Magpie. "Next I take some twigs and arrange them about the mud."

Blackbird. "Now I know all about it. Here I go, I'm off to make my nest in the cherry-tree in Mr. Smith's cornfield!

Sticks upon mud, mud upon sticks,
Caw, caw! I'll make a nest for six!"

Magpie. "See, here I put another layer of mud over the twigs."

Wise Owl. "Oh! That's quite obvious. Strange I never thought of that before. Farewell, come to see me at the old elm-tree beside the gray church!

Mud over twigs! To-whit, to-whoo!
No better nest than that ever grew!"

Magpie. "See these long twigs. I just twine them round the outside."

Sparrow. "The very thing. I'll do it this very day. I can pick some up on my way home. I'll choose the spout that looks down over the school-yard; then I can see the children at play. They must like me for they never chase me away or hit me.

A nest with twigs twined round and round,
Chip, chip! No fear that would fall to the ground!"

Magpie. "And see these little feathers and soft stuff. What a comfortable, cosy lining for the nest they make!"

Starling. "That suits me! Off I go, I like a cosy warm nest. It shall be in that old plum-tree in the orchard, on the side of the hill.

Feathers and down to make cosy and warm,
That's the nest to keep us from harm!"

Magpie. "Well, Birds, have you seen how I made my nest? Do you think you know how? — Why, where are all the Birds? They could n't wait until I'd finished. Only you, Turtle-Dove, left!"

Turtle-Dove. "Take two, Taffy, take two—o—o—o!"

Magpie. "Here I put a twig across. But not two — one 's enough!"

Turtle-Dove. "Take two, Taffy, take two—o—o—o!"

Magpie. "One's enough I tell you, do you not see how I lay it across?"

Turtle-Dove. "Take two, Taffy, take two—o—o—o!"

Magpie. "Here I fly away from my nest for awhile! I will teach no more Birds to build nests. I cannot teach a silly Turtle-Dove who will not learn. I heard him sing just now as I turned around,

Turtle-Dove. "Take two, Taffy, take two—o—o—o,
Take two, Taffy, take two—o—o—o!"

Laura F. Kready.

TYPES OF TALES

An Animal Tale[1]

The Good-Natured Bear

"I shall never forget the patience, the gentleness, the skill, and the firmness with which she first taught me to walk alone. I mean to walk on all fours, of course; the upright manner of my present walking was only learned afterwards. As this infant effort, however, is one of my earliest recollections, I have mentioned it before all the rest, and if you please, I will give you a little account of it."

---

[1] *See* note, p. 217.

"Oh! do, Mr. Bear," cried Gretchen; and no sooner had she uttered the words than all the children cried out at the same time, "Oh, please do, sir!"

The Bear took several long whiffs at his pipe, and thus continued, —

"My Mother took me to a retired part of the forest (of Towskipowski, Poland) where few animals ever came; and telling me that I must now stand alone, extended both paws, and slowly lowered me towards the earth. The height as I looked down, seemed terrible, and I felt my legs kick in the air, with fear of I did not know what, till suddenly I felt four hard things and no motion. It was the fixed earth beneath my four infant legs. 'Now,' said my Mother, 'you are what is called standing alone!' But what she said I heard as in a dream. With my back in the air as though it rested on a wooden trussel, with my nose poking out straight snuffing the fresh breeze and the many secrets of the woods, my ears pricking and shooting with all sorts of new sounds to wonder at, to want to have, to love, or to tumble down at, — and my eyes staring before me full of light and confused gold and dancing things, I seemed to be in a condition over which I had no power to effect the least change, and in which I must remain fixed till some wonderful thing happened. But the firm voice of my Mother came to my assistance and I heard her tell me to look upon the earth beneath me and see where I was. First I looked up among the boughs, then side-ways at my shoulder, then I squinted at the tip of my nose — all by mistake and innocence — at last I bent my nose in despair and saw my forepaws standing, and this of course was right. The first thing that caught my attention, being the first thing I saw distinctly, was a little blue flower with a bright jewel in the middle, which I afterwards found was a drop of dew. Sometimes I thought this little blue darling was so close that it almost touched my eyes and certainly the color of it was up in my head; sometimes I thought it was deep down, a long way off. When I bent my face towards it to give it a kiss it seemed just where it was though I had not done what I had thought to do.

"The next thing I saw upon the ground was a soft-looking

little creature that crawled along with a round ball upon the middle of its back, of a beautiful white color, with brown and red curling stripes. The creature moved very, very slowly, and appeared always to follow the opinion and advice of two long horns on its head, that went feeling about on all sides. Presently it slowly approached my right forepaw and I wondered how I should feel or smell or hear it as it went over my toes; but the instant one of the horns touched the hair of my paw, both horns shrunk into nothing and presently came out again, and the creature slowly moved away in another direction. While I was wondering at this strange proceeding — for I never thought of hurting the creature, not knowing how to hurt anything, and what should have made the horns think otherwise? —while then I was wondering at this, my attention was suddenly drawn to a tuft of moss on my right near a hollow tree trunk. Out of this green tuft looked a pair of very bright round small eyes, which were staring up at me.

"If I had known how to walk I should have stepped back a few steps when I saw those bright little eyes, but I never ventured to lift a paw from the earth since my Mother had first set me down, nor did I know how to do so, or what were the proper thoughts or motions to begin with. So I stood looking at the eyes and presently I saw that the head was yellow and that it had a large mouth. 'What you have just seen,' said my Mother, 'we call a snail; and what you now see is a frog.' The names however did not help me at all to understand. Why the first should have turned from my paw so suddenly and why this creature should continue to stare up at me in such a manner I could not conceive. I expected however that it would soon come slowly crawling forth and then I should see whether it would also avoid me in the same manner. I now observed that its body and breast were double somehow, and that its paws were very large for its size, but had no hair upon them, which I thought was probably occasioned by its slow crawling having rubbed it all off. I had scarcely made these observations and reflections, when a beam of bright light breaking through the trees, the creature suddenly gave a great hop right up under my nose; and I, thinking the world was at an end, instantly fell flat down on one side and lay there waiting!" —

With this glimpse of an old-time modern animal tale we shall have to say with "Mr. Titmarsh," "Those who wish to know more about him must buy the book for themselves," — and add: Or they must get some enterprising publisher to reprint it.

A Few Romantic Tales[1]

Puss-in-Boots and Lord Peter

Puss-in-Boots, a romantic tale suited to the first grade, delights with its strong sense of adventure and of the heroic. Puss is a Master-Cat, a hero clever and quick, and with fine imagination to see what would happen and prepare for it. He is successful, combining initiative and motivation delightfully. His devotion to his master seems like disinterested loyalty, love, and sacrifice. While it is true the plot is based on a lie, the moral effect is not bad because we recognize Puss as a match-making character similar to the matchmaking Jackal of India; and in love "all is fair." Moreover Puss-in-Boots was only true to his cat-nature in playing a trick, and we admire the cleverness of his trick in behalf of a master really deserving. The underlying philosophy of the tale, "That there is a power in making the best with what you possess," appeals to all, and has the ability to lend dignity and force to the light intrigue of the tale.

The setting in *Puss-in-Boots* gives a touch of nature beauty. First we have the Miller's poor home, and from there we are led in succession to the brambles through which Puss scampered; the rabbits' warren where he lay in waiting to bag the heedless rabbits; the palace to which he took the rabbits caught by the Marquis of Carabas; the cornfield where he bagged the partridges; the river-side where the Marquis bathed; the meadow where the countrymen were mowing; the cornfields where the good people were reaping; until at last we are escorted to the stately castle where the Ogre dwelt.

---

[1] *See* note, p. 232.

The plot of the tale is very pleasing as it easily arranges itself into a simple drama of three acts: —

Act I,	*Scene i.*	Revery of the Master. The Cat's promise to help.
	Scene ii.	Puss in the rabbits' warren with his bag.
	Scene iii.	Puss takes the rabbits to the King in his palace.
Act II,	*Scene i.*	Puss with his bag in the cornfield.
	Scene ii.	Puss takes partridges to the King.
	Scene iii.	Puss and his Master. Puss gives advice.
Act III,	*Scene i.*	The Marquis bathing and Puss by the river-side.
	Scene ii.	The Drive. Puss runs before and meets the mowers.
	Scene iii.	The Ogre's Castle. Puss's reception of the coach. Marriage of the Marquis of Carabas. Puss becomes a Lord.

The tale possesses an appeal to the emotions, we want Puss-in-Boots to accomplish whatever scheme he invents, and we want the Miller's son to win the Princess. Its appeal to the imagination is an orderly succession of images, varied and pleasing. The invention of Puss and his successful adventures make the tale one of unusual interest, vivacity, and force. The transformation of the Ogre into a Lion and again into a Mouse, and the consequent climax of Puss's management of the Mouse, bring in the touch of the miraculous. A similar transformation occurs in Hesiod, where the transformed Metis is swallowed by Zeus. This transformation may be produced by a witch, when the help of another is needed, as in *Beauty and the Beast* and in *Hansel and Grethel;* or the transformation may come from within, as in this case when the Ogre changes himself into a Mouse, or when a man changes himself into a Wolf. A situation which parallels the theme of Puss-in-Boots occurs in *The Golden Goose* where Dummling gets as his share only a goose, but having the best disposition makes his fortune out of his goose. Grimm's *Three Feathers* also contains a similar motif. D'Aulnoy's *White Cat*, the feminine counterpart of *Puss-in-Boots*, is a tale of pleasing fancy in which the hero wins the White Cat, a transformed Princess, who managed to secure for him, the youngest son, the performance of all the tasks his father had set for him.

But the most interesting parallel of *Puss-in-Boots* is the Norse *Lord Peter* told by Dasent in *Norse Tales*. Here the helpful Cat does not use a bag, but in true Norse fashion catches game in the wood by sitting on the head of the reindeer and threatening, "If you don't go straight to the King's palace, I'll claw your eyes out!" The Norse tale omits the bathing episode. The King wants to visit Lord Peter but the Cat manages that Lord Peter shall visit the King. The Cat promises to supply coach, horses and clothes, not by craft — their source is not given — but they are furnished on the condition that Peter must obey to say always, when he sees fine things in the Castle, that he has far finer things of his own. In the Norse tale Peter and the Cat work together, Peter is in the secret; while in the Perrault tale Puss does all the managing, Carabas is simply being entertained by the King. In the Norse tale, on the way home the coach meets a flock of sheep, a herd of fine kine, and a drove of horses. The Cat does not threaten that the caretakers shall be "chopped as fine as herbs for the pot," if they do not say all belongs to Lord Peter, but he cunningly bribes the shepherd with a silver spoon, the neat-herd with a silver ladle, and the drover with a silver stoop. In place of the Ogre's Castle, there is a Troll's Castle with three gates — one of tin, one of silver, and one of gold. The Norse Cat wins the victory by craftily playing upon the troll-nature. He gains the Troll's attention by meeting him at the gate and telling him about the secrets of agriculture, one of the secrets of men the trolls wanted to learn. Then at the height of interest, he plays upon his curiosity by getting him to look round. Whereupon, the Troll, meeting the glare of the full sun, burst; for trolls cannot bear the sight of the sun, and live. In the Norse tale, the Cat, after Lord Peter at her request cuts off her head, becomes the Princess and marries Lord Peter. In Perrault's tale, the King, with French etiquette and diplomacy, invites the Marquis to be his son-in-law.

The *Story of Puss-in-Boots* appeared in *Straparola*, 11, 1, and in *Basile*, 2, 4. Laboulaye, in his *Last Fairy Tales*, has retold the Pentamerone tale, *Gagliuso*, in which the Cat is a crafty advocate of his Master's interests, but the Master is ungrateful and forgets the Cat. The effect of the tale is not pleasing, it is a satire on gratitude.

The *Story of Puss-in-Boots* is also told by Ludwig Tieck, with twelve etchings by Otto Speckter, published in Leipzig, in 1843. A critic, writing for the Quarterly Review in 1844, "An Article on Children's Books,"[1] recommended this edition of *Puss-in-Boots* as the beau ideal of nursery books. *Puss-in-Boots* appeared also in the Swedish of Cavallius. A monograph on the Carabas tale has been written by Andrew Lang.

Tom Thumb and Little Thumb

Tom Thumb, another romantic tale suited to the first grade, is one of the most entertaining of tales. The germ of *Tom Thumb* exists in various forms in the books of the far East, among American Indians, and among the Zulus of South Africa. Tom Thumb is one of the oldest characters in English nursery literature. In 1611, the ancient tales of Tom Thumb were said to have been "in the olde time the only survivors of drouzy age at midnight. Old and young, with his tales chim'd mattens till the cock's crow in the morning. Batchelors and maids have with his tales compassed the Christmas fireblocke till the curfew bell rings candle out. The old shepheard and the young plowboy, after a days' labour, have carol'ed out a *Tale of Tom Thumb* to make them merry with, and who but little Tom hath made long nights seem short and heavy toyles easie."

Tom Thumb, as has been previously mentioned, most probably was transmitted to England by the early Norsemen. *The Tale of Tom Thumb*, as told by Jacobs, was taken from the chap-book version in *Halliwell*. The first mention of Tom is in Scot's *Discoverie of Witchcraft*, in 1584. Tradition says that Tom died at Lincoln, which was one of the five Danish towns of England. A little blue flagstone in the cathedral, said to be his tombstone, was lost and has never been replaced during recent repairs early in the nineteenth century. *Tom Thumb* was first written in prose by Richard Johnson, in 1621. In Ashton's *Chap-Books of the Eighteenth*

---

[1] Reprinted in *Living Age*, Aug. 13, 1844, vol. 2, p. 1.

Century we have a facsimile of the chap-book, *The Famous History of Tom Thumb*. The tale is in three parts. The first part, which is much superior to the rest of the tale, was taken from a copy printed for John Wright, in 1630. The second and third parts were written about 1700. The first part closes with the death of Tom from knightly feats. He was buried in great pomp, but the fairies carried him to Fairy Land. The first part closed with a promise of the second: —

> The Fairy Queen, she lov'd him so
> As you shall understand,
> That once again she let him go
> Down to the Fairy Land.
>
> The very time that he return'd
> Unto the court again,
> It was as we are well inform'd
> In good King Arthur's reign.
>
> When in the presence of the King,
> He many wonders wrought,
> Recited in the Second Part
> Which now is to be bought
>
> In Bow Church Yard, where is sold
> Diverting Histories many;
> And pleasant tales as e'er was told
> For purchase of One Penny.

The second part opens with Tom's return to Fairy Land. His second death is caused by a combat with a cat. Again he is taken to Fairy Land. In the third part the Fairy Queen sends Tom to earth in King Thunston's reign. His final death occurred from the bite of a spider.

The Life and Adventures of Tom Thumb appeared in the *Tabart Collection of Fairy Tales*, noted before, and a version entirely in verse was included in *Halliwell*. A monograph on *Tom Thumb* was written by M. Gaston Paris. *Little Thumb* as it appeared in *Perrault* and in *Basile*, was a tale similar to the German *Hansel and Grethel*. *Thumbling*, and *Thumbling as Journeyman* are German variants. Andersen's *Thumbelina* is a feminine counterpart to *Tom Thumb*, and in Laboulaye's *Poucinet* we have a tale of the successful younger brother, similarly diminutive.

There were current many old stories of characters similar to Tom Thumb. A certain man was so thin that he could jump through the eye of a needle. Another crept nimbly to a spider's web which was hanging in the air, and danced skillfully upon it until a spider came, which spun a thread round his neck and throttled him. A third was able to pierce a sun-mote with his head and pass his whole body through it. A fourth was in the habit of riding an ant, but the ant threw him off and trampled him. In a work written in 1601, referred to in Grimm's *Household Tales* a spider relates: —

Once did I catch a tailor proud
Heavy he was as elder wood,
From Heaven above he'd run a race,
With an old straw hat to this place,
In Heaven he might have stayed no doubt,
For no one wished to turn him out.
He fell in my web, hung in a knot,
Could not get out, I liked it not,
That e'en the straw hat, safe and sound,
Nine days ere him came to the ground.

A delightful little rhyme, *Tom Thumb*, is among Halliwell's *Nursery Rhymes*. It may refer to the Danish *History of Tom Thumb:* —

I had a little husband
No bigger than my thumb;
I put him in a pint pot
And there I bade him drum:
I bridled him and saddled him,
And sent him out of town;
I gave him a pair of garters
To tie up his little hose;
And a little handkerchief
To wipe his little nose.

The English version of *Tom Thumb* as we know it today, opens with a visit of the magician Merlin at the cottage of an honest and hospitable ploughman. Merlin rewarded the Goodman and his Wife for their hospitality by calling on the Queen of the fairies, who brought to the home, Tom Thumb, a boy no bigger than a man's thumb.

The time of the tale is in the days of Merlin and King Arthur's court. The tale is marked by a number of distinct English elements. The introduction of the Queen of the Fairies, of Fairy Land and the visit there, and of the fairy clothes they make for Tom, are all decidedly English. The sly ways of Tom, his tricks and his cleverness are distinctly English humor. He played with the boys for cherry-stones, and took theirs. He had so much curiosity that he fell into his mother's pudding. He was so light that on a windy day he had to be tied to a thistle when his mother went to milk the cow; and so, with his oak-leaf hat, he got caught in the cow's one mouthful. After other strange adventures he arrived at King Arthur's court where he became the favorite. His feats at tilts and tournaments give a glimpse of English court life, with its pastime of hunting; and fighting with the sword brings in the knight element. The story has little plot, being a succession of many episodes and a repetition of some. It shows little constructive ability, promises to be a perpetual tale, and is ended only by sudden death at the poisonous breath of the spider. *Tom Thumb* is one of the tales of pure fancy, with no underlying meaning, created for pure entertainment, to please children and grown-ups by its little people and little things. The moral is in the effect of Tom's character.

Perrault's *Little Thumb* tells how a poor Fagot-maker and his Wife sat by the hearth, sad with famine, and Little Thumb overheard their words. When they started to the wood to gather fagots, Little Thumb, like Hansel, scattered pebbles. The parents left the seven children in the wood but little Thumb guided them home by his pebbles. They set out a second time, when Little Thumb scattered bread-crumbs; and as the birds ate them, the children were lost. Little Thumb climbed a tree and saw the light of the Ogre's cottage afar off. The children reached the Ogre's cottage where Little Thumb changed the golden crowns of the seven little Ogresses, and putting them on his brothers, saved their lives. Then they all fled through the wood and hid in a rock, while the Ogre in his seven-league boots, pursued them and lay down to rest at the rock in which they were hidden. Little Thumb sent his brothers home, stole the fairy boots, and through craft, persuaded the Ogre's Wife to give him all the Ogre's gold. So, rich and happy, he returned to his father's home.

This tale shows a number of common motifs that appear in other tales: —

(1) The design of distressed parents to expose children to the forest.
(2) The discovery and prevention of the scheme by a child.
(3) The repetition of incident; the clew spoiled by the birds. The trail motif, similar to the one in *Hansel and Grethel*.
(4) The arrival of children at the home of the Ogre.
(5) The shifting of crowns to the heads of his brothers.
(6) The flight of the brothers pursued by the Ogre in seven-league boots.
(7) Little Thumb, stealing the boots and winning court favor, or the Ogre's treasure.

Some say that in this tale, symbolically, the forest represents night; the crumbs and pebbles, stars; and the Ogre, the sun. Little Thumb, because of his cunning and invention, has been called the Ulysses of the fairy tales. His adventure with the Ogre at the rock, while not a parallel one, reminds one of Ulysses and Polyphemus. Both succeeded in getting the better of the giant. An English edition of this tale was illustrated by William Blake.

Snow White and Rose Red

Snow White and Rose Red, besides blending the romantic and the realistic, illustrates rather completely how the old tale may stand the tests which have been emphasized here. As a romantic type, it contains adventure and the picturesque. It arouses emotion. It contains objects of beauty; and the strange Bear and the stranger Dwarf, about both of whom there is a sense of mystery. It exaggerates character and incidents beyond the normal, — the Mother and Daughters were more lovely than mortals usually are, — and the harmony between man and beast may belong to the millennium rather than to this common earth. This is one of the most romantic of fairy tales in that it is a highly idealized type.

The story was current in Germany before the time of the Grimms, and appeared in the collection of Caroline Stahl. The rhyme, —

Snowy-white, rosy-red,
Will ye strike your lover dead?

was taken from a popular song, and is found in a child's story in *Taschenbüch Minerva* for 1813.

Snow White and Rose Red is full of many beauties; the characters are beautiful, the setting is beautiful, and the spirit of the whole is full of beauty. There is sister-love; and mother-love — not the selfish kind that loves but its own, but that similar to the rich growth of our modern times, when mother-love seeks to include those without the home. There is genuine kindness that pours its sweetness on the Bear or on the Dwarf, that falls like the rain on the deserving and on the ungrateful; there is devotion to animals and a lack of enmity between man and beast; and there is a portrayal of the beauty of domestic life and of the charms of childhood in simple life — its play, its pleasure, and its tasks. This is all set as in two pictures whose sky is the golden glow of passion for the sun and the spring-time and summer it brings. In the first picture, on the edge of the forest stands a little cottage before whose gate grow two rose-trees, a red rose-tree and a white rose-tree, not only symbols of the beauty of the spring-time and of the rich fruitage of summer, but also symbols typifying the more wondrous beauty of the character of the two children, Snow White and Rose Red. In the second picture, a tall palace rears itself, before whose gate grow two rose-trees also, a red rose-tree and a white rose-tree, not only symbols of the same beauty of spring-time and fruitage of summer, but also symbols typifying the beauty of loveliness and the fairness of happiness and prosperity that guarded from harm the lives of the deserving Snow White and Rose Red, and continued to bless them to the close.

First, looking at the characters in this tale, we see a Mother who illustrates the richness of womanhood. She managed her own home and kept it a place of beauty and cheer. She had two daughters, both lovely, but very different. She recognized this difference and respected it, and permitted each child to enjoy a delightful freedom to grow as was her nature. She permitted the children to play but she also commanded willing obedience. She arranged their work with fairness so that each had her share and each seemed free in doing that work to use her individual taste and judgment. She taught her children to spin and to sew, and she read to them. She told them about the guardian Angel who watched over them to keep them from harm. She was not anxious when they were out of sight, for even when Snow White and Rose Red stayed in the wood all night and slept on the leaves, she had no fear, for no accident ever happened to them. As a strong, noble woman, without fear, and full of love, pity, and fairness, — George Eliot's ideal of highest character, — the Mother of Snow White and Rose Red has no equal in the fairy tales.

The two Children, beautiful as the roses that grew outside the cottage, were both industrious, good, amiable little girls, who in their natural sweetness showed the spirit of the Golden Age when peace and good-will dwelt among men. They were natural children and they loved to play. They gathered berries in the forest, they played hide-and-seek among the trees, they waded in the river, went fishing, made wreaths of flowers, and played with their animal friends. They fed the hares cauliflower, or watched the fawns grazing and the goats frisking; and even the birds loved them and did not fly away when they were near. In the home they kept things not only clean but beautiful; they not only did work but took pleasure in doing that work. Now at a time when domestic life in the home is being threatened, *Snow White and Rose Red* gives a realistic picture of the beauty of domestic life, its simple joys and charm. In summer there was always a nose-gay for the Mother, and in winter there was a cheery fire with a copper kettle over it, shining like gold. And in the evening when the snow fell fast outside, inside was warmth and comfort. The Children sat sewing and the Mother reading, while a lamb and a white dove beside them enjoyed their protection and care.

The entrance of the Bear gave the Children a natural thrill of fear. But the Mother, with beautiful hospitality, gave the Bear protection and kindness and led them to overcome that fear. To the Bear they showed that good nature which willingly serves; and in the tricks they played with their comrade they showed a great strength of vitality and that freedom which grows where there is no repression.

The Bear departed at spring-time; and as he left Snow White thought she saw glittering gold under his coat. This seems to hint that the tale is symbolic, typifying the change of seasons. Spring, the Bear, took refuge in the cottage during the cold winter months; but in the spring he had to go abroad into the forest, to guard his treasures from the evil Dwarf of winter.

The Children again showed their sweetness and good nature when, while gathering sticks, they came upon the Dwarf, with his wrinkled face and snow-white beard, the end of which was caught in a split of a tree. The contrast is delightful, between the cross and impatient Dwarf and Rose Red who offered to fetch help, and Snow White who politely tried to soothe his impatience by cutting off the end of his beard with her scissors. This time the Dwarf snatched a sack of gold which lay at the foot of the tree, and fled, most ungrateful, not even thanking the Children. The Children had two other adventures with the Dwarf; and these, together with their adventure with the Bear, make up the plot of the story. They met the Dwarf a second time, one day when they went fishing. Then Rose Red told him to be careful or he 'd fall into the water, because a great fish was pulling on the bait and his beard became entangled in the fishing-line. Snow White again cut off the end of his beard to free him and again he snatched his bag — this time of pearls, lying among the rushes — and fled. One day, on going to town to buy thread, needles, laces, and ribbons, they met the Dwarf a third time. This time an eagle had caught him and was about to carry him off. The Children, with compassion, held on and freed him; but again he scolded, seized his bag of precious stones, and slipped away to his cave. On their return from town, the Children again met the Dwarf, in the wood, counting his treasure. Again he was very angry, but just then the Bear arrived out of the forest and demanded the life of the Dwarf. The Dwarf offered up in his stead, Snow White and Rose Red. But the Bear, faithful to his old comrades, slew the Dwarf, and then becoming a beautiful Prince, went home with the Sisters. Snow White married the Prince and Rose Red his Brother, and they all lived with their Mother happily in the beautiful palace.

When the Bear slew the Dwarf spring returned to the land. The Dwarf with his snow-white beard seems to typify winter. Each time the Dwarf's beard was cut the beard of winter became shorter, another winter month was gone, and there remained a shorter season. The bag of gold which the Dwarf first took might signify the golden fruit of autumn, and the pearls and diamonds which he next took, the ice and snow of winter. The Dwarf's beard became entangled in the fishing-line when the icy winds of winter began to give the pond its frozen coat; and then the animals of the wood were compelled to seek a refuge. When the Bear came out of the wood to meet the Dwarf and slew him, the time for the departure of winter was at hand, and spring returned to the land.

This fairy tale evidently shows a good, interesting plot, with something happening all the time. The climax is very distinctly marked, everything leads up to the meeting of the Bear and the Dwarf in the forest. The characters present interesting variety and strong contrasts. The setting is unusually beautiful: the cottage, the wood, the lake, the town, the hillside, the palace, and the two symbolic rose-trees. The tale appeals to the emotions of love, kindness, compassion, and gratitude. It presents to the imagination distinct episodes: the home-life of the Children in the cottage, their life in the wood, their adventure with the Bear, their three adventures with the Dwarf, and the meeting of the Bear and the Dwarf. The conclusion follows closely upon the climax, — the Bear, grateful to the kind Children, saved their lives and re-transformed, became a Prince. The happy marriage brings the tale to a close, with the palace home guarded by the two rose-trees. The message of the tale is the possible beauty of woman's love and character, and the loveliness of spring and of summer.

A Modern Tale[1]

The Elephant's Child

The Elephant's Child might be examined here more particularly because it is unusually interesting as an example of the complete test applied to the child's fairy tale. One need not test it as to interest for it was written especially for children by one who could play with them. As to literature it certainly has mind and soul; there is no doubt about its structure or its appeal to the sympathies. The quantity of good humor and fun it bestows upon childhood is a permanent enrichment; for even a child's world has need of all the good cheer and fun that can be given to it.

This tale is especially interesting also because it might be classed as almost any one of the types of tales. It is not accumulative though it possesses to a marked degree three characteristics of the accumulative tale, repetition, alliteration, and all sorts of phonic effects. And it is not an old tale. But it is not only one of the most pleasing animal tales we possess but one of the best humorous tales having the rare quality of freshness. It is realistic in its portrayal of animal life; and it is highly romantic in its sense of adventure, the heroic, the strange, and the remote.

As a short-story it shows the essentials, originality, ingenuity, and compression. The single interest is how the Elephant got his trunk, and everything points to the climax of his getting it. The plot is "entertaining, novel, comical and thrilling." The structure is very easily seen in these ten episodes: —

1. The introduction; the family; the Child; his home; his questions; the new, fine question.
2. The Elephant's Child set out to answer his own question.
3. The Elephant's Child met Kolokolo Bird.
4. The Elephant's Child journeyed to the Limpopo.
5. The Elephant's Child met the Python.
6. The Elephant's Child met the Crocodile. He got his trunk. (Climax.)
7. The Elephant's Child gained experience from the Python.

---

[1] *See* p. 239.

8. The Elephant's Child's journey home.
9. The Elephant's Child's return home.
10. Conclusion. How all elephants got trunks. Peace.

The characters are unique and interesting. They are usual animals but unusual in what they say. They exhibit animal traits and motives but they also show us a hidden meaning in their actions and words. They seem living, they speak directly; yet they preserve the idea of the fable for they are symbolic. The Elephant's Child typifies human innocence, the inexperience of youth; the Kolokolo Bird, a friend; the Python, experience or wisdom; and the Crocodile, guile or evil. All the animals become very interesting because we are concerned to know their particular reason for spanking the "'satiable Elephant's Child." What they say is so humorous and what they do is consistent, in harmony with their natural animal traits. The Child is the hero. He is a very attractive character because he has that rare charm we call temperament. He is curious, polite, and sweet, and follows his own nose in spite of everything. He wins out with strength, experience, and a new nose; and we are rejoiced at his triumphs. His questions are so funny and yet they seem quite what any elephant with a bump of curiosity might ask. To the Giraffe — "What made his skin spotty?" To the Hippopotamus — "Why her eyes were red?" To the Baboon — "Why melons tasted just so?" And at last, "What does the Crocodile have for dinner?"

The setting of the tale is suggested continually in expressions which show visual imagination of a high order: such as, "And he lived in Africa"; "dragged him through a thorn bush"; "blew bubbles into her ear"; "hove him into a hornet's nest"; and "from Graham's Town to Kimberley and from Kimberley to Khama's Country, and from Khama's Country east by north to the Limpopo."

The tale possesses most delightful humor. A verbal magic which fairly scintillates with the comic spirit, and clinging epithets of which Kipling is a master, suggest the exact picture needed. Humor is secured largely through the use of the unique word; as, "*spanked*," "*precisely* as Kolokolo Bird had said," and "for he was a *Tidy* Pachyderm." Often it is increased by the use of newly coined words; as, "hijjus," "curtiosity," "scalesome, flailsome, tail," "fever-trees," "self-propelling man-of-war," and "schloop of mud." Another element of humor in the tale is the artistic use of repetition, which has been previously referred to as one of the child's interests. Sometimes one meaning is expressed in several different ways; as, "immediately and directly, without stopping, for a long time." Or we are given contrasted terms; as, "a little warm but not at all astonished," and then later, "very warm and greatly astonished." One main element of humor is this way in which expressions reflect back on preceding ones. Sometimes we are given very surprising, startling, expressions; as, "wait-a-bit-thorn-bush" — which reminds us of the "all-alone-stone" in *Water Babies* — and "he sang to himself down his trunk."

As to imagination, *The Elephant's Child* is a delightful illustration of the appeal to the associative, the penetrative, and the contemplative imagination. While its philosophy may be understood in part by the child it has a deeper meaning for the adult. It seems to imply that it is the way of life to spank somebody else. It is the stronger who spank the weaker until they become strong enough to stand up for themselves. Then nobody spanks anybody any more and there is peace. When the Child asked a question that no one would answer he set out to find his own answer just as in life it often is best to work to answer one's own questions. When the Elephant trusted the Crocodile he got something to keep just as in life the innocent may bear the marks of a contest though in no sense responsible for the contest. Experience in the guise of the Python helped the Child in his contest for life with the advice his own common sense would have offered. As an allegory of Experience *The Elephant's Child* does not view life as a whole; it gives but a glimpse of life. It would say: Experience teaches us to make the best with what we have. The way to get experience is to try a new power, just as the Child with his trunk tried to kill the fly and eat grass. As soon as he had received his new power he tested it on the Hippopotamous. He won the respect of his kind by beating them at their own game.

The emotional appeal in *The Elephant's Child* would repay study. The dominant emotional tone is that of the adventurous hero with his "'satiable curtiosity." There is vividness of emotion, steadiness of emotion, and a rich variety in the contrasts of feeling. Emotion of a moral quality is characteristic of its implied message of worldly wisdom but it does not leave one exactly satisfied.

The form of the story is a splendid example of a literary classic style. A pleasing humorous touch is given to the unity of the tale by making the Elephant's Child pick up with his new trunk, on his way home, the melon-rinds he had scattered on his journey to the Limpopo. The coherence in the tale is unusually fine and is secured largely by expressions which look backward or forwards; as, "By and by when that was finished," or "One fine morning," or "That very next morning." Any study will show that the tale possesses the general qualities of form and has its parts controlled by the principles of composition.

OUTLINE

I. THE WORTH OF FAIRY TALES

I. Two public tributes 1
II. The value of fairy tales in education........... 3
1. They bring joy into child-life................ 3
2. They satisfy the play-spirit of childhood...... 4
3. They give a power of accurate observation.... 6
4. They strengthen the power of emotion, develop the power of imagination, train the memory and exercise the reason.......................... 6
5. They extend and intensify the child's social relations 7
6. In school they unify the child's work or play.. 8
7. In the home they employ leisure time profitably 9
8. They afford a vital basis for language-training 10
III. References 12

II. PRINCIPLES OF SELECTION FOR FAIRY TALES

I. The interests of children 13
1. Fairy tales must follow the law of composition and must contain the interests of children..... 13
a. A sense of life 14
b. The familiar.......................... 14
c. The surprise.......................... 15
d. Sense impression........................ 17
e. The beautiful.......................... 18
f. Wonder, mystery, magic................ 19
g. Adventure 19
h. Success............................. 20
i. Action.............................. 20
j. Humor.............................. 21
k. Poetic justice.......................... 22

l. The imaginative 23
m. Animals 24
n. A portrayal of human relations, especially with children 24
o. The diminutive 25
p. Rhythm and repetition 26
q. The simple and sincere 28
r. Unity of effect 29
2. Fairy tales must follow the law of the emotions and avoid elements opposed to the interests of the very young child 30
a. The tale of the witch 31
b. The tale of the dragon 31
c. Giant tales 31
d. Some tales of transformation 32
e. The tale of strange animal relations and strange creatures 33
f. Unhappy tales 34
g. The tale of capture 34
h. The very long tale 35
i. The complicated or the insincere tale 36
II. The fairy tale as literature 37
1. The fairy tale must be a true classic 38
2. The fairy tale must have mind and soul 39
3. The fairy tale must have the distinguishing marks of literature 40
a. A power to appeal to the emotions 41
1) Literary emotion is not personal 41
2) Literary emotion must have justness 41
3) Literary emotion must have vividness 41
4) Literary emotion must have steadiness 41
5) Literary emotion must have variety 41
6) Literary emotion must have moral quality 41
7) Application of the test of emotion to the fairy tales 41
8) The value of fairy tales in the development of emotion 44
b. A power to appeal to the imagination 45
1) Appeal to the creative imagination 45

2) Appeal to the associative imagination... 46
a) Appeal to fancy.................... 46
3) Appeal to the penetrative imagination... 47
4) Appeal to the contemplative imagination. 47
a) Philosophy in the fairy tales......... 48
b) Proverbs in the fairy tales........... 50
c) Relation of the contemplative imagination to science..................... 52
c. A basis of truth, or appeal to the intellect.. 53
1) The truth must be idealistic............ 53
a) It may be realistic.................. 53
b) It may be romantic 53
2) Value of the appeal of literature to the intellect.............................. 53
d. A form more or less perfect.............. 54
1) The elements of form: words, sentences, paragraphs, and wholes................ 58
a) Words, the medium of language must have two powers.................. 54
(1) Denotation, to name what they mean......................... 54
(2) Connotation, to suggest what they imply 54
b) Suggestive power of words illustrated. 55
2) General qualities characteristic of perfect form.............................. 57
a) Precision or clearness 57
(1) Precision demands that words have denotation 57
(2) Precision appeals to the intellect.. 57
b) Energy or force.................... 57
(1) Energy demands that words have connotation 58
(2) Energy appeals to the emotions and holds the attention.............. 58
c) Delicacy or emotional harmony...... 58
(1) Delicacy demands that words have the power of adaptation 58
(2) Delicacy demands that form appeal to the æsthetic sense 58

(3) Delicacy is secured by selection and arrangement of words according to emotional associations 58
d) Personality 58
(1) Personality gives the charm of individuality 58
(2) Personality suggests the character of the writer 58
3) Principles controlling the elements of form, principles of composition 58
a) The principle of sincerity 58
(1) Sincerity demands a just expression 58
b) The principle of unity 59
(1) Unity demands a central idea 59
(2) Unity demands completeness 59
(3) Unity demands no irrelevant material 59
(4) Unity demands method, sequence and climax 59
c) The principle of mass 59
(1) Mass demands that the chief parts readily catch the eye 59
(2) Mass demands harmonious proportion of parts 59
d) The principle of coherence 59
(1) Coherence demands unmistakable relation of parts 59
(2) Coherence demands this unmistakable relation be preserved by the order, forms and connections 59
4) Form characterized by perfect adaptation of words to thought and feeling is called style 59
a) Style demands that form possess the four general qualities of form in perfection: precision, energy, delicacy, and personality 59
b) Style demands that form have its elements controlled by the four general

principles: sincerity, unity, mass, and coherence.......................... 59
c) *Oeyvind and Marit*, a modern tale illustrating style...................... 60
d) *Three Billy-Goats Gruff*, a folk-tale illustrating style...................... 64
e) The folk-tale generally considered as to literary form........................ 65
f) The tale by Grimm, Perrault, Dasent, Harris, Jacobs, Lang, and Andersen considered as to literary form............ 67
g) The tale of to-day considered as to literary form........................ 69

III. The fairy tale as a short-story................. 70
1. Characters................................ 71
a. Characters must be unique, original, and striking 72
b. Characters of the fairy tales.............. 72
2. Plot 73
a. Plot must be entertaining, comical, novel, or thrilling 73
b. Plot must show a beginning, a middle, and an end................................ 73
c. Plot must have a distinct climax 74
d. Introduction must be simple.............. 74
e. Conclusion must show poetic justice....... 74
f. Plot must be good narration and description 74
1) Narration must have truth, interest, and consistency 74
2) Description must have aptness and concreteness 75
g. Structure illustrated by *Three Pigs* and *Briar Rose* 76
3. Setting................................ 77
a. Setting must give the time and place, the background of the tale................. 77
b. Setting must arouse sensation and feeling ... 77
c. Effect of transformation of setting......... 77
1) Story sequence preserved by setting illustrated by *Robin's Christmas Song* 78

d. Setting and phonics, illustrated. *The Spider and the Flea* 79
e. Setting illustrated. *Chanticleer and Partlet* .. 81
4. A blending of characters, plot, and setting illustrated by *The Elves and the Shoemaker* 82
5. Tests to be applied to fairy tales 84
6. Tales examined and tested by the complete test of interests, classic, literature, short-story, narration, and description 84
a. *How the Sun, Moon, and West Wind Went to Dinner* (Indian) 84
b. The Straw Ox (Cossack) 86
IV. References 87

III. THE TELLING OF FAIRY TALES

Story-telling as an Art. Introductory 90
1. Story-telling as an ancient art 90
2. The place of the story in the home, library, and the school 93
3. Principles of story-telling 94
I. The teacher's preparation. Rules 94
1. Select the tale for some purpose 94
a. The teacher's problem of selecting the tale psychologically or logically 95
2. Know the tale historically as folk-lore, as literature, and as a short-story 96
a. The various motives contained in the fairy tales listed 97
3. Master the structure of the tale 99
4. Dwell upon the life of the story 99
5. Secure the message 100
6. Master the form 100
II. The presentation of the tale 102
1. Training of the voice 103
a. Study of phonetics 103
2. Exercises in breathing 104
3. A knowledge of gesture 105
a. Gesture precedes speech 106

b. Gesture begins in the face................ 106
c. Hands and arms lie close to the body in controlled emotion......................... 106
4. A power of personality........................ 106
5. Suggestions for telling........................ 107
a. The establishment of the personal relation between the teacher and the listener.........108
b. The placing of the story in a concrete situation for the child 110
c. The consideration of the child's aim in listening, by the teacher in her preparation...... 112
6. The telling of the tale 112
a. The re-creative method of story-telling. Illustrated by a criticism of the telling of *The Princess and the Pea*...................... 114
b. The re-creative method illustrated by *The Foolish, Timid Rabbit* 116
7. Adaptation of the fairy tale. Illustrated by *Thumbelina* and by *The Snow Man*.......... 118
III. The return from the child......................... 119
Story-telling as one phase of the art of teaching. Introductory.................................. 119
1. Teaching as good art and as great art; and fairy tales as subject-matter suited to accomplish high purposes in teaching............ 120
2. The part the child has to play in story-telling 121
3. The child's return, the expression of his natural instincts or general interests............ 125
1. The instinct of conversation 125
a. Language expression, oral re-telling........ 125
b. The formation of original little stories...... 126
c. Reading of the tale a form of creative reaction................................. 127
2. The instinct of inquiry......................... 127
a. Appeal of the folk-tale to this instinct...... 128
b. The instinct of inquiry united to the instinct of conversation, of construction, and of artistic expression, illustrated................ 128
3. The instinct of construction.................. 129

a. Clay-modelling.......................... 129
b. Construction of objects.................. 129
4. The instinct of artistic expression........... 130
a. Cutting of free silhouette pictures. Illustrated 130
b. Drawing and crayon-sketching. Illustrated 132
c. Painting. Illustrated.................. 132
d. Song. Illustrated...................... 133
e. Dance, rhythm plays. Illustrated......... 134
f. Game. Illustrated...................... 135
g. Representation of the fairy tale. Illustrated by *The Steadfast Tin Soldier*............. 135
h. Free play and dramatization.............. 138
1) Virtues of dramatization.............. 138
a) It develops voice.................. 138
b) It gives grace of movement.......... 138
c) It develops control and poise........ 138
d) It strengthens attention and power of visualization...................... 138
e) It combines intellectual, emotional, artistic, and physical action............ 138
f) It impresses many pieces of literature effectively......................... 138
g) It is the true Direct Moral Method and may establish a habit............... 143
2) Dangers of dramatization............. 139
a) Dramatization often is in very poor form............................ 139
b) Dramatization may develop boldness in a child 141
c) Dramatization may spoil some literature 142
d) Dramatization has lacked sequence in tales used from year to year......... 142
i. Illustrations of creative return........... 144
1) *The Country Mouse and the City Mouse* as expression in language, dramatization, drawing, and crayon-sketching......... 144
2) *The Elves and the Shoemaker* as expression in the dramatic game................. 145
3) *Little Two-Eyes* as expression in dramati-

zation. A fairy-play outline. (See *Appendix*) 145
4) *Snow White* as expression in dramatization. (See *Appendix*) 145
5) *Sleeping Beauty* as expression of partial narration, dramatic game, and dramatization combined 146
6) *The Little Lamb and the Little Fish*, an original tale developed from a Grimm fragmentary tale, illustrating expression in folk-game and dramatization. (See *Appendix*) 147
7) *The Bird and the Trees*, an original play illustrating expression in rhythm play and dramatization 149
8) *How the Birds came to Have Different Nests*, an original play illustrating language expression and dramatization. (See *Appendix*) 151
9) Andersen's *Fir Tree* as expression in dramatization, illustrating organization of ideas through a play 152

IV. References 154

IV. THE HISTORY OF FAIRY TALES

I. The origin of fairy tales 158
1. The fairy tale defined 159
2. The derivation and history of the name, *fairy*. . 159
a. Four senses in which *fairy* has been used . . . 160
3. The theories concerning the origin of fairy tales 161
a. Fairy tales are detritus of myth 161
1) The evolution of the tale 161
b. Fairy tales are myths of Sun, Rain, Dawn, Thunder, etc., the Aryan Theory 162
c. Fairy tales all arose in India, the Philological theory 165
d. Fairy tales owe their origin to the identity of early fancy 167
e. Fairy tales owe their origin to a combination of all these theories 167

II. The transmission of fairy tales.................. 167
1. The oral transmission of fairy tales.......... 167
a. Examples of transmission of fairy tales: *Jack the Giant-Killer, Dick Whittington,* etc...... 168
2. Literary transmission of fairy tales........... 170
a. An enumeration of the literary collections and books that have handed down the tales; as *Reynard the Fox,* the *Persian King-book, The Thousand and One Nights,* Straparola's *Nights,* Basile's *Pentamerone,* and Perrault's *Tales of Mother Goose*.................... 170
b. French publications of fairy tales.......... 179
1) The tales of Perrault 179
2) Tales by followers of Perrault.......... 181
3) A list of tales from the time of Perrault to the present time...................... 183
c. English and Celtic publications of fairy tales 183
1) Tales of Scotland and Ireland.......... 184
2) English tales and books............... 184
3) A list illustrating the history of the English fairy tale, including chap-books: *Jack the Giant-Killer, Tom Hickathrift;* old collections; etc. 184
4) A list illustrating the development of fairy-tale illustration in England............ 188
d. German publications of fairy tales......... 192
1) A list of tales from the time of the Grimms to the present...................... 193
e. Fairy-tale publications of other nations.... 193
f. American publications of fairy tales....... 195
1) A list of tales from the earliest times to 1870.............................. 196
g. Recent collections of folk-lore............ 200
III. References.............................. 201

V. CLASSES OF FAIRY TALES

I. Available types of tales...................... 204
1. The accumulative or clock story............. 205
a. Tales of simple repetition................ 206

1) The House that Jack Built............ 206
2) The Key of the Kingdom.............. 207
b. Tales of repetition with an addition....... 208
1) The Old Woman and Her Pig.......... 208
2) Titty Mouse and Tatty Mouse......... 208
3) Johnny Cake.................... 209
4) The Gingerbread Man............... 209
5) The Straw Ox...................... 209
c. Tales of repetition and variation.......... 209
1) The Three Bears................... 209
2) The Three Billy Goats.............. 211
2. The animal tale.......................... 211
a. The evolution of the animal tale 211
b. The animal tale may be an old beast tale... 211
1) Henny Penny...................... 213
2) The Foolish Timid Rabbit............ 214
3) The Sheep and the Pig............... 215
4) Medio Pollito...................... 215
5) The Three Pigs..................... 216
c. The animal tale may be an elaborated fable, illustrated........................... 211
d. The animal tale may be an imaginary creation, illustrated....................... 211
e. The Good-Natured Bear, a modern type. (See *Appendix*)........................... 217
3. The humorous tale........................ 217
a. The humorous element for children........ 218
b. The Musicians of Bremen, a humorous type 219
c. Humorous tales mentioned previously...... 221
d. Drakesbill, a humorous type............. 221
4. The realistic tale......................... 223
a. Lazy Jack, a realistic type of common life.. 224
b. The Old Woman and Her Pig, a realistic type 225
c. How Two Beetles Took Lodgings, a realistic tale of scientific interest............... 226
d. Titty Mouse and Tatty Mouse, a realistic theme transformed into a romantic tale.... 227
5. The romantic tale......................... 228
a. Cinderella............................ 228

b. Sleeping Beauty........................ 231
c. Red Riding Hood........................ 232
d. Puss-in-Boots. (See *Appendix*)........... 232
1) The Norse Lord Peter (See *Appendix*) .. 232
e. Tom Thumb, a romantic tale of fancy. (See *Appendix*)........................ 232
1) The French Little Thumb. (See *Appendix*) 232
2) The English Tom Thumb. (See *Appendix*) 232
f. Snow White and Rose Red, a highly idealized romantic type tested by the standards included here. (See *Appendix*) 232
6. The old tale and the modern tale............ 234
a. The modern tale often lacks the great art qualities of the old tale, unity and harmony, sincerity and simplicity................. 235
b. The modern tale often fails to use the method of suggestion........................ 235
c. The modern tale often does not stand the test of literature........................ 235
d. The modern tale gives richly to the primary and elementary field.................... 235
e. Criticism of a few modern tales........... 236
1) Little Beta and the Lame Giant, a good modern tale........................ 236
2) The Cock, the Mouse, and the Little Red Hen, a good modern tale............... 238
3) Peter Rabbit, a classic; other animal tales 239
4) The Elephant's Child, a modern animal tale. (See *Appendix*)................ 239
5) A Quick-Running Squash, a good modern tale........................ 240
6) A few St. Nicholas fairy stories......... 241
7) The Hop-About-Man, a romantic modern fairy tale........................ 241
f. What the modern fairy tale is............. 243

VI. SOURCES OF MATERIAL FOR FAIRY TALES: A LIST OF FAIRY TALES, FOLK-TALES, PICTURES, PICTURE-BOOKS, POEMS, AND BOOKS

Basis on which lists are made. Introductory.......... 245
I. A list of fairy tales and folk-tales suited to the kindergarten and first grade.................. 246
1. Tales of Perrault.................... 246
2. Tales of the Grimms.................. 246
3. Norse tales.......................... 247
4. English tales, by Jacobs............... 247
5. Modern fairy tales, by Andersen.......... 248
6. Uncle Remus tales, by Harris............ 248
7. Miscellaneous tales.................... 249
II. Bibliography of fairy tales.................. 253
III. A list of picture-books.................... 254
IV. A list of pictures.......................... 255
V. A list of fairy poems 256
VI. Main standard fairy-tale books.............. 256
VII. Fairy tales of all nations................... 258
VIII. Miscellaneous editions of fairy tales........... 259
IX. School editions of fairy tales.................. 262

APPENDIX

Illustrations of creative return...................... 265
Tales suited for dramatization.................... 265
Little Two-Eyes.............................. 265
Snow White.................................. 266
The Little Lamb and the Little Fish............ 267
How the Birds came to Have Different Nests.... 270
Types of tales.................................. 272
An animal tale.............................. 272
The Good-Natured Bear....................... 272
A few romantic tales.......................... 275
Puss-in-Boots and Lord Peter.................. 275
Tom Thumb and Little Thumb................ 278
Snow White and Rose Red..................... 282
A modern tale 287
The Elephant's Child 287

INDEX

Accumulative or clock story, 205–11.
Action, 20–21.
Adaptation of fairy tales, 117–19.
Adventure, 19–20.
Adventures of Chanticleer and Partlet, 81–82.
American fairy tales, 195–99.
Andersen, Hans C.: tales by, tested as literary form, 69; Steadfast Tin Soldier, 46, 49, 135–38; Fir Tree, 151–53; list of tales by, 248; editions, 256–57.
Animal tale: class, 211–17; evolution of, 211–13; types of, 213–17, 272–75, 287–90.
Animals: an interest, 24; tale of strange, 33–34.
Appendix, 265–90: Little Two-Eyes, 265–66; Snow White, 266–67; The Little Lamb and the Little Fish, 267–70; How the Birds came to Have Different Nests, 270–72; The Good-Natured Bear, 272–75; Puss-in-Boots and Lord Peter, 275–78; Tom Thumb and Little Thumb, 278–82; Snow White and Rose Red, 282–86; and The Elephant's Child, 287–90.
Arabian Nights, Thousand and One Nights, 176–78, 190, 196.
Art: of teaching, 119–20; in teaching, good, 120; in teaching, great, 120-21; in literature, good, 39–40; in literature, fine, 39–40; of story-telling, 90–91, 93–94; ancient, of story-telling, 91–93.
Artistic expression, instinct of, 130–54.
Aulnoy, Comtesse d', tales of, 181–82.

Basile, 178–79.
Beaumont, Madam de, 182.
Beautiful, the, 18–19.
Beauty and the Beast, dramatization of, 140–41; editions of, 189, 198.
Bibliography of fairy tales, 253-54.
Bird and the Trees, 148–51.
Books, main standard fairy tale, a list, 256–58. *See* Sources of material.
Breathing, exercises in, 104–05.
Briar Rose, 77. *See also* Sleeping Beauty.

Capture, tales of, 34–35.
Celtic fairy tales, 183–84.
Chap-books, 185–87, 188, 196, 198.
Characters, 71–73.
Child: his part in story-telling, 121–25; interests, 13–37; instincts, 125–54; growth: in observation, 6, 47–48; in reason, 6–7, 53–54; in language, 10; in emotion, 44–45; in imagination, 45–53; in experience, 54; in intellect, 53–54; in self-activity, 121–22; in consciousness, 122–23; in initiative, 122; in purpose, 123–25; in creative return possible to him, 123–54; in self-expression, 124–54; in organization of ideas, 153.
Child's Own Book, The, 190.
Cinderella, a chap-book, 187, 188, 198; a romantic type, 228–31.

Classes of tales, 204–44: accumulative, 205–11; animal, 211–17; humorous, 217–23; realistic, 223–28; romantic, 228–34; old and modern, compared, 234–43; references, 243–44.
Classic, fairy tale as a, 38–39.
Cock, the Mouse, and the Little Red Hen, 238–39.
Coherence, principle of, 58–59; illustrated, 62, 65.
Complicated or insincere, the, 36.
Composition: general qualities of, 57–58; precision, 57; energy, 57–58; delicacy, 58; personality, 58; principles of, 58–59; sincerity, 58–59; unity, 59; mass, 59; coherence, 59; style in, 59–60.
Comte de Caylus, 182.
Concrete situation, placing of story in, 94–95, 110–11.
Connotation, 54–57.
Consciousness, development of, 122–23.
Construction, expression of instinct of, 129–30.
Conversation, expression of instinct of, 125–27.
Country Mouse and City Mouse, 144–45.
Crayon-sketching, as expression, 132.
Creative return, illustrated, 144–54. *See* Return.
Criticism: of life, teaching, a, 120–21; of Oeyvind and Marit, 60–64; of Three Billy-Goats Gruff, 64–65; of How the Sun, Moon, and West Wind went out to Dinner, 84–86; of Straw Ox, 86–87; of Steadfast Tin Soldier, 135–38; of Musicians of Bremen, 219–20; of Drakesbill, 221–23; of Puss-in-Boots and Norse Lord Peter, 275–78; of Tom Thumb and Little Thumb, 278–82; of Snow White and Rose Red, 282–86; and of Elephant's Child, 287–90.

Danish tales, 194.
Dasent, Sir George W., tales by, as literary form, 68–69; Norse tales by, 194, 247, 257.
Delicacy, or emotional harmony, quality of, 57–58; illustrated, 60, 61, 64.
Denotation, 54.
Description, 75.
Dick Whittington, illustrating oral transmission of tales, 169; a chap-book, 185, 188, 196, 198.
Diminutive, the, 25–26.
Dragon tales, 31.
Drakesbill, 221–23.
Dramatic game: Elves and the Shoemaker, 145; Sleeping Beauty, 146–47.
Dramatization, as expression, 138–54; virtues of, 138, 143; dangers of, 139–43; of Sleeping Beauty, 146–47; of Bird and the Trees, 149–51; of Fir Tree, 152–53; of Little Two Eyes, 265–66; of Snow White, 266–67; of How the Birds came to have Different Nests, 270–72; and of Puss-in-Boots, 276.
Drawing, as expression, 132.
Dwarf's Tailor, 237.

Editions, main fairy tale, 256–58; fairy tale, of all nations, 258–59; illustrated, 254–55; miscellaneous, of fairy tales, 259–62; school, of fairy tales, 262–64.
Elements to be avoided, 30–36.
Elephant's Child, illustrating: repetition, 27–28; suggestion, 56–57; form, 100–01; modern animal tale, 239, 287–90.
Elves and the Shoemaker, illustrating: structure and short-

story, 82–84; creative return, 145.
Emelyan the Fool, 170.
Emotion, appeal to, distinguishing literary trait, 40–41; qualities of literary, 41; literary, in fairy tales, 41–44; growth of, 44–45; comparison of, in fairy tales and Shakespeare's dramas, 7, 43–44.
Energy or force, quality of, 57–58; illustrated, 61, 64.
English fairy tales, 184–92; collections of, 184–88; illustrating development of illustration, 188–92; by Jacobs, list, 247–48; editions, 257.
Expression in: language, 125–27; reading, 127; inquiry, 127–29; construction, 129–30; art, 130–54; paper-cutting, 130–31; drawing, 132; painting, 132; rhythm play, 133–34; song, 132–33; game, 134–35; representation, 135–38; dramatization, 138–54, 265–72.

Fairy, derivation of, 159–60; history of the name, 160.
Fairy tales: worth of, 1–12; principles of selection for, 13–89; telling of, 90–157; history of, 158–203; classes of, 204–44; sources of material for, 245–64; tributes to, 1–3; interests in, 13–37; as literature, 37–70; as classics, 38–39; possessing mind and soul, 39–40; distinguished by marks of literature, 40; as emotion, 41–45; as imagination, 45–53; philosophy in, 48–52; proverbs in, 50; as truth, 53–54; as form, 54–70; powers of words in, 54–57 general qualities of form in, 57–58; general principles controlling form in, 58–59; style in, defined, 59–60; tested as literary form, 60–70; as a form of short-story, 70–87; characters, 71–73; plot, 73–77; narration, 74–75; description, 75; structure, 76–77; setting, 77–82; three elements blended, 82–84; tested by complete standards, 84–87; teacher's preparation for telling, 94–102; presentation of, by teacher 102–19; return of child from, 119–54; rules for preparation of, 94–102; selection of, 95–96; motifs in, 96–98; re-telling of, 101–02; training of voice in telling, 103–04; breathing in telling, 104–05; gesture in telling, 105–06; power of personality, in telling, 106–07; suggestions for telling, 107–12; establishment of personal relation in telling, 107–10; placing of, in a concrete situation, 110–11; conception of child's aim in listening to, 112; re-creative method of telling, 112–17; adaptation of, 117–19; art of teaching, in telling, 119–25; as expression of conversation, 125–27; as expression of inquiry, 127–29; as expression of construction, 129–30; as expression of art, 130–54; origin of, 158–67; transmission of, 167–200; French, 179–83; Celtic, 183–84; English, 184–92; German, 192–93; tales of other nations, 193–95; American, 195–99; collections of folklore, 200; accumulative, 205–11; animal, 211–17; humorous, 217–23; realistic, 223–28; romantic, 228–34, 275–86; old and modern, 234–43; of Perrault, 246; of the Grimms, 246–47; Norse, 247; English, by Jacobs, 247–48; modern, by Andersen, 248; Uncle Remus, by Harris, 248–49; miscellaneous, 249–53; bibliography of,

253–54; in picture-books, 254–55; in pictures, 255; in poems, 255–56; in standard books, 256–58; of all nations, 258–59; in miscellaneous editions, 259–62; in school editions, 262–64; in Appendix, 265–90.
Familiar, the, 14–15.
Fancy, 46, 47.
Fir Tree, 151–53.
First-grade fairy tales, 231–34, 265–86.
Folk-game, illustrated by Little Lamb and the Little Fish, 147–48, 267–70.
Folk-tales, generally, as literary form, 65–67; tested as literary form, 60–70; characters of, compared with those of Shakespeare, 7, 43–44; recent collections of, 200.
Foolish, Timid Rabbit, illustrating method in story-telling, 116–17; an animal type, 214.
Form, a distinguishing literary trait, 40, 54; perfect, 57–60; general qualities of, 57–58; precision, a quality, 57; energy, a quality, 57–58; delicacy, a quality, 58; personality, a quality, 58; principles controlling, 58–60: sincerity, 58–59; unity, 59; mass, 59; coherence, 59; style in, 59–60; illustrated: by Oeyvind and Marit, 60–64; by Three Billy-Goats Gruff, 64–65; folk-tales as literary, 65–70; mastery of tale as, 100–02.
French fairy tales, 179–83.

Game, as expression, 134–35.
Gardens of the Tuileries, 1.
German fairy tales, 192–93.
Gesta Romanorum, 174–75.
Gesture, knowledge of, 105–06; library pamphlet relating to, 106.
Giant tales, 31–32.
Golden Egg and the Cock of Gold, 237–38.
Good-Natured Bear, a modern animal type, 217, 272–75; a book, 190.
Grimm, William and Jacob, 67–68; list of tales by, 246–47; editions by, 257; tales by, as literary form, 67.

Harris, J. C., list of Uncle Remus tales by, 248–49; tales by, as literary form, 69; editions by, 257.
Henny Penny, 214.
History of fairy tales, 158–203; origin of fairy tales, 158–67; transmission of fairy tales, 167–200; oral transmission, 167–70; literary transmission, 170–200; references, 201–03.
Hop-About-Man, 241–43.
House that Jack Built, 206–07.
How the Birds came to Have Different Nests, 151; 270–72.
How the Sun, Moon, and West Wind went out to Dinner, 84–86.
How Two Beetles Took Lodgings, 226.
Humor in fairy tales: an interest, 21–22; 217–19.
Humorous tales, 217–23; types of, 219–23.

Imagination, a distinguishing literary mark of fairy tales, 40, 45–53; creative, 45; associative, 46; penetrative, 47; contemplative, 47–53; fancy, 46, 47; exhibited in child's return, 122, 125–54.
Imaginative, the, 23.
Initiative, development of, 122, 123–25.
Instincts of child, expression of: conversation, 125–27; inquiry, 127–29; construction, 129–30; artistic expression, 130–54.

Intellect, appeal of fairy tales to, 53–54.
Interests of children, 13–37; sense of life, 14; the familiar, 14–15; surprise, 15–17; sense impression, 17–18; the beautiful, 18–19; wonder, mystery, magic, 19; adventure, 19–20; success, 20; action, 20–21; humor, 21–22; poetic justice, 22–23; the imaginative, 23; animals, 24; portrayal of human relations, 24–25; the diminutive, 25–26; rhythm and repetition, 26–28; the simple and the sincere, 28–29; unity of effect, 29–30; opposed to, 30–36; witch tales, 31; dragon tales, 31; giant tales, 31–32; some tales of transformation, 32–33; tales of strange creatures, 33–34; unhappy tales, 34; tales of capture, 34–35; very long tales, 35–36; complicated or insincere tales, 36.
Introduction, i–iii.
Inquiry, instinct of, 127–29.

Jack the Giant-Killer, 185, 186, 188, 190.
Jacobs, Joseph, list of tales by, 247–48; tales by, as literary form, 69; editions by, 257.
Jatakas, 170.

Key of the Kingdom, 207–08.
Kindergarten: play in, 5–6; work in, unified by the fairy tale, 8–9; language-training in, 10–11; interests of child in, 13–37; standards for literature in, 37–87; standards for composition in, 54–60; story-telling in, 94–119; return to be expected from child in, 119–54; standards of teaching for teacher in, 119–25; instincts of child in, 125–54; history of fairy tales to be used in, 158–203; classes of tales used in, 204–44; sources of material for fairy tales to be used in, 245–64.
King-book, Persian, The, 175–76.

Lang, Andrew, tales by, as literary form, 69.
Lambikin, 21.
Language, expression in, 125–27.
Lazy Jack, 224–25.
Life, a sense of, 14; criticism of, 120–21; fairy tale a counterpart to, 8–9.
Lists: of tales, 246–53; *See* Sources of material.
Literature, mind and soul in, 39–40; qualities of, 40; fairy tale as, 37–87.
Little Lamb and the Little Fish, 147–48, 267–70.
Little Two-Eyes, 145, 265–66.
Little Thumb, editions, 189; tale, 232, 281–82.
Literary collections of tales, 170–200.
Logical method of selecting tales, 95–96.
Long tales, opposed to child's interests, 35–36.
Lord Peter, 232, 277.

Magpie's Nest, 151, 270–72.
Märchen Brunnen or Fairy-tale Fountain, 2–3.
Mass, principle of, 58–59; illustrated in: Oeyvind and Marit, 61–62; Three Billy-Goats Gruff, 65.
Medio Pollito, 215–16.
Memory, development of, 226.
Message, of the tale, 100; of this book. *See* Summaries.
Method of story-telling, the re-creative, 113–17; criticism of, 114–16; illustration of, 116–17; direct moral, 143.
Mind, in literature, 40.
Miscellaneous, tales, a list, 249–53; editions, 259–62.

Modern tale, compared with old tale, 234–43; types of, 235–43; what it is, 243; tales, by Andersen, 28–29, 234, 248, 256–57.
Motifs in folk-tales, classified, 97–98.
Mother Goose, tales of, 179–81; her Melodies, 187, 195, 197, 198.
Musicians of Bremen, 130–31, 219–20.

Narration, in fairy tales, 74–75; illustrated by Sleeping Beauty, 146–47.
Norse tales, 194; a list of, 247; editions, 257.

Objectification in fairy tales, 135–38.
Oeyvind and Marit, 60–64.
Old Woman and Her Pig, accumulative type, 207, 208; realistic type, 225–26; an exercise of memory, 226.
Organization of ideas, accomplished through Fir Tree, 152–53; social, of tale, 153–54.
Origin of fairy tales, 158–67.
Outline, 291–303.

Paper-cutting, 130–31.
Painting, as expression, 132.
Panchatantra, the Five Books, 171.
Pause, in story-telling, 104–05.
Pentamerone, The, 178–79.
Perrault, Charles, statue of, 1; list of tales by, 180; tales by, tested as literary form, 68; editions by, 257–58.
Personality, quality of, 57–58; in Oeyvind and Marit, 60; in Three Billy-Goats Gruff, 64; power of, 106–07.
Personal relation, establishment of, 107–10.
Peter Rabbit, 239.
Philosophy, in fairy tales, 48–52; of Uncle Remus Tales, 51–52; of Laboulaye's Tales, 51; of Cat and Mouse in Partnership, 48; of Emperor's New Suit, 48–49; of Ugly Duckling, 49–50; of Elephant's Child, 49; child's, 50–51.
Phonics in fairy tales, 79–81.
Pictures, list, 255.
Picture-Books, list, 254–55.
Plot, element of fairy tale as short-story, 73–77; structure illustrated, 76–77.
Poems, fairy, list, 255–56.
Poetic justice, 22–23.
Poetry, of teaching, 120.
Portrayal of human relations, especially with children, 24–25.
Position, of story-teller, 107.
Precision, quality of, 57; illustrated in: Oeyvind and Marit, 60; Three Billy-Goats Gruff, 64.
Preparation, teacher's, in story-telling, 94–102; rules for telling, 94–102.
Presentation, teacher's, of tale, 102–19: training of voice, 103–04; exercises in breathing, 104–05; gesture, 105–06; power of personality, 106–07; suggestions for telling, 107–12; establishment of personal relation, 108–10; placing of story in concrete situation, 94–95, 110–11; conception of child's aim, 112; telling of tale, 112–19; re-creative method of story-telling, 113–17; adaptation of fairy tales, 117–19.
Princess and Pea, 114–16.
Principles, of selection for fairy tales, 13–89: interests of children, 13–37; fairy tale as literature, 37–70; fairy tale as short-story, 70–87; references, 87–89.

Principles, of composition, 58–60; of story-telling, 94; of teaching, 119–25; concerning instincts of children, 124–25.
Problem, a means of developing consciousness, 122–25.
Proverbs in fairy tales, 50.
Purpose, growth in child's, 123–25.
Puss-in-Boots, 232, 275–78.
Psychological method of selecting tales, 95–96.

Quick-Running Squash, 240.

Realistic, tale, 223–28; types of, 224–28.
Reading, as expression, 127; relation of, to literature, 10–11, 127.
Reason, growth in, 6–7, 10; development of, 53–54.
Re-creative method of story-telling, 113–17.
Red Riding Hood, chap-book, 189; a romantic type, 232–34.
References; chapter I, 12; chapter II, 87–89; chapter III, 154–57; chapter IV, 201–03; chapter, V, 243–44.
Relation, of contemplative imagination to language-training, 47–48; of contemplative imagination to power of observation, 47–48; of contemplative imagination to science, 52–53; of literature to intellect, 53–54; of sound to sense or meaning, 55; of sound to action, 55–56; of phonics and emotional effect, 55; of gesture to story-telling, 105–06; personal, between the story-teller and listener, 107–10; of reading to story-telling, 127; of reading to literature, 10, 11, 38, 127; of rhyme to meaning, 56; of fairy tales to nature study, 6, 47–48; of fairy tales to industrial education, 71–73; of fairy tales to child, 3–11; of dramatization to story-telling, 138–54; of fairy tales to literature, 37–70; of fairy tales to composition, 54–70; of fairy tales to story-telling, 90–91.
Repetition, 26–28, 205–11.
Representation, 135–38.
Re-telling of fairy tales, 101–02.
Return, creative, from child, in telling of fairy tales, 119–54: in language, 125–27; in inquiry, 127–29; in construction, 129–30; in artistic expression, 130–54; in paper-cutting, 130–31; in drawing, 132; in painting, 132; in song, 132–33; in rhythm, 133–34; in game, 134–35; in dance, 137, 145, 147; in dramatization, 138–54; illustrated, 145–54, 265–72.
Reynard the Fox, place in the animal tale, 212; history, 172–74; chap-book, 185, 186, 190, 196.
Rhyme, 56.
Rhythm, in fairy tales, 26–28; plays, 133–34.
Robin's Christmas song, 78–79.
Romantic tale, 228–34; types of, 228–34, 275–86.

St. Nicholas, Stories retold from, 241.
Sanskrit Tales, 171.
School editions of fairy tales, 262–64.
Science, relation of contemplative imagination to, 52–53.
Sea Fairy and the Land Fairy, 236–37.
Selection of fairy tales by teacher, psychological or logical, 95–96.
Sense impression, 17–18.
Setting, element of fairy tale as short-story, 77–82; sequence in, 78–79; story told by, 81–82; and phonics, 79–81.
Sheep and Pig, 215.

Short-story, fairy tale as, 70–87: elements of, 70–71; ways of writing, 71; characters, 71–73; plot, 73–77; narration in, 74–75; description in, 75; setting, 77–82; elements of, blended, 82–84. Tales tested as, 84–87; telling of, 90–154.
Silhouette pictures, cutting of, 130–31.
Simple and sincere, 28–29.
Sincerity, principle of, 58–59; illustrated in: Oeyvind and Marit, 60, 61; Three Billy-Goats Gruff, 64–65.
Sindibad, The Book of, 172.
Sleeping Beauty, romantic type, 231–32; uniting partial narration, dramatization, and dramatic game,146–47.
Snow White, 145, 266–67.
Snow White and Rose Red, 232, 282–86.
Song, as expression, 132–33.
Soul, in literature, 39–40.
Sources of material for fairy tales, 245–64: list of fairy tales and folk-tales, 246–53; bibliography of fairy tales, 253–54; list of picture-books, 254–55; list of pictures, 255; list of fairy poems, 255–56; main standard fairy-tale books, 256–58; fairy tales of all nations, 258–59; miscellaneous editions of fairy tales, 259–62; school editions of fairy tales, 262–64.
Sparrow and the Crow, as expression, 125–26.
Spider and the Flea, 79–81.
Standards, for testing fairy tales, 84; for selecting tales, 204–05; for making lists, 245–46. *See* Summaries.
Standard fairy-tale books, a list, 256–58.
Story, place of, in home, library, and school, 93–94; formation of original stories, 126–27.
Story-telling, an ancient art, 91–93; principles governing, 94; teacher's preparation for, 94–102; rules for, 94–102; presentation in, 102–119; voice in, 103–04; breathing in, 104–05; gesture in, 105–06; re-creative method of, 113–17; return from child, in, 119–54; child's part in, 121–25.
Straparola, 178.
Straparola's Nights, 178.
Straw Ox, 86–87.
Structure, illustrated, 76–77; study of, in story-telling, 99–100.
Study of tale as folk-lore and as literature, 96–99.
Style, defined, 59–60; illustrated, 60–65; qualities of, 59–60; principles controlling, 59–60.
Success, 20.
Suggestion, illustrated by Pope, 55; by Andersen, 136; by Kipling, 56–57; through gesture and sound, 55; through arrangement of words and speech-tunes of voice, 56–57.
Summaries: giving message of book, 13, 37–38, 40, 70–71, 84, 158, 204–05, 235.
Surprise, 15–17.
Swedish tales, 193.

Tales: of Mother Goose, 179–81; of Perrault, 246; of the Grimms, 246–47; Norse, 247; English, by Jacobs, 247–48; modern fairy, by Andersen, 248; Uncle Remus, 248–49; miscellaneous, 249–53; fairy, of all nations, 258–59; literary collections of, 170–200. *See* Fairy tales.
Teaching, story-telling, a part of the art of, 119–25; poetry of, 120; good art in, 120; great art in, 120–21; a criticism of life, 120–21.
Telling, of fairy tales, 90–154;

art of story-telling, 90–94; principles controlling, 94; preparation by teacher for, 94–102; presentation by teacher, in, 102–19; suggestions for, 107–12; return by child, from, 119–54; re-creative method of, 113–17; adaptation of tales for, 117–19; references, 154–57.
Theories of origin of fairy tales: detritus of myth, 161–63; sun-myth theory, 163–64; common Indian heritage, 165–67; identity of early fancy, 167.
Three Bears, illustrating surprise, 16–17; a chap-book, 190; accumulative, 209–11.
Three Billy-Goats Gruff, 64–65.
Three Pigs, illustrating structure, 76; animal type, 216.
Thumbelina, illustrating adaptation, 118; illustrating rhythm play, 134.
Tin Soldier, Steadfast, as emotion, 42; tale of imagination, 46; as representation, 135–38; as a game, 135, 138.
Titty Mouse and Tatty Mouse, 81, 208–09, 227–28.
Tom Hickathrift, 185, 186, 187, 196.
Tom Thumb, chap-book tale, 185, 188, 190, 196; romantic type, 278–81.
Tone-color, in story-telling, 105.
Training of voice, 103–04.
Transformation, tales of, 32–33; kinds of, 276.
Transmission, of tales: oral, 167–170; literary, 170; illustrated by: Dog Gellert, 166; Dick Whittington, 169; Peruonto, 169–70.
Tributes, two public, 1–3.
Truth, basis of, in fairy tales, a distinguishing literary mark, 40, 53–54.
Tuileries, gardens of. *See* Gardens.

Uncle Remus Tales, by Harris, 248–49; editions, 257.
Unhappy tales, 34.
Unity, of effect, 29–30; principle of composition, 58–59; illustrated in: Oeyvind and Marit, 61; Three Billy-Goats Gruff, 65.

Value, of fairy tales in education, 3–12, 119–25; to give joy. 3–4; to satisfy the play-spirit, 4–6; to develop observation, 6; to give habits of mind, 6–7; to strengthen emotion, 6–7, 44–45; to extend social relations, 7–8; in home, library, and school, 8–9; to give language-training, 10–11; to develop imagination, 45–53; to develop reason, 53–54; to develop power of creative return, 119–54; to develop self-activity, 121–22; to develop consciousness, through problems, 122–23; to develop initiative, 122; to develop purpose, 123–25; to develop self-expression, 124–54; to strengthen originality, 127–29; to develop organization of ideas, 153; and to exercise memory, 226.
Version, of tale, 101–02.
Villeneuve, Madam, 182.
Voice, training of, 103–04.

Witch tales, 31.
Wolf and the Seven Kids, expression in painting, 132; in song, 132–33.
Words, powers of, 54–55; denotation, 54; connotation, 54–55; suggestion, 54–57.
Wonder, mystery, magic, an interest, 19.
Worth of fairy tales, 1–12: two public tributes, 1–3; value of fairy tales in education, 3–12; references, 12.